Why We Hate Politics

For Ailsa and Ian

Why We Hate Politics

COLIN HAY

polity

First published in 2007 by Polity Press

Reprinted 2007, 2008, 2009, 2010

Polity Press
65 Bridge Street
Cambridge CB2 1UR, UK

Polity Press
350 Main Street
Malden, MA 02148, USA

ISBN-13: 978-07456-3098-4
ISBN-13: 978-07456-3099-1 (pb)

A catalogue record for this book is available from the British Library

Typeset in 11.25 / 13 pt Dante
by Servis Filmsetting Ltd, Manchester
Printed and bound in Great Britain by the MPG Books Group

For further information on Polity, visit our website www.politybooks.com

Contents

Figures and Tables

Figures

Tables

Preface and Acknowledgements

This book has taken rather longer to write than I had hoped, just like the last one, and the one before that . . . and, almost certainly, the one before that (I forget). When the idea for this book, or at least a book somewhat like this, was first put to me by Louise Knight, I was about to begin a three-year tenure as Head of the Department of Political Science and International Studies (POLSIS) at the University of Birmingham. I accepted enthusiastically the offer to submit a proposal, both because I was excited about the prospect of sorting out in my own mind the nature of the contemporary condition of political disaffection and disengagement and because this was the kind of book that I could imagine writing as Head of Department. That was to prove a forlorn hope. It has been far more difficult and more challenging intellectually to sort out my previously rather disparate thoughts on the issues addressed in this volume than I had thought likely. And the process has taken me in some genuinely new directions. It also became clear, rather early on, that I was profoundly naïve to think that I was going to write anything very much as Head of Department. But the book is probably better for its rather lengthy gestation. It is certainly the case that when I eventually sat down to consign my thoughts to paper at the start of my period of sabbatical in the Department of Government at the University of Manchester, I was far clearer about what I was seeking to do. The months that have followed have proved unusually cathartic.

As this perhaps already implies, I have, as usual, amassed a great variety of debts, both personal and intellectual, in writing this book. I must first thank my colleagues in POLSIS. It is not their fault that I failed to write this book whilst acting as their Head of Department – indeed, they have contributed greatly to making that a far less legitimate excuse for my inability to meet my publisher's deadlines than it would normally be in British higher education today. I must also thank my friends, new and old, in the Department of Government at the University of Manchester, who have accommodated my sabbatical but who have, by virtue of this book, seen rather less of me than they might have expected. Now that it is completed,

I hope to rectify that and to repay as best I can their generosity. An innumerable array of friends and colleagues have shaped, often unbeknownst to them, my ideas on the issues that I address in this volume. Amongst those who spring immediately to mind are the following, whom I thank profusely: Sam Ashman, Stephen Bates, Mark Blyth, Jim Buller, Pete Burnham, Keith Dowding, Alan Finlayson, Matthew Flinders, Andrew Gamble, Bob Goodin, Peter Hall, Andrew Hindmoor, Chris Howell, Laura Jenkins, Steven Lukes, Ross Maloney, Dave Marsh, Mick Moran, Pippa Norris, Craig Parsons, Ben Rosamond, Heather Savigny, Nicola Smith, Hugh Ward and Matthew Watson. It is almost inevitable that the day this book goes to press I will recall another dozen names that should be on this list – I thank them too, equally profusely – and trust that they will excuse my notoriously appalling memory. I am also immensely indebted to three anonymous readers for Polity, each of whose thoughtful, supportive and yet probing comments led to significant improvements, I think, in the final manuscript. I must also thank Louise Knight, Ellen McKinlay and, latterly, Emma Hutchinson at Polity. It was Louise who first put the idea to me for this volume, and I am immensely grateful to her for that – especially now that the book is complete! But I would also like to thank all three for their dedication, support and, above all, their enthusiasm for the project as it has developed and for their patience and perseverance. Whilst on the subject of patience and perseverance, this book, like all the others, would simply not have been written without the love and support of Elspeth. It is testimony to her generosity, kindness and tolerance that she has read almost every word and commented on almost every page.

Finally, it is now well over four years since the completion of my last single-authored book, *Political Analysis*. Since then I have become a father – twice. This book is, appropriately enough, dedicated to Ailsa (now four) and Ian (six months). I guess that, like any father and author, I hope that one day they will be interested to see what I have written. Yet I have one further hope – namely, that if they do, they will scarcely recognize the description of the condition of political disaffection and disengagement from which it builds.

Colin Hay
May 2006, Macclesfield

1

Political Disenchantment

Politics, or so it seems, is not all that it was once cracked up to be. Despite its near global diffusion, democracy motivates a seemingly ever smaller proportion of the electorate to exercise its right to vote in the states in which that right has existed the longest. Levels of electoral participation amongst the young are particularly low, and, it appears, each successive cohort of new voters has a lower propensity to vote than the previous one. Moreover, despite the bitter, often bloody and almost always protracted struggle to acquire the right to vote in free, fair and open elections, levels of participation in the new democracies are scarcely less depressing. Nowhere, it seems, does politics animate electorates consistently and *en masse* to enthusiastic participation in the democratic process. It should come as no surprise, then, that membership of political parties and most other indices of participation in formal politics are down – in established democracies to unprecedented levels.

For most commentators, this is depressing enough in itself.[1] Yet, arguably, such trends are merely the symptoms of a more worrying and deep-seated condition. For each individual pathology might be seen as indicative of a more pervasive – indeed, near universal – disdain for 'politics' and the 'political'. Once something of a *bon mot*, conjuring a series of broadly positive connotations – typically associating politics with public scrutiny and accountability – 'politics', has increasingly become a dirty word. Indeed, to attribute 'political' motives to an actor's conduct is now invariably to question that actor's honesty, integrity or capacity to deliver an outcome that reflects anything other than his or her material self-interest – often, all three simultaneously.

Politics and the collective good

There is, of course, a certain irony about this, the more detailed analysis of which will concern us throughout much of this volume. Stated most simply, politics responds to the need in complex and differentiated societies for collective and ultimately binding decision making. In the language of rational choice theory, contemporary societies are characterized by the proliferation of so-called collective action problems to which politics is, in some sense, a response. A collective action problem exists whenever the common or collective interest of a group or society is not best served by the narrow pursuit by individuals of their own (perceived) self-interest. Facing pervasive environmental degradation, the pursuit of material self-interest by profit-driven corporations will, in the absence of a collective and authoritative decision-making body, result in the continued exploitation of the natural world. No individual corporation can afford to impose upon itself unilaterally the costs of environmental sustainability unless it is entirely confident that others will do likewise. Rationality at the level of the individual unit (here the corporation) translates into collective irrationality – an outcome, environmental degradation, from which all suffer. Politics, here in the form of an authoritative environmental regulatory agency, is capable (in theory at least) of providing a solution to such collective action problems, negotiating and enforcing a set of binding environmental standards and, in so doing, imposing collective rationality where otherwise it would not prevail.[2]

As this perhaps suggests, politics is concerned, almost by definition, with the construction and, ideally, the realization of a sense of the collective good. The contemporary association of politics with the pursuit of the material self-interest of politicians is, then, oddly antithetical to its very *raison d'être*. The prevalence of such attitudes raises a whole host of questions. Together these frame a considerable part of the analysis and argument to follow.

Amongst the most important of these are the following.

- Are electorates right to discern in contemporary politics an increase in the prevalence of instrumental, self-interested behaviour on the part of those vested with political power?
- Whether they are right or wrong to do so, how have electorates come to conceive of politics in this way?
- To what extent is politics today less able than it once was to provide solutions to collective action problems?
- Is any failure to supply political solutions to contemporary societal problems attributable to the nature, prevalence and character of such problems, to the quality, capabilities, motivations or moral calibre of politicians, or to the ideas which inform contemporary political strategy?

This, to be fair, is a far from innocent set of questions. There are a variety of ways of approaching these issues, and the agenda mapped out above is by no means neutral with respect to such choices. Indeed, there are no doubt hints as to the analysis to be presented in subsequent chapters in the questions posed, the order in which they are presented, and the manner in which they are expressed. Nonetheless, were we able to furnish ourselves with a complete set of answers to these questions, we would know a great deal about the nature of our current political predicament, the disaffection and disengagement to which it has given rise, and the character of politics more broadly. My aim in this book is to provide some answers to these questions. In so doing, I restrict myself, quite consciously and explicitly, to a consideration of the contemporary condition of the advanced liberal democracies. Whilst some of the answers that I offer may potentially prove generalizable beyond Europe, North America, South-East Asia, Australia and New Zealand, it is with these cases that I am principally concerned.

Dissecting disaffection: an agenda for political analysis

Tackling this list of questions, even for a limited number of cases, is no small task, however. And although political science has much to contribute to an analysis of each, as we shall see, it is a very long way from providing definitive answers to any of them. Moreover, despite a recent proliferation of literature concerned to identify the malaise afflicting the advanced liberal democracies, such questions remain rather further from the heart of contemporary political science than one might imagine. Indeed, part of the normative content of this book is the claim that political analysts should pay rather greater attention to this set of issues than they have tended to do to date. That is likely to prove contentious. It is justified in part by two potentially no less contentious claims.

The first is that political analysts should pay rather greater attention to the understandings of politics of 'real-world' political participants and non-participants. Such understandings change over time and are themselves highly consequential – becoming contributory factors in the development of the 'politics' they purportedly reflect. There is a danger, as with any specialist field of inquiry, that the analyst, whose inherent interest in the intricacies of the political is presumably not in doubt, simply takes for granted a similar level of innate interest on the part of political subjects more generally. As should now be clear, that would be a very grave mistake – and one which can only distort the character of contemporary politics as it appears through the analyst's lens.

The second relates to the responsibilities of political analysts towards their chosen subject matter. It would, of course, be massively to overstate both the influence and the significance of contemporary political science to assume that it can bear any direct responsibility for whatever pathologies afflict the contemporary polity. Nonetheless, political analysts surely have some responsibility towards their subject matter – particularly, one might reasonably surmise, when it comes to diagnosing and seeking solutions to clearly articulated political pathologies. The contemporary condition of disengagement and disenchantment with politics itself is as clear an instance as one could conceivably imagine of such a situation. Yet it is a topic which has received somewhat less attention than this significance might lead one to expect (perhaps the most systematic treatment to date is that provided by Dalton 2004).

Moreover, as we shall see presently, political analysis is not, perhaps, as totally innocent as one might at first assume in the generation of this condition of disenchantment and disengagement. It is important not to overstate this role, but arguably the systematic questioning of the motives of political actors and public servants has its origins in the projection of instrumental assumptions on to such actors. This, in turn, can be traced to the development of public choice theory within political science in the 1960s and 1970s, and its growing influence on public policy from the 1980s. The extent to which such assumptions are true is an index of the degree to which it is irrational to trust politicians and public servants to act in the collective interest. Consequently, the extent to which such assumptions are believed is likely to be an index of the rational disengagement of the electorate from the political process. It would certainly seem as though public choice theory's cynicism with respect to the motivations of political actors is now deeply shared.[3]

Yet this is perhaps to get ahead of ourselves. Before we can diagnose the contemporary political condition, we need to know rather more about its symptoms. That is the principal task of this lengthy introductory chapter. In it, my aim is both to set out in some detail the problem to be explained in later chapters and to introduce the key themes of the volume as a whole. I do so by reflecting upon the associations and connotations of the term 'politics' in popular discourse. Such associations are suggestive of the complex and contested nature of the phenomena they serve to label. In recent years the term 'politics' has become synonymous, for many, with notions of duplicity, corruption, dogmatism, inefficiency, undue interference in essentially private matters, and a lack of transparency in decision making. To label an activity or process 'political' is, it seems, invariably to deride and to distance oneself from it. This immediately raises a series of important questions about the nature and content of political processes and the place, purpose and value of political analysis today.

In this chapter I reflect upon the sense of political disenchantment that has arisen in recent years, seeking to trace its origins, gauge its extent, and assess the degree to which it might genuinely be seen as a recent phenomenon. I contrast the largely negative contemporary connotations of politics in popular discourse with the rather idealized depiction of politics as an arena of deliberation, public scrutiny, accountability and responsiveness which has tended to characterize the academic discourse about politics. If politics is, indeed, about holding power to account, how has it come to be associated with duplicity, corruption and undue interference? There are many reasons for this contemporary disenchantment with politics. However, two in particular are important in establishing the agenda for this volume. The first has already been alluded to – the rise of public choice theory and its natural affinities with neoliberalism. The second I have yet to mention – the challenges associated with globalizing tendencies. To the former's deep distrust of the inherent interventionism and inefficiency of political processes, the latter has added a plausible account of the ever diminishing capacity of political actors. The result is a profound crisis of both legitimacy and confidence in processes of political deliberation. Neoliberalism, informed by public choice theoretical assumptions, suggests the value of a tightly delimited political sphere which does not encroach upon the essentially private realms of economic and social exchange, encouraging a profoundly suspicious, sceptical and anti-political culture; the globalization thesis suggests the increasingly anachronistic nature of political intervention in an era of external economic constraint, inviting a fundamental reappraisal of the previously unquestioned capacity of political processes to shape societal trajectories. Both conspire to discredit the 'political' in contemporary societies, raising a series of questions about the nature of politics, the space for political deliberation in an era of globalization, and the role of political analysis in holding power to account. These issues frame the discussion of subsequent chapters.

Contextualizing political disenchantment

I started by noting that, if current levels of political cynicism, disengagement and disaffection with the political are anything to go by, then politics is not all that it was once cracked up to be. Yet, from the outset, it is important not to get this totally out of proportion. There is plenty to concern us in contemporary patterns of political participation and non-participation without having to exaggerate the extent to which current trends are unprecedented historically.

Stated most bluntly, ostensibly democratic political systems require at least a minimal level of participation if the democratic legitimacy they claim is to be anything other than a façade. As Carole Pateman suggests, 'for a democratic polity to exist it is necessary for a participatory society to exist' (1970: 43). Arguably, levels of participation in at least some established and new democracies alike are low enough to give considerable cause for concern on this count. The picture is bleaker still if we allow ourselves a differentiated view of the democratic polity. For it is certainly no exaggeration to suggest that certain sections of the electorate – typically, in the established democracies and most obviously in the US, the black urban poor – are effectively disenfranchised altogether. Democracy is, for them, a privilege enjoyed by others; politics, an essentially external yet life-course-shaping imposition.

The point is that in making such arguments we do not have to rely upon the nostalgic construction of a mythical past of near total participation and near perfect democratic political legitimacy. Such a world never existed, politics has always had its detractors, and there have been other times when disdain and cynicism for politics have proved dominant. Indeed, John Dunn is surely right to note in characteristically sombre tones that politics has proved 'consistently disappointing'. Yet what is remarkable here – for Dunn at least – is less that politics should disappoint than that, given its tendency to disappoint, it should 'repeatedly nourish such high hopes' (2000: p. xii). Whether it will continue to nourish such high hopes is an interesting question. But, in so far as it has and does still, there is arguably something rather positive, even endearing, about this. That politics might continue to generate expectations that it can seemingly only ever fail to realize is testimony to a certain triumph of the human will over human capabilities. It also suggests a degree of political animation and engagement that has arguably both served to elevate levels of political participation in the past and is now on the wane. For Dunn, however, this triumph of hope over experience is less endearing than irritating. If we understood politics rather better, we would expect less of it. Consequently, we would be surprised and dismayed rather less often by its repeated failures to live up to our over-inflated and unrealistic expectations. We would, in turn, be better placed to set for ourselves political ambitions that we had some chance of achieving. This may well be true, but such a rational recalibration of our expectations might also lead us to lose our sense of political ambition, animation and engagement. Indeed, does that not describe the contemporary political condition rather well?

If politics is not all what it was once cracked up to be, then we should not lose sight of the fact that for many it has never lived up to its billing and has always been rather less than it was cracked up to be. Indeed, as we shall see, a crucial factor in the development of contemporary political disaffection has been the growing political influence of those for whom politics is, at best, a necessary evil. This kind of argument does not differentiate between a past – in which politics was a good in itself – and the present day – in which it has become an increasingly malevolent force. In a sense, it is timeless and, so its proponents would contend, of universal relevance. What varies is not so much the content of the argument as its ability to shape attitudinal dispositions towards politics – and it is no more likely to mould such dispositions than when, as today, it has direct access to political power.[4] And whilst there is a certain irony about this capture of the political system by those committed to an avowedly anti-political agenda, it hardly lessens the significance or pervasiveness of the effects.

We would be wrong, then, to attribute current political disaffection solely to the critique of *contemporary* political personnel, their conduct and their motivations; it is just as much a product of a more general and timeless critique of politics as a practice or vocation. Similarly, we would be wrong to assume that the predominantly negative associations and connotations of politics today are unprecedented historically. Politics has been seen as the problem rather than the solution at various historical junctures. We might note, for instance, that all references to 'politics' in the work of Shakespeare are distinctly and overtly negative in their connotations. Not unrepresentative is King Lear's remark, 'Get thee glass-eyes, and like a scurvy politician, seem to see things thou dost not' (Act IV, scene 6). No less scathing is Hotspur's contempt for 'this vile politician Bolingbroke' (*Henry IV Part I*, Act I, scene 3). What is more, the association between Bolingbroke's vileness and his identification as a 'politician' is clearly not incidental – vileness is in the very nature of the 'politician'. Mine Host of the Garter in *The Merry Wives of Windsor* adds a further and possibly more familiar dimension to the odiousness of the politician in asking, 'Am I politic? Am I subtle? Am I a Machiavel?' (Act III, scene 2, all cited in Sparks 1994: 76). The capacity for manipulation, duplicity and deception is here added to a growing list of objectionable traits which set political actors apart from their peers.

It might, of course, be objected that, whatever its connotations, the term 'politics' was not employed in quite the same way in Elizabethan England as it is today. That is undoubtedly true, but it merely serves to demonstrate the timelessness of the critique of politics, however much the practice to which it refers may have changed over time. Thus Isaac D'Israeli's summary (cited in Crick 2000: 16), several centuries later, of what he took to be the pervasive misrepresentation of politics as 'the art of governing people by deceiving them' seems entirely in keeping with Shakespeare's attribution of Machiavellian motives to the political subject. That, of course, may be no coincidence. For the influence of Machiavelli's *Il Principe* (*The Prince*), published in 1513 – both for what it says and for what it is assumed to say – on the pejorative connotations of the 'term politics' is considerable.[5]

Yet, for present purposes, what is perhaps both most interesting and most easily forgotten about Machiavelli's writings is the extent to which they were part of a far broader reconfiguration of societal attitudes towards politics that was occurring in late sixteenth- and early seventeenth-century Italy. In a number of key respects this parallels more contemporary developments. As Maurizio Viroli suggests, 'having enjoyed for three centuries the status of the noblest human science, politics emerged . . . as an ignoble, depraved and sordid activity: it was no longer the most powerful means of fighting corruption, but that art of conforming to, and perpetuating it' (1992: 1). In fact, two rather different conceptions of politics were at work here. The first, dominant until the late sixteenth century but with its origins in Aristotle, conceived of politics as the noble art of preserving the republic, largely through the subordination of sectional interests to the common interest of the community as a whole. Politics, in this conception (or discourse), was very much about the resolution of collective action problems and the delivery of public goods – such as security, social cohesion and societal well-being more generally.[6] The second conception, which gradually came to replace and supplant it was, strictly speaking, not a discourse of politics at all – but of *raison d'état*, literally 'reason of state'. Where the discourse of politics had drawn attention to the authentically political art of managing the republic to satisfy the collective needs of the many against the parochial desires of the individual, that of *raison d'état* highlighted a rather different and darker art – that of preserving *l'état*, the 'state'. By this was meant the art of stabilizing, insulating and crystallizing the political power and authority of a person or group (for Machiavelli, 'the prince') through the strategic deployment of access to, and control over, public institutions. Whereas politics had been concerned with the defence of the collective interest of society through the development of public authority, *raison d'état* was concerned to promote – invariably in the name of the public good – the self-interest of the ruling group or elite. In this sense it was *raison d'état* rather than politics that was the art of governing people by deceiving them.

This is an important point, for Machiavelli and other writers of the time sought to differentiate very clearly between politics and *raison d'état*. Indeed, though now invariably cast as a cynical and dispassionate advocate of the dark arts of government through duplicity, strategic deception and, where necessary, outright tyranny, Machiavelli was himself a staunch defender of politics as the art of the republic. Moreover, as Viroli again notes, 'by not using the word *politico* when he spoke about the art of the state, and by using it only for the art of the republic . . . [he] helped to preserve the conventional republican meaning of politics' (1992: 6). It was only later on that politics would become synonymous with the art of the state, the positive associations and connotations that it had derived from Aristotelian republicanism now largely overwritten with the decidedly bleaker and more instrumental assumptions of the latter. The transition took the best part of a century. Once complete, *raison d'état* had essentially replaced civic republicanism as the 'new politics'. In the process, the public discourse of politics and its popular connotations and associations had been totally reconfigured.

Though it is important not to exaggerate them, the parallels with the more contemporary demonization of the political in public discourse are striking. In late sixteenth-century Italy, just as today, the motivational assumptions we project on to political actors and public officials largely determine whether we see politics as a good, a necessary evil or an innately malevolent force. More specifically, the extent to which we project on to such actors instrumental and self-interested preferences is the extent to which we will find it hard to conceive of politics as a process capable of delivering public goods. Machiavelli's *The Prince* is, in essence, a thought experiment exploring the implications of conceiving of 'the prince' as an instrumental and self-serving rational actor keen to preserve the privileges and power bestowed by his status.[7] Then, as now, our conception of human nature itself underpins our judgement as to whether politicians can be trusted and whether politics can indeed serve the collective interest of the community. The largely implicit insight for which Machiavelli is famous is the idea that rational, self-interested, strategic 'princes' are, at best, erratic and dishonest guarantors of the public interest. As this suggests, in the end, whether politics is a good or a bad boils down to the simple question of whether we are optimists or pessimists about the human condition. Today, as in sixteenth-century Italy, it seems that we have been overcome with pessimism. It is with elucidating the reasons for this that much of the present book is concerned.

There is, however, one potential objection to the above analysis. For it assumes that, whether optimists or pessimists, we can be confident about attributing motives and preferences to political actors. It is not at all clear that Machiavelli was so sure. For, as already suggested, *The Prince* is, as much as anything else, a thought experiment – an exploration of the consequences of assuming a particular type of (instrumental) rationality on the part of the prince. Machiavelli nowhere asserts, far less defends, the claim that all princes are so motivated. Instead, much like modern-day rational choice theorists, he explores (through a process of logical deduction) the consequences of adopting such an assumption – providing, in so doing, something of a lesson in the art of government to those prepared to act in such an instrumental fashion. The point is that we do not necessarily have to believe all political actors to be motivated in this way in order to think it prudent to protect ourselves from the scenario in which they are.

Here we come to a key point with considerable contemporary significance. Given that human nature hardly presents an open book to the political analyst, given that the motivations of political actors are likely to vary (over time and from one to the next), and given that at least some potential princes are likely to behave in something akin to the narrowly instrumental fashion depicted by Machiavelli, are we not right to assume the worst possible motives of those seeking political power? After all, why take any kind of risk with the motivations of political actors when we do not have to do so? Are we not right, in other words, to adopt a strong *precautionary principle*?

This is, in fact, a rather more difficult question to answer than it might at first appear. Presented in this way, it is certainly tempting to answer it in the affirmative. More to the point, it *has* been answered in the affirmative with very significant consequences. And this perhaps offers us a rather different perspective on things. For, arguably, the Madisonian and Jeffersonian tradition of liberal republicanism on which the US Constitution is constructed is predicated on precisely such an assumption.[8] As Madison himself stated in *The Federalist Papers*, 'it is in vain to say that enlightened statesmen will be able to adjust . . . clashing interests. Enlightened statesmen will not always be at the helm' (Hamilton, Jay, and Madison 1901: 47). No clearer statement of a precautionary principle could be imagined. And without this precautionary principle, the US Constitution would not be so codified, or so characterized by checks and balances; nor would elections to the House of Representatives be more frequent than in any other national legislative system (Birch 2001: 75–6). That may be fine and good – and there is certainly nothing innately wrong with frequent elections. Yet designing one's political institutions to protect citizens from the presumed proclivity of politicians to 'corruption, plunder and waste', in Thomas Jefferson's terms, may have a series of unintended consequences. It is, for instance, hardly likely to breed trust in elected officials, whilst arguably limiting their capacity to earn trust. Nor is it conducive to building confidence in the ability of the state to resolve the collective action problems that complex societies invariably generate. Yet, such confidence may itself be a condition of – and is certainly likely to prove a contributory factor to – providing effective solutions to such collective action problems. If the state is not trusted to uphold and enforce the law in a fair, competent and effective way, for instance, because lawmakers and law-enforcers cannot be trusted, it is unlikely that such law will prove effective in regulating societal behaviour. Finally, as we shall see presently, assuming the worst of political actors and other public officials has something of a tendency to become a self-fulfilling prophecy – since it invariably involves incentivizing (and thereby rewarding) instrumental behaviour. A vicious circle is all too easily established. That the US is characterized by some of the lowest levels of formal political participation and has a Constitution and associated democratic culture that projects instrumental assumptions on to political actors may not be entirely unrelated.

Yet we need to be extremely careful here. As I have sought to indicate, there are potential dangers in simply assuming the worst of those seeking public office. By the same token, however, naïvety, deference to authority, and a willingness to accept at face value every political appeal to the rhetoric of the common good are certainly no more conducive to an effective and participatory democratic culture. As in most things, there is a balance to be struck.

Mapping political disaffection

Thus far we have simply assumed that contemporary societies are characterized by low and declining levels of formal political participation and by a more pervasive and deep-seated sense of political disenchantment and disengagement. That, of course, is an empirical proposition. So, before turning to potential causes of this condition, it is first important to establish that the diagnosis is an accurate one.

Here there is a vast and growing body of work to draw upon, the merest surface of which we can only hope to scratch in the pages that follow. What helps is the relatively high degree of consensus amongst commentators, both as to the nature and extent of the current political condition and the appropriate indices of political disaffection and disengagement. Attention has tended to focus on three separate but related sets of issues:

- The extent to which citizens avail themselves of opportunities to engage in the formal political process – through voting, membership of political parties, attendance at public meetings and so forth.
- The extent to which citizens engage in informal and/or extra-parliamentary forms of political conduct and the extent to which they consider themselves, in so doing, to be expressing themselves 'politically'.
- The extent to which attitudes towards politics, democracy and government have changed and, more specifically, the extent to which recent decades have seen a significant decline in levels of trust and confidence in politicians and public officials.

Given the substantial empirical effort required to generate comparative time-series data on any one of these sets of issues, it is perhaps unremarkable that very little of the existing literature addresses all three sets of issues simultaneously. Yet, if we are to map the nature and extent of contemporary levels of political disaffection, it is necessary to engage in precisely such an exercise. Before doing so, however, it is important to consider both the evidence itself and the rather different inferences drawn from it in each relatively discrete body of literature. Accordingly, in the sections which follow, we consider, first, the evidence itself, then the various interpretations offered of it in the existing literature, before turning to some alternatives.

Trends in formal political participation – voter turnout

No single issue has prompted greater concern or received greater empirical scrutiny in the broad literature on political disaffection than the question of voter turnout. That should not surprise us. Elections lie at the heart of the liberal democratic conception of politics. Indeed, politics, as we know it, draws its legitimacy largely from this form of political participation. Consequently, levels of formal political participation are likely to be monitored closely. And in this respect what the empirical evidence shows is an alarming and consistent trend. This is summarized in figure 1.1, which shows average turnout levels in OECD member states (the advanced liberal democracies) plotted over time. The data series is constructed as an annual rolling average of the most recent election in each OECD member state, and shows turnout in national parliamentary elections as a proportion of

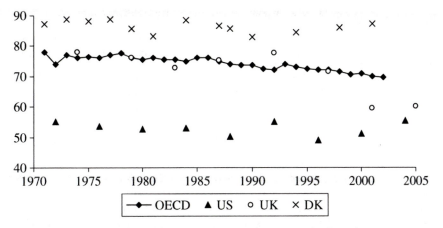

Figure 1.1 Trends in electoral turnout, OECD average and selected countries
Source: Calculated from *The International IDEA Database* (Stockholm, 2005)

total registered voters. The raw data for the US, the UK and Denmark are also plotted to offer some comparative perspective.

What the data series reveals is a consistent and long-standing trend for electoral turnout to fall over time. Though the graph shows only the period from the early 1970s, this decline is widely held to date from the 1960s. Yet the effect is not a massive one. Average turnout for the OECD states has fallen by only about 8 percentage points between 1970 and 2005 – a seemingly modest annual rate of decline of less than a quarter of a percentage point per year. This might make the apocalyptic pronouncements that have often accompanied the identification of this trend appear unwarranted. Should we really be that concerned about average turnout levels falling by less than 1 percentage point in an (OECD average) four-year electoral cycle? Yet what is most remarkable and potentially alarming about this trend is not the rate of decline itself. What worries commentators far more is the consistent and seemingly now accelerating nature of the trend and its cumulative consequences over a number of decades. If declining formal political participation threatens to destroy the legimacy that liberal democracy has come both to enjoy and to rely upon, this will not prove a rapid death. But that does not make the process any less potentially pathological.

The graph also shows the significant variation in average turnout levels between cases, with average turnout levels in Denmark, for instance, some 30 percentage points higher than in the US over this period of time. There is no evidence of this gap being closed by turnout decline – in other

Table 1.1 Decline in electoral turnout, 1945–2005, selected OECD countries

	Maximum (Year)	Minimum (Year)	Decline (% of maximum)	Annual rate of change
Japan	74.7 (1980)	44.9 (1995)	29.8 (40)	−1.99
UK	83.6 (1950)	59.4 (2001)	24.2 (29)	−0.47
Canada	75.4 (1958)	54.6 (2000)	20.8 (28)	−0.50
France	82.7 (1956)	60.3 (2002)	22.4 (27)	−0.49
New Zealand	95.1 (1951)	72.5 (2002)	22.6 (24)	−0.44
Netherlands	95.5 (1956)	73.1 (1998)	22.3 (24)	−0.53
United States	62.8 (1960)	49.0 (1996)	13.8 (22)	−0.38
Ireland	76.9 (1969)	62.6 (2002)	14.3 (19)	−0.43
Austria	96.8 (1949)	80.4 (1999)	16.4 (17)	−0.33
Germany	91.1 (1972)	77.8 (1990)	13.3 (15)	−0.74
Italy	93.7 (1958)	81.4 (2001)	12.3 (13)	−0.29
Norway	85.4 (1965)	75.0 (2001)	10.4 (13)	−0.29
Denmark	89.3 (1968)	80.6 (1953)	−8.7 (−10)*	+0.58
Sweden	91.8 (1976)	77.4 (1958)	−14.5 (−16)*	+0.81

* Note that turnout increased between these two dates.
Source: Calculated from *The International IDEA Database* (Stockholm, 2005)

words, turnout levels have not fallen more rapidly in those democracies characterized by the highest initial levels.

Table 1.1 offers a little more comparative detail, showing maximum and minimum levels of turnout in national elections during the post-war years for a number of advanced liberal democracies. The figures again express turnout as a percentage of the total number of registered voters. The table also displays both the extent and the annual rate of the decline in voter turnout between the maximum (peak) and minimum (trough). The states are listed in rank order of decline in turnout between peak and trough.

We need, of course, to be extremely cautious in the inferences we draw from data such as these. Maximum levels of turnout, for instance, may well be the product of one-off factors quite specific to the national context in which an election takes place and to the lie of the political landscape at a particular moment in time. Such factors are likely to include the closeness of the competition between the principal parties and the perceived stakes of the contest. Indeed, concentrating on turnout maxima and minima arguably magnifies the significance of such case- and time-specific factors. This should make us wary of extrapolating too easily from such data to discern more general patterns and trends. Nonetheless, a number of observations can tentatively be made.

First, turnout has indeed declined in most cases over the post-war period. With only a couple of exceptions, peaks in electoral participation occurred relatively early in the period (the average date is 1962) and troughs relatively late in the period (the average date is 1993). Indeed, in precisely half the cases the minimum turnout level was recorded in elections held in 2000 or later. Again, however, we see significant variations between cases – in maxima and minima, in the extent of decline and in the rate of decline. Thus, whilst Japan has seen a recent precipitous decline in turnout from a peak as late as 1980, New Zealand has seen a rather more steady and pro-tracted process of decline dating from the early 1950s, and Denmark and Sweden have actually seen turnout increase from minima in the 1950s to maxima in the late 1960s and 1970s respectively, only for turnout to fall again in the 1980s and 1990s. As this suggests, if the norm is for a lengthy process of decline over several decades, then there are exceptions. The most obvious and perhaps most significant of these are the Nordic / Scandinavian countries –Norway, Denmark and Sweden – clustered at the bottom of the table. Although they, too, have suffered some decline in turnout in recent decades, it has been less pronounced, generally later in its onset and from a higher initial level. As a consequence, the Nordic countries enjoy some of the highest – and most stable – levels of turnout amongst advanced liberal democracies. We might well ask ourselves what these archetypally social democratic regimes are doing right. A clue is perhaps contained in the marked contrast between their experience and that of the rather more market-oriented regimes of the Anglophone world – Canada, New Zealand, the US, the UK and Ireland. This group of so-called liberal market economies (see Hall and Soskice 2001) is characterized by a low and com-paratively early peak in levels of turnout (their average maximum is 78.8 per cent in 1957), amongst the highest levels of decline in turnout (with the exception of Ireland, they are all in the top half of the table), and, as a con-sequence, some of the lowest current levels of electoral participation (with an average minimum of 59.6 per cent in 2000). Though the evidence of figure 1.1 is hardly decisive in adjudicating such a proposition, it might well be that the contrasting political cultures characteristic of liberal and social democratic regimes has something to do with it. The greater willingness, for instance, to see politics as an effective means of delivering public goods in a social democratic polity might plausibly be reflected in higher levels of political engagement – especially when contrasted to liberalism's charac-teristic cynicism about the motivations of political actors. Yet, for now, this is little more than an untested proposition, though one to which we will return.

Thus far we have looked at trends in electoral participation exclusively in aggregate terms. Yet a significant body of literature now exists that dissects this general picture, thereby sharpening our analytical purchase on the factors driving falling electoral turnout. Two issues emerge from this literature. The first relates to the role of demographic factors in declining electoral participation, the second to the uneven nature of electoral participation and to the significance in this of a range of socio-economic and educational factors.

Demographic factors

The demographic picture is in fact very clear, and highly conserved between cases. It can be summarized in two simple and widely noted trends.

1 Groups (or 'cohorts') of potential voters eligible to vote for the first time at a particular election display a remarkable consistency in their patterns of electoral participation at subsequent elections – as if a potential voter's very first decision whether to vote or not exerted a powerful influence on each subsequent decision.
2 Levels of electoral participation amongst successive cohorts of first-time voters tend to fall from one election to the next, with each successive cohort carrying that lower propensity to vote forward into subsequent elections.

Put slightly differently, one of the very best predictors of a potential voter's propensity to vote at the next election is whether or not she decided to vote when first eligible to do so. And the longer ago that was, the more likely she was to have decided to cast a vote then, and the more likely she is to cast a vote when next given the opportunity to do so. Both of these important findings are displayed for the British case in figure 1.2.

This at first rather complex-looking graph, compiled from data assembled by Mark Franklin (2004), shows the level of turnout for each British general election between 1964 and 1997. Turnout levels are shown for each age cohort and for each election. Each voter is placed in an age cohort corresponding to the election at which he or she was first eligible to vote.

The graph suggests a strong and positive correlation between the number of elections for which voters have been registered to vote and their levels of electoral participation – a finding reinforced by Franklin's analysis of the five other countries for which data are available (2004: 71–4). In the 1997 British general election, for instance, nearly nine out of ten of those

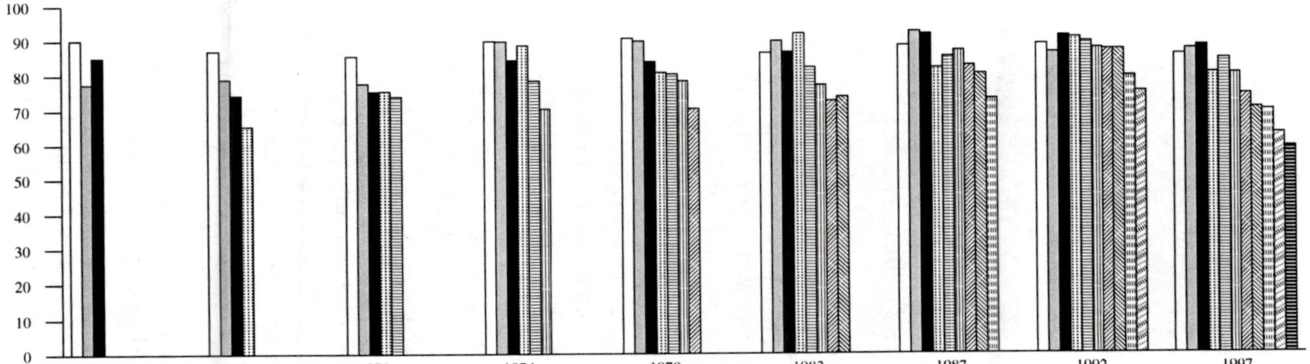

Figure 1.2 Average British voter turnout by age cohort and year, 1964–97
Source: Compiled from Franklin 2004: 69, table 3.1, with permission of the author and Cambridge University Press

	1964	1966	1970	1974	1979	1983	1987	1992	1997
Pre-1955	90.1	87	85.5	89.8	90.6	86.4	88.5	88.9	86
1959 cohort	77.4	78.8	77.6	89.7	89.8	89.8	92.5	86.5	87.6
1964 cohort	85.1	74.2	75.3	84.3	83.9	86.6	91.8	91.3	88.6
1966 cohort		65.5	75.4	88.6	80.8	91.9	82	90.8	80.7
1970 cohort			73.9	78.4	80.3	82.2	85.3	89.6	84.8
1974 cohort				70.3	78.3	77.1	87.1	87.8	80.5
1979 cohort					70.3	72.5	82.7	87.4	74.5
1983 cohort						73.7	80.3	87.4	70.6
1987 cohort							73.2	79.7	70
1992 cohort								75.3	63.2
1997 cohort									59.4

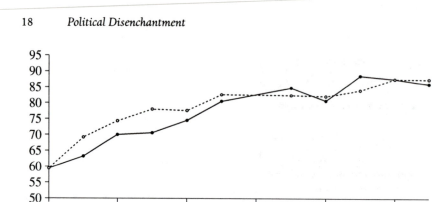

Figure 1.3 Electoral participation and duration of voter eligibility, UK 1997. For voters eligible to vote prior to 1964, average turnout between 1964 and 1997 is given instead of average lifetime turnout; average lifetime turnout here refers to average turnout in all elections for which the citizen was registered to vote up to and including the 1997 general election
Source: Calculated from Franklin 2004: 69, table 3.1

citizens first eligible to vote before 1964 exercised their right to vote, compared to fewer than six out of ten of those newly eligible to vote. This is shown even more clearly in figure 1.3, in which, again for the 1997 general election, turnout levels are plotted against the number of elections since the voter was first entitled to vote. A very clear positive association between levels of electoral participation and the number of electoral cycles for which the citizen has been eligible to vote is revealed.

There are, of course, two potential and rather different explanations for such a trend: (i) that as voters age, or acquire greater political experience, they become more and more likely to vote; (ii) that voting is a habit established early and that, as a consequence, voters carry with them the legacy of their very first decision whether or not to participate electorally. To help adjudicate between these contending explanations, the graph also shows, on the same axis, the propensity of voters to exercise their right to electoral participation averaged over all (national parliamentary) elections in which they were eligible to vote.

What is particularly interesting, then, about figure 1.3 is the closeness of the two plots; the figures for average lifetime turnout and for turnout in 1997 do not differ markedly for any age cohort. This indicates a quite remarkable degree of consistency in turnout levels from one election to the next for cohorts of voters first eligible to vote at the same election. On the basis of this evidence, it would seem, we should reject the first hypothesis in favour of the second. The initial decision to vote or not to vote would indeed appear highly consequential. Voting and, indeed, non-voting would appear to be habits established early that prove difficult to shake.

This is a most important finding when it comes to understanding the decline in electoral participation in advanced liberal democracies in recent decades, offering us a rather richer and more nuanced description of the phenomenon. If Franklin is right, and age cohorts acquire a propensity to vote or not to vote that proves 'sticky' over time, then the burden of accounting for declining electoral participation must fall disproportionately on explaining the disaffection of first-time voters with politics. It also suggests that we should expect to see turnout continue to decline for some time to come, since with each passing election a young cohort of citizens with a low propensity to vote effectively replaces the most elderly cohort of citizens with the greatest propensity to vote. Until the turnout level of first-time voters exceeds that of those they replace, aggregate electoral participation will continue to fall.[9] This 'generational replacement' effect also helps to account for the generally slow but cumulative nature of shifts in levels of electoral participation over time. It should perhaps lead us to be sceptical of any quick fix to the problem of declining turnout.

At the same time, however, we should be wary of the fatalism that the above analysis might be seen to imply. Identifying the sources of youth political disaffection is clearly crucial to understanding decline in electoral participation over time, but this does not mean that solutions to the problem of low electoral participation should be confined to efforts to engage the first-time voter politically, important though these clearly are. Patterns of electoral participation amongst seasoned citizens may well have proved sticky during periods in which, for the most part, turnout has received very little political attention. But this does not mean that they must necessarily continue to prove so sticky during times when turnout is identified as a problem requiring a political solution. Indeed, it would be rather perverse if the more accurate diagnosis of the problem of voter disaffection offered by this demographic perspective served only to increase its perceived intractability.

Socio-economic and educational factors

A second theme of the existing literature is the influence of socio-economic and educational factors as determinants of levels of electoral participation. Here, again, there is a fair degree of consensus. By and large, levels of educational attainment are associated positively with political participation of all kinds, including voting (Parry et al. 1992; Franklin 2002: 152; 2004: 154). Though the effect is not as strong as it once was, this remains the case despite the mounting evidence that the most educated are also the most cynical with respect to politics in general and the most critical of politicians' motivations (van Deth and Scarborough 1995; Dalton 2004: 86–91, 95; cf. Almond and Verba 1963; Stokes 1962). Important though these more recent finding are, however, they should not lead us to lose sight of the still strong correlation between educational experience / attainment, on the one hand, and formal political participation, on the other. Given this persistent relationship, and the significant increase in average levels of both educational experience and attainment in the advanced liberal democracies over recent decades, we would expect to have seen a marked increase in levels of formal political participation. That we have not merely emphasizes the extent of the contemporary disaffection and disengagement of citizens with formal politics.

The picture is very similar with respect to socio-economic factors. As is long established, the most marginalized from society are also the least likely to participate in formal politics (Pattie et al. 2004). The unemployed black urban poor remain the least likely of all to vote in US elections, for instance. They are effectively disenfranchised as a consequence – since both major political parties can essentially discount their participation. Again, though, the more recent trend is for voter cynicism to be growing most rapidly amongst sections of the population previously characterized by the highest levels of political engagement, party identification and participation. This has led some to identify the rise of a new group of often young, well-educated and affluent 'critical citizens' (Norris 1999a).

Trends in formal political participation – party membership

Voting is, of course, not the only form that political participation of a formal kind may take, though understandably perhaps, it has tended to receive the most attention from analysts, commentators and professional politicians alike. But if we are to assess accurately trends in formal political participation, it is important that we consider the numerous other forms it may take – most notably membership of political parties and attendance at political meetings. Here the empirical evidence reveals effects that are both substantial in their magnitude, certainly when compared to trends in levels of electoral participation, and just as persistent.

Figure 1.4 presents standardized data for both turnout levels and party membership for the OECD countries from the mid-1950s. The data are those of Robert D. Putnam, who has perhaps done more to draw our atten-

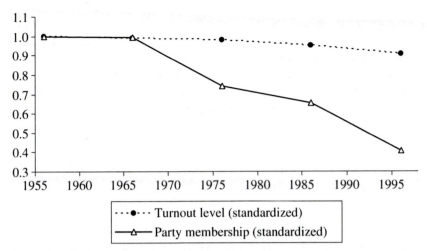

Figure 1.4 Decline in turnout and party membership, OECD countries
Source: Calculated from Putnam 2002: 405–6

tion to these trends than anyone else. His data points are constructed as rolling averages of turnout levels. They have been standardized such that all other data points are expressed as a proportion of turnout level in the first two elections of the 1950s.

A number of important observations can be made from this graph:

- Party membership has fallen precipitously throughout the OECD countries.
- It has fallen at a far greater rate than levels of electoral participation.
- Like decline in turnout, this would appear to be an accelerating trend.
- Both trends seem to exhibit a similar temporality – having their origins in the 1960s and accelerating since then in a seemingly unchecked manner.

Of course, party membership has always been something of a minority pursuit, but what is clear is that only a small and ever declining section of the population is now animated sufficiently by political competition to become party members. When the (ageing) demographics of party membership are taken into consideration, and when it is noted that according to the World Values Survey, only some 40 per cent of party members in the Anglophone democracies would claim to be activists (Scarrow 2000: 96), the picture looks bleak indeed. It is perhaps unsurprising that a number of commentators have been led to suggest the death of the political party as an effective campaigning organization altogether (e.g. Lawson and Merkl 1988). This is almost certainly premature, and something of an exaggeration (for a collection of rather more sanguine alternative views see Dalton and Wattenberg 2000). But the trends in the data are nonetheless alarming. For, when turnout decline is considered alongside these figures, we see unequivocal evidence that formal politics today is capable of consistently animating *neither* those with a moderate interest in politics to electoral participation *nor* those most engaged politically to party membership. To return to an earlier theme, politics (or at least formal politics) would seem not to be all that it was once cracked up to be. Moreover, the decline in party membership, whether it entails the death of the party as an effective campaigning organization or not, does have consequences for the ability of political parties to mobilize citizens to participate electorally. In 1964 the combined membership of the British Labour and Conservative parties stood at 3.4 million; today it stands at less than 500,000. Even on the most optimistic of estimates, that leaves Britain's two principal parties with fewer than 200,000 party activists between then. That level of activism is simply insufficient to maintain constituency campaigning in national elections in all but a limited number of target seats. Yet, as a growing body of recent evidence demonstrates, constituency campaigning is highly effective, both in raising turnout and in improving party performance (Denver et al. 2004; Whiteley and Seyd 2003). As this suggests, the rapidly diminishing capacity of political parties in most advanced liberal democracies to mount co-ordinated local campaigns may be a further mechanism contributing to ever lower electoral participation. Indeed, it may serve further to entrench a spiral of diminishing mobilization, participation and engagement at all levels.

If figures for party membership are likely to make fairly depressing reading for political elites, then the figures for a range of other indices of political participation are unlikely to lighten the mood. Table 1.2 summa-

Table 1.2 Trends in political participation in the US and the UK

	US (1974)	US (1994)	UK (1984)*	UK (2000)
Signed petition	36	26	63	42
Attended political meeting	32	18	9	6
Written to politician	16	12	30	13
Boycotted products	–	–	4	31
Contacted media	–	–	4	9
Engaged in illegal protest	–	–	1	2

* Respondents asked to itemize participation over five years; in all other surveys they were asked to do so over twelve months.
Source: Assembled from Parry et al. 1992: 44; Pattie et al. 2003b: 631; Wuthnow 2002: 74

rizes the findings of attitudinal surveys in the US and the UK in which respondents were asked to itemize their participation, indicating whether or not they had engaged in a variety of political acts in the preceding twelve-month or five-year periods.

Given the tenor of the discussion thus far, this evidence will come as no great surprise. In the US (where the data for 1974 and 1994 are directly comparable) and even for the UK (where they are not), there is clear evidence of decline in most indices of conventional political participation. It should also be noted that since these data are based on respondents' self-reporting of political participation, and since respondents have something of a tendency to over-report what they take to be positive attributes in survey responses, these figures almost certainly exaggerate actual levels of participation.[10] The key point, however, is not the levels of participation these surveys report but the downward trend in levels of formal political participation that they indicate.

Yet this is not the whole picture. For the UK data show, in addition to this now rather familiar tendency, something new and different. This is not simply a story of declining levels of political engagement and participation. Such a decline is undoubtedly under way, but it would seem to be accompanied by a simultaneous rise in other forms of political expression – notably, those which bypass conventional/formal political channels. This, it seems, may take a variety of forms, from contacting the media, rather than writing to politicians, to boycotting products and engaging in (often illegal) forms of public protest, rather than lobbying public authorities. It is perhaps indicative less of a decline in political participation than a change in its form. This, as we shall now see, is precisely the argument of those who have not restricted their analysis of contemporary trends to formal/conventional modes of political participation.

From formal to informal political participation?

Though the subject has, perhaps understandably, received far less attention from political analysts, changes in patterns of informal political participation are a crucial aspect of the contemporary reorientation of political conduct in the advanced liberal democracies. By and large, those with the most restrictive and conventional conceptions of political participation identify a strong and consistent pattern of declining political participation and engagement over time, whilst those with a more inclusive conception discern instead a change in the *mode* of political participation. These may sound like mutually incompatible descriptions of current trends, and in a sense they are. But, odd though it may seem, they are both consistent with the empirical evidence. On the face of it, the dispute would appear to be almost entirely semantic – for what counts as declining political participation in the first place depends on what political participation is taken to mean. Yet such semantic disputes are far from innocent theoretically – reflecting prior normative concerns about the nature of 'good' political participation. And this, in turn, raises the question of what politics *is* and how it should be defined. That is the subject of the next chapter, and cannot concern us further at this point. Suffice it to note for now that much is at stake in resolving the semantics of this debate, and the normative and theoretical issues which lie just below its surface.

To illustrate this, consider the highly influential thesis that (formal) political disaffection and disengagement are a product of political apathy on the part of (largely contented) citizens. Such a description is perfectly compatible with a narrow and formal definition of politics and, it might be noted, is rather convenient for political elites. For it suggests that the problem is one of demand rather than supply. As a consequence, if there is any culpability to apportion for declining levels of political participation, the lion's share must surely rest with feckless citizens rather than with those responsible for their government. This is an issue to which we will return in some detail presently. The key point for now is that if politics is understood solely in such formal terms, then evidence of declining political participation is unequivocal; it is but a short step to accounting for this in terms of mounting political apathy (see also O'Toole et al. 2003a: 350). Yet, if politics is understood in a rather more inclusive way, it becomes far more difficult to explain the exhibited decline in formal political participation in terms of voter apathy – since there is plenty of other evidence that citizens continue to behave politically whilst bypassing conventional/ formal channels of political expression. It is to that body of evidence that we now turn.

The picture that emerges of informal/extra-parliamentary political participation is by no means simple. Indeed, such political conduct is multidimensional. Yet one of the clearest trends that emerges is the development of a new repertoire of non-collective political conduct and communication centred on the individual (Pattie et al. 2004). Much of this seems to be associated with the rise of politicized consumption in a more or less conspicuous form. As the results of the UK Economic and Social Research Council's Citizen Audit show, when contrasted to Parry et al.'s earlier findings, the use of consumption to indicate political preferences has increased markedly since the mid-1980s. Only 4 per cent of survey respondents in 1984 reported that they had boycotted products in the previous five-year period (Parry et al. 1992: 44). This compares with 31 per cent in 2000 who reported that they had done so in the previous twelve months. In the same survey, 28 per cent of respondents indicated that, again during the last year, they had 'bought products for political, ethical or environmental reasons', whilst 22 per cent reported that they had 'worn or displayed a campaign badge or sticker' (Pattie et al. 2003a, 2003b). What this certainly suggests is the rise of a new individuated lifestyle politics in which ethically informed consumer choices are the key to a form of atomized yet mass political expression. As Pattie et al. note, 'well-publicised examples of companies modifying their policies, apparently in response to consumer behaviour . . . no doubt encourage this type of political engagement' (2003b: 622). Whatever inferences we might draw from this about democratic governance, it is clear that formal and conventional political channels are being bypassed altogether by such strategies. And, if Pattie et al. are correct, such strategies would appear no less effective in influencing outcomes because they have bypassed formal political channels – quite the opposite.

The examples of such outcomes that they list are interesting, however, and indicate something of the complexity of this kind of ethical consumption-based identity politics. They are 'the supermarkets' increased stocks of organic and fair-trade products, Nestlé's modification of its policy towards Ethiopian debt', and 'Shell Oil's reversal of its policy regarding the disposal of its Brent Spar oil-drilling platform' (Pattie et al. 2003b: 622). What is particularly interesting about this list is that it is only really with the first of these examples that the desired outcome could be achieved in the absence of a co-ordinated campaign. It would be wrong, then, to see this new mode of political expression as totally atomistic and individualized. Indeed, it is here that one of the distinguishing features of such new modes of political protest becomes especially significant – namely, the use of new digital technologies (notably the Internet) to facilitate the loose co-ordination of otherwise individuated protest often over considerable distances. Small numbers of activists may here play a crucial role in identifying, promoting and channelling appropriate consumer choices to maximize their symbolic and political significance. Here non-governmental organizations (both international and domestic) come to play an increasingly crucial role, acting as intermediaries between citizens whose atomized choices they seek to co-ordinate and corporations whose behaviour they seek to tame or influence.

Not all forms of alternative politics are so atomistic, however. A mounting body of recent research suggests that, far from being apathetic politically, a significant proportion of those who regard themselves as having disengaged entirely from formal politics are actively engaged in other modes of informal yet collective political conduct (Margetts 2000; O'Toole et al. 2003a). Such political actors typically feel let down or even betrayed by the formal political system, which they perceive as alienating, uninterested in the issues which motivate them to behave politically, and unresponsive. Bypassing conventional channels of political influence, they are far more prone to take matters into their own hands, contributing significantly to the exhibited recent rise in levels of direct, sometimes even illegal, political protest in most advanced liberal democracies. These protests should perhaps be seen less as an attempt to lobby public authorities for specific concessions than as an expression of political exasperation at the seeming failure of existing political institutions both domestically and internationally to deal effectively with issues such as climate change, poverty and Third World debt. Recent high-profile examples in the British context include the Poll Tax 'riots' of 1990, Greenpeace's direct action campaign against the disposal of the Brent Spar oil platform in the North Sea in 1995, protests against the export for slaughter of veal calves in 1995, the Snowdrop Appeal (following the Dunblane massacre) which led to the abolition of hand-guns in 1996, the campaign against the second runway at Manchester airport in 1997, opposition to the proposed ban on fox hunting in 1998 and 2004, protests against fuel price rises in 2000, the mass demonstrations against the Iraq War in 2003, and the protests around the G8 summit of 2005 (Maloney, W. 2006).

Recent research shows that those who have largely disengaged from conventional politics to engage in these alternative forms of political expression regard their own decision not to participate in formal politics as itself a highly political act. Their non-participation is itself a form of politics, and, as those who have drawn our attention to this mode of political expression argue, one that should be acknowledged as such (O'Toole et al. 2003a, 2003b).

Conventionally, it has simply been assumed that participation in formal politics is linked – in many accounts, causally – with other forms of civic/extra-political participation. This assumption, for instance, lies at the heart of Robert D. Putnam's highly influential 'social capital' thesis, which explains declining levels of political participation in the US by reference to declining levels of civic engagement more generally (Putnam 2000).

Table 1.3 Arenas of political participation and non-participation

	Formal politics	Informal politics
Participation	1	2
Non-participation	3	4

Arguably, such a view underpins the convenient myth that political disaffection is a product of voter apathy. It would suggest that those who inhabit arena 3 in table 1.3 are also likely to be found in arena 4. Yet, recent findings, like those reviewed above, suggest otherwise. Many, especially young, citizens who have chosen either to disengage, or never to engage in the first place, in formal politics are active in informal politics – they inhabit arenas 2 and 3 in table 1.3. Whatever they are, they are not apathetic politically.

This provides an important corrective to much of the conventional wisdom about political participation. But such findings need to be interpreted cautiously. They certainly problematize the ease with which we might identify an aggregate decline in levels of political participation, but they do not so do so by challenging the view that levels of formal political participation have fallen. Instead, they contextualize such an observation within a broader and richer understanding of contemporary patterns of political participation. We may well be right to redefine political participation to include activities beyond the formal political arena. But we cannot afford, in so doing, to forget that levels of formal political participation have declined and continue to decline. This matters. That those most disaffected and disengaged from formal politics have found alternative modes of political expression is certainly important, but it is as much a symptom of the condition we are seeking to diagnose as is declining formal participation itself.

Put slightly differently, alternative modes of political participation are neither a substitute for, nor incompatible with, formal political participation. But they are most definitely an indication that we cannot simply read disaffection and disengagement from formal politics as an index either of political apathy or of the demise of politics itself.

Democracy, legitimacy and trust in political actors

The third distinct source of evidence that needs to be considered in mapping the form and character of contemporary political disaffection and disengagement is attitudinal. Relatively high-quality survey data are now available for most advanced liberal democracies, in many cases going back several decades. These data are often assembled as part of official national election studies, and they offer an important window on citizens' attitudes towards political institutions, politicians and politics in general. Though they are not always comparable between cases, since the need to ask the same or equivalent questions in national surveys has only been recognized relatively recently, they still provide the most reliable basis from which to

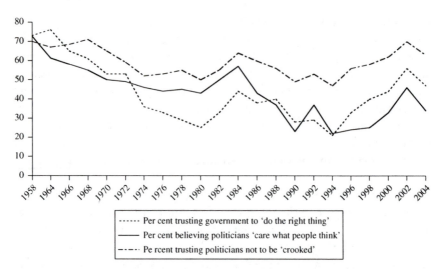

Figure 1.5 Levels of trust in politicians and government in the US, 1958–2004
Source: Compiled from American National Election Studies (University of Michigan, various years)

gauge comparatively changing attitudes towards politics, democracy and government. In particular, they allow us to assess the extent to which recent decades have seen a trend decline in levels of trust and confidence in politicians and public officials.

In keeping with the tenor of the analysis thus far presented, none of these data make very attractive reading to politicians or public officials. Figure 1.5 displays time-series data on levels of trust in politicians and government amongst American citizens of voting age. The data are drawn from consecutive American National Election Studies between 1958 and 2004, and show attitudinal changes in three separate, if clearly related, aspects of political trust. Respondents were asked to indicate how much of the time they thought 'they could trust government in Washington to do the right thing – just about all of the time, most of the time, or only some of the time'. The graph shows the proportion responding 'always' or 'most of the time'. Similarly, they were asked whether they agreed or disagreed with the statement, 'Public officials don't care much what people like me think'. The graph shows the percentage expressing disagreement with the statement. Finally, they were asked what proportion of 'the people running the government are crooked'. The graph shows the share of respondents answering 'not many' or 'hardly any'.

Each data series shows a consistent and, until the early 1980s, an uninterrupted decline. Thereafter the data fluctuate rather more, with three clear periods in which levels of trust are temporarily restored (in the early 1980s, briefly from 1990, and again between 1994 and 2002). It is notable, however, that each of these episodic recoveries in levels of political trust is followed by an equally precipitous decline. Indeed, in the first two cases, this decline takes levels of political trust to an all-time low. In 2004, despite the significant recovery in each measure of political trust to a twenty-year high following the events of September 11, only a third of US citizens believed politicians cared what they thought, an equivalent proportion believed that 'many' of their politicians were 'crooked', whilst fewer than half believed that government could be trusted to 'do the right thing' more often than not. This is hardly an edifying image of the institutions of American democracy, especially when it is noted that commercial polls do not show the same recovery in levels of political trust between 1994 and 2000 (though September 11 did bring a temporary boost in 2001–2, albeit one which has long since subsided).[11]

Given what we know about levels of formal political participation in the US, and the concern it has generated, it may well be tempting to question the broader relevance of such findings, dismissing them as another case of American exceptionalism. Alternatively, and rather more pessimistically, we might see US trends as offering advanced warning of the path down which most other advanced liberal democracies are now heading. In fact, neither reaction is appropriate, as a look at the evidence makes alarmingly clear. Sadly, few national election studies ask their respondents so directly to indicate their levels of political trust. And even those that do have not done so as consistently, in such depth, or for so long. This leaves us with only one dimension of political trust for which comparative time-series data are available, and even then, only for a handful of countries and for a limited period of time. Figure 1.6 presents the proportion of respondents in the US, France and Sweden expressing disagreement with the statement, 'Public officials don't care much what people like me think' (suitably translated).

As figure 1.6 suggests, the US is very far from being the exception. The strong and persistent downward trend in levels of political trust is clearly exhibited in all three cases. Moreover, the rate and timing of the decline and, perhaps more surprisingly, the levels of trust/distrust recorded are remarkably similar between these (very different) cases. The Swedish data are perhaps the most difficult to explain here. Sweden, like other Nordic/ Scandinavian countries, has amongst the highest and most consistent levels of formal political participation of any advanced liberal democracy. Yet 70 per cent or so of respondents in 1994 found themselves agreeing with the statement that 'Public officials don't care much what people like me think'.

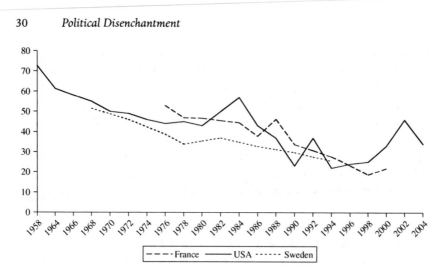

Figure 1.6 Do politicians care? Comparative attitudinal trends
Source: Compiled from National Election Studies (various years)

That this figure was recorded in a year in which close to 90 per cent of them voted in the national parliamentary election makes it all the more remarkable; indeed, it might lead one to ask why they bothered. Of course, it might well be suggested that the legitimacy of the social democratic tradition of government rests rather less than that of its liberal counterpart on the claimed responsiveness to societal opinion. Indeed, in placing far greater emphasis on the state's role in safeguarding the collective interest of society as a whole, it might even be argued that social democracy entails a willingness to tolerate a certain indifference to public opinion on the part of government.[12] That is all very well, but it remains unlikely that many of those expressing what they saw as the consistent failure of government to respond to their wishes did so approvingly.

If anything, the point works the other way around. For if the American liberal democratic system of governance cannot deliver or, more importantly, *be seen to deliver*, representativeness and responsiveness, then what can it deliver? These are, after all, its self-declared defining traits and its *raison d'être* – this is, quite simply, what it is *for*. If it can no longer deliver, or be seen to deliver, that which it values above all else, then one might imagine that its very legitimacy would be seriously in doubt. Yet that is not what the evidence shows. Whatever its exhibited failings in the minds of those it claims to represent, American citizens do not blame liberal democracy itself. And, once again, they are by no means alone in absolving the democratic system of responsibility for their lack of trust in political institutions.

This is the message of table 1.4, which shows current levels of satisfac-

Table 1.4 Satisfaction with democracy

Country	Democracy as good system of government	Democracy as best form of government
Canada	87	87
Denmark	98	99
Finland	88	90
France	89	93
Germany (West)	95	97
Great Britain	87	78
Ireland	92	93
Italy	97	94
Japan	92	92
Luxemburg	92	95
Netherlands	97	86
Sweden	97	94
United States	89	87

Source: World Values Survey (2000–2)

tion with democracy for a number of OECD member states. The data come from the most recent iteration of the World Values Survey conducted between 2000 and 2002. Respondents in each country were asked whether 'having a democratic system' was 'a very good, fairly good, fairly bad or very bad way of governing' their country. The first column of the table shows the proportion answering 'very good' or 'fairly good'. Respondents were also asked whether they 'agreed strongly, agreed, disagreed or disagreed strongly' with the statement 'Democracy may have problems, but it's still better than any other form of government'. The second column of the table shows the proportion expressing agreement or strong agreement.

What these attitudinal data show very clearly is the very considerable support for democracy, both as an abstract ideal and as the most appropriate system of government in the countries in which each set of respondents reside. Sadly, there is little by way of good time-series data available on trends over time in levels of satisfaction with democracy. Yet, what limited evidence there is has generally been taken to indicate that, if anything, support for democracy has increased in recent years. Russell J. Dalton summarizes the consensus well when he writes, 'even though contemporary publics express decreasing confidence in democratic politicians, parties and parliaments, these sentiments have not been carried over to the democratic principles of these regimes' (2004: 47; see also Klingemann 1999; Norris 1999a). The conclusion is not unfounded, but it does not do full justice to the complexity of the issues involved, as I now hope to show.

Table 1.5 Trends in the evaluation of democracy

Country	Democracy as good system of government			Democracy as best form of government		
	1994–7	2000–2	Change	1994–7	2000–2	Change
Denmark	98	98	0	93	99	+6
Finland	–	88	–	75	90	+15
France	95	89	−6	78	93	+15
Germany (W)	96	95	−1	82	97	+15
Great Britain	93	87	−6	76	78	+2
Ireland	93	92	−1	65	93	+28
Italy	93	97	+4	74	94	+20
Japan	–	92	–	88	92	+4
Luxemburg	98	92	−6	83	95	+12
Netherlands	98	87	−1	85	86	+1
Sweden	–	97	–	93	94	+1
United States	–	89	–	88	87	−1
Average (N)	95.5 (8)	92.7 (12)	−2.1 (8)	81.6 (12)	91.4 (12)	+9.8 (12)

Sources: Calculated from World Values Survey (1994–7, 2000–2);
European Values Survey (1999)

Table 1.5 compares levels of support for democracy, both as an ideal and as a practical system of government, in consecutive World Values Surveys (the only two to ask comparable questions). The table shows the proportion of respondents in 1994–7 and 2000–2 regarding democracy as a good system of government; a third column shows the change in response between these two surveys. Similarly, it shows the proportion of respondents in 1994–7 and 2000–2 identifying democracy as the best system of government; again, a third column shows the change in response between the two surveys. On the face of it, this would appear to show a significant strengthening in support for democracy as the *best* available form of government, yet a certain waning in support for the abstract ideal of democracy as an innately *good* system of government. This may sound somewhat contradictory – how, after all, can democracy be the best system of government if it is not regarded as a good system of government? Yet this seeming paradox is perhaps not as difficult to explain as might at first appear. Indeed, it may well reveal something very interesting about contemporary attitudes towards democracy.

To start with, however, it is important to note that the interpretation of these data is made rather more difficult by subtle changes in the wording of the questions posed to respondents in the 1994–7 and 2000–2 surveys. In the earlier survey respondents were asked whether 'in principle' they were 'for or against the idea of democracy'; in the later survey they were asked whether democracy was a good or bad system of government. Similarly, in the earlier survey respondents were asked to pick between one of three options – (1) 'Democracy is the best form of government, whatever the circumstances may be'; (2) 'In certain cases a dictatorship can be positive'; and (3) 'It doesn't make any difference whether we have a democracy or a dictatorship' – whereas in the later survey they were asked merely to agree or disagree with the statement that whatever its problems, democracy is better than any other form of government. Whilst it would be remarkable if these changes in the construction of the survey did not affect respondents' answers, it seems unlikely that they can account fully for the significant changes in the evaluation of democracy between the two surveys. That is presumably also the view taken by Dalton, who uses precisely the same data to draw the conclusion cited above. Indeed, what is perhaps remarkable is that more than a quarter of respondents in Britain, Italy, Ireland and Finland in the earlier survey thought either that dictatorship could be preferable to democracy or that there was little to choose between them.

The crucial point, however, is that if the differences summarized in figure 1.5 cannot simply be dismissed as methodological artefacts, then they would seem to suggest a rather different interpretation to that placed upon them by Dalton. For what they appear to show is that citizens may well regard democracy as the best available system of government – indeed, they may well do so in increasing numbers – but that they do so at a time when they are increasingly pessimistic about what it can deliver. What the evidence would suggest is a rising tide of cynicism and fatalism about the capacity of even the best – democratic – system of government to provide good outcomes. It is certainly true that, as Hans-Dieter Klingemann notes, 'persons dissatisfied with the current performance of the regime . . . do not necessarily constitute a reservoir of anti-democratic sentiment' (1999: 43). But this is arguably because they perceive no alternative, and are simply resigned to a form of government they no longer associate with the satisfaction of their most basic political desires.

Another rich vein of attitudinal evidence comes in the form of public opinion poll data. Particularly interesting here are polls which seek to gauge comparatively the public's perception of a variety of key professions and institutions. Data such as these allow us to assess the extent to which perceptions of politicians are broadly representative of attitudes towards citizens in general and the extent to which such perceptions are shifting over time. Table 1.6 presents the latest snapshot picture (from 2004) of levels of trust in political and other institutions in the US and the European Union.

Table 1.6 Trust in public institutions in the US and the EU, 2004

	US	EU (25)	UK	France	Germany
Political parties	−69	−63	−68	−66	−70
National government	−28	−35	−50	−34	−45
Congress/parliament	−34	−25	−36	−18	−31
United Nations	−14	+15	+12	+2	+7
Legal system	−11	−2	−14	−9	−20
Police	+44	+28	+20	+14	+55
Military	+40	+37	+47	+25	+36
Church	+14	−3	−8	−19	−11
Trade unions	−32	−16	−8	−19	−30
Large corporations	−58	−34	−45	−32	−45
Voluntary sector	+37	+31	+43	+44	+19
Press	−40	+1	−53	−24	−5

Sources: Calculated from Harris Poll (2004); Eurobarometer (2004)

Respondents (more than 27,000 in total) were asked to indicate whether they tended to trust or not to trust a range of public institutions. The table shows net levels of trust – the proportion of respondents indicating a tendency to trust minus those indicating a tendency not to trust – for each type of institution.

Such data offer a fascinating glimpse into the relative standing of various public institutions in the US and the EU. They show, as one might expect, a very wide variation in levels of trust between different public institutions – political parties being almost universally distrusted, whilst the police are almost universally trusted. With a few interesting exceptions, they also show that variations between institutions are rather more important than variations between national publics. The police, the military and the voluntary sector receive strong net positive evaluations, and would appear to be trusted by a significant proportion of the public throughout the EU and the US. Evaluations of the United Nations and the press are rather more mixed. The former receives a modest endorsement in EU public opinion, but a rather more negative judgement from the US public. The evaluation of the press varies the most between countries, being trusted and distrusted in almost equal measure in the EU taken as a whole, yet attracting almost universal distrust in the US and the UK. Yet the public's greatest and most consistent contempt is left, predictably perhaps, for domestic-level political institutions, large corporations and, if to a somewhat lesser extent, trade unions and the legal system. The most consistent and the most negative evaluations are received by political parties. Those expressing distrust out-

Table 1.7 Changing UK public trust in the professions, 1983–2005

	1983	1993	1997	1999	2001	2003	2005	Change (1983–2005)
Doctors	+68	+73	+76	+84	+82	+85	+85	+17*
Teachers	+65	+75	+72	+82	+76	+79	+80	+15
Judges	+59	+47	+53	+61	+63	+53	+60	−1
Clergy/priests	+74	+67	+57	+66	+63	+51	+55	−19*
Scientists	−	−	+41	+36	+43	+43	+52	+11*†
Police	+29	+37	+31	+30	+36	+38	+26	−3
Ordinary people	+30	+43	+28	+32	+18	+21	+25	−5
Civil servants	−38	−13	−14	+6	−2	+5	+1	+39*
Trade union officials	−53	−22	−29	−8	−7	−20	−9	+44*
Business leaders	−40	−25	−31	−32	−34	−32	−39	+1
Government ministers	−58	−70	−68	−47	−53	−53	−51	+7
Politicians, generally	−57	−65	−63	−49	−57	−57	−51	+3
Journalists	−54	−74	−61	−64	−57	−57	−51	+3

* Significant at the 0.05 level, † Change 1997–2005.
Source: Calculated from BMA/MORI, various years

number those expressing trust for political parties by a staggering ten to one in the US and a scarcely less appalling six to one in the EU as a whole. The figures for national governments and parliaments are somewhat better, though even here the equivalent ratios for the former range from four to one in the UK to two to one in the US. Once again, a very depressing picture presents itself of levels of trust and confidence in political institutions in the supposed cradle of democracy.

Given the trend decline in levels of political participation and, indeed, other indices of confidence in politicians in recent years, one might be forgiven for thinking that the widespread lack of trust in political institutions is a relatively recent phenomenon. Table 1.7, however, suggests otherwise. This shows trends in public attitudes towards the professions in the UK from 1983 to the present day. The data was assembled by the MORI polling agency in a series of surveys largely funded by the British Medical Association (BMA). As in the data previously considered, respondents were asked to indicate whether they tended to trust or not trust a range of professionals. Once again, the table shows net levels of trust (the proportion indicating trust minus that indicating distrust). Changes in such net approval ratings over time are also shown, as are indications of the statistical significance of any exhibited trend in the data.

It is not difficult to see why it is the BMA rather than the government or the British Association of Journalists that funds this series of polls. For doctors emerge as the most trusted profession in all but two of the polls conducted, being narrowly relegated to second place by clergy and priests in 1983 and by teachers in 1993. Since then, the very high levels of public confidence that they command as a profession have merely been consolidated. At the other end of the spectrum, journalists, politicians in general, and government ministers in particular continue to fight it out for the dubious honour of being the least trusted profession in the UK – in 2005 achieving a (presumably dishonourable) draw. Yet what is most interesting about these data for our present concerns is that they show no significant decline in trust for politicians in general or government ministers in particular since the early 1980s. If anything, there has been a modest recovery in levels of trust (though this is not statistically significant). This suggests either that levels of trust in politicians and government ministers have always been low or, perhaps more plausibly, that the decline in levels of trust to their present (parlous) level occurred rather earlier.

This latter proposition is rendered all the more plausible by the findings of the classic Civic Culture study conducted in 1959. This showed very high levels of pride amongst British citizens in their political institutions and practices. As its authors concluded, 'the attachment to the [political] system is a balanced one: there is general system pride as well as satisfaction with specific governmental performance' (Almond and Verba 1963: 455). The same could most definitely not be said today, nor at any point since at least the early 1980s.

That is an important point. For it suggests that although low levels of trust in politicians and political institutions may be a significant contributory factor to the decline in political participation that we have witnessed in recent years, they are by no means the only factor, nor arguably the most important. It is, after all, the period since the early 1990s that has witnessed the most precipitous decline in political participation. Yet levels of trust in politicians have been relatively static since the early 1980s.

Thus far we have concentrated largely on the substantial and ever growing body of evidence to suggest that levels of trust and confidence in politicians and political institutions are low. What we have only touched upon are the reasons for this. Sadly, there is surprisingly little attitudinal data on which we might draw in approaching this question inductively. Pollsters have mapped, often in great depth, levels of dissatisfaction with politics, but for the most part they have not probed the reasons for this to anything like the same extent. To be fair, political scientists and commentators have not been short of answers to this important question, and it is to these that we turn in the next section. But before doing so, it is import-

Table 1.8 Primary interests served by MPs

	1994 (per cent)	1996 (per cent)
Own interests	52	56
Party's interests	26	27
Constituents' interests	11	7
Country's interests	5	5
Other interests	1	1
No opinion	5	1

Sources: MORI (1994, 1996)

ant first to consider those few rare insights into the reasons for contemporary disaffection with formal politics offered in public opinion polling data.

In fact, there are but two pieces of evidence that would seem to be relevant here. Moreover, the absence of reliable comparative time-series data in each case means that we have to be extremely cautious in the inferences we might draw from this attitudinal evidence. The first source of data is a question posed by MORI in two surveys of public attitudes towards sleaze and corruption conducted in the UK in 1994 and 1996. Respondents were asked whose interests Members of Parliament (MPs), in general, put first: their own, those of the country, those of their party, or those of their constituents. The findings are summarized in table 1.8.

Whilst we should be cautious not to over-interpret the answers to one question in an opinion poll conducted over a decade ago, this is a potentially significant piece in the jigsaw. It is strongly suggestive of a thesis introduced earlier – that citizens do not trust politicians and political parties, since they project on to them instrumental motives. That 88 per cent of respondents in 1996 (and 84 per cent in 1994) should feel unable to attribute to their elected representative a primary interest in pursuing collective as distinct from sectional interests reveals a quite staggering breakdown in political trust. For presumably almost 100 per cent of MPs would profess to putting the collective interests of the country or their constituents above narrow party or self-interest. The finding also stands in marked contrast to Almond and Verba's (1963) description of British political culture as one of mutual respect and deference on the part of citizens towards those they elected. This was based on extensive research conducted in the late 1950s. Yet what is perhaps most interesting about these more recent data is not so much the proportion of respondents failing to see MPs as motivated by collective interests, as the distribution of those responses attributing more instrumental motives to MPs. That more than 50 per cent of respondents in both surveys should identify not party interest but self-interest as MPs' primary

Table 1.9 US perceptions of the interests that government serves

	1964	1974	1984	1994	2004
Few big interests	29	66	55	76	56
Benefit of all	64	24	39	19	40
Don't know	7	10	6	5	4

Source: Compiled from American National Election Studies (various years)

Table 1.10 US perceptions of wastage of taxpayers' money by government

	1964	1974	1984	1994	2004
A lot	47	74	65	70	61
Some	44	22	29	27	37
Not very much	7	1	4	2	2
Don't know	2	2	2	1	1

Source: Compiled from American National Election Studies (various years)

motivation is remarkable. Indeed, were the majority of respondents correct in their attribution of motives to MPs – and it is of course impossible to assess the accuracy of such judgements – it is difficult to see how democratic government could function at all. For, as argued earlier, politics is about the capacity to deliver collective/public goods; were politicians motivated solely by self-interest, it is difficult to see how they could do anything other than subvert that capacity.

The second piece of evidence comes from consecutive American National Election Studies. Since the mid-1960s, in some cases earlier, these have asked respondents for a variety of evaluations of government. Some of the resulting data we have already considered (see figures 1.5 and 1.6). But two further questions merit closer inspection at this point, supplementing in a way the evidence presented above. Table 1.9 shows responses, at ten-year intervals between 1964 and 2004, to the question 'Is government run for the benefit of all or for the benefit of a few big interests?'

Table 1.10 shows responses, again at ten-year intervals from 1964 to 2004, to the question 'Do people in government waste taxpayers' money?' As is often the case with opinion polls, these questions are hardly posed innocently. Indeed, they may well prompt respondents not especially enamoured of government to pick the first and most critical answer. Nonetheless, whilst we should perhaps be cautious about inferring too much from the precise distribution of answers between the options available, the trend over time cannot readily be dismissed as a methodological artefact. Some time between 1964 and 1974, a period seeing both the débâcle of the Vietnam War and the Watergate affair, the American public's perceptions of government seem to have changed decisively. Prior to that point, a significant majority of respondents saw government as for the benefit of all; after that point, a significant majority come to see government as principally for the benefit of a few large interests. Similarly, whilst it seems that the US public has always been fairly cynical or sanguine (depending on one's view) about government wastage of tax revenue, levels of concern rose significantly in the 1970s and stabilized thereafter. From this point onwards, virtually all of the US public perceive of some significant wastage of tax revenue by government, with a very significant majority seeing that wastage as substantial. They may well be right to do so, though it seems unlikely that levels of inefficiency in government increased as rapidly in the 1970s as the opinion poll data would suggest. The key point, however, is the insight into the determinants of voter dissatisfaction and distrust that such data offer us.

Taken together, the UK and US data suggest three key sources of voter dissatisfaction and distrust of politicians. These are: (1) the (perceived) tendency of political elites to subvert the collective public interest in the narrow pursuit of party or self-interest whilst proclaiming themselves disingenuously to be guardians of the former; (2) the (perceived) tendency for political elites, in pursuit of such narrow party or self-interest, to be captured by large (often corporate) interests; and (3) the (perceived) tendency of government to the inefficient use of public resources.

Accounting for political disenchantment – the demand side

Having now mapped in some detail contemporary levels of political disaffection, disenchantment and disengagement, we are rather better placed to evaluate the contending explanations of such trends offered in the existing literature. There are many. Yet, surprisingly perhaps, what most of these share is a common emphasis on what might be termed the *demand side* rather than the *supply side* of the problem. By and large, those political scientists and commentators who have sought to map and diagnose the contemporary condition of disaffection and disengagement with the political have tended to see its origins as resting not with changes in the supply of political goods so much as with changes in the responsiveness to, and desire for, such goods by their potential consumers. One might even discern a tendency to assume that the content of politics – the supply of political goods, as it were – has remained constant or can essentially be discounted, leaving the lion's share of the explanatory work to be done by demand-side factors. With respect to political participation, the suggestion would appear to be that if there is any blame to apportion for falling electoral turnout, it must lie with potential voters rather than with the purveyors of political goods.

This almost exclusive emphasis on the demand side I reject for three reasons. First, as I will seek to demonstrate in the pages that follow, the theories to which it has led are in fact quite difficult to reconcile with the empirical evidence set out in the preceding section, certainly when taken as a whole. Second, there is something of a tendency in conventional accounts to shoot the messenger without heeding the message. It is exceptionally convenient for political elites to be able to pass off voter disaffection and disengagement as a product of the moral fecklessness or simple contentedness of those citizens who failed to participate in their election. For, in so doing, they can detract attention from any failure on their part to provide something capable of animating voters to higher levels of participation. That demand-side explanations are politically expedient is, of course, not in itself a reason to reject them. Yet it does suggest that we cannot afford to provide political elites with such a convenient alibi until such time as the supply-side alternatives have been rather more exhaustively considered and dismissed. And as we shall see presently, they cannot easily be dismissed. Finally, many such demand-side explanations are dangerously circular (or tautological) in character. In effect, they often merely re-describe the phenomena to be explained by, for instance, accounting for voter turnout by appeal to voter apathy – where apathy is understood as little more than the propensity of potential voters not to vote. Labelling those who fail to participate apathetic is certainly to pass a moral judgement on their conduct, but it should not be mistaken for an explanation of that conduct.

At the risk of some inevitable simplification, the plethora of explanations of contemporary political disenchantment and disengagement can be distilled down to three core theories. Of these, the 'social capital' thesis, associated in particular with Robert D. Putnam, has proved by far the most influential amongst political analysts and, indeed, amongst those with a more professional interest in voter disaffection. Its defining statement is Putnam's best-selling work *Bowling Alone: The Collapse and Revival of American Community* (2000). It is this account of the problem of political participation that is arguably responsible for the moralizing tone of much of the popular literature on the subject. The latter tends to associate declining voter participation with a diminished sense of civic/public duty on the part of citizens. It is nonetheless important to note that Putnam's thesis is itself rather more subtle than this. The term 'political apathy', though it is often attributed to him, appears nowhere in his work.

The second core theory to account for voter disaffection and disengagement is rather more optimistic in tone. It has found considerable support amongst more empirically minded political scientists, and charts the rise of what Pippa Norris terms 'critical citizens', who are generally better informed, less deferential and more realistic in their expectations of government and politics than their parents and grandparents (Norris 1999a, 1999b; see also Klingemann 1999; Klingemann and Fuchs 1995). Though the thesis takes a variety of different forms, its advocates tend to be united in discerning nothing particularly sinister in what others would see as the rise of political apathy. Indeed, for the most part, it seems, declining political participation is simply a product of a more educated and more savvy electorate passing an appropriately critical judgement on institutions of representative government invented in the eighteenth and nineteenth centuries and now long in need of reform. Though this might appear to bring a range of supply-side variables into consideration, the explanatory emphasis continues to stress the socio-economic, cultural, educational and demographic factors which might account for the growing prevalence of critical citizens. Rather less analytical and empirical attention is lavished upon the focus of such citizens' increasingly critical concerns. It is the *disposition to be critical*, rather than the appropriateness of that critique, in other words, that is emphasized.

A third perspective also emphasizes demographic change. In a bold, original and meticulously researched study, Mark N. Franklin (2004) suggests that, taken together, the lowering of the voting age (to 18) in most advanced liberal democracies and what we know about the habit-forming nature of early decisions about voting participation, can account almost entirely for exhibited trends in turnout decline. It is tempting to dismiss this as another, albeit highly sophisticated and significant, re-description of the phenomenon of declining electoral turnout. But that won't quite do. For Franklin offers an imaginative and compelling explanation of why it is that the new electoral cohorts generated by the lowering of the voting age should be less inclined to vote than earlier cohorts of first-time voters. This is, in effect, a variant of Putnam's social capital thesis. Franklin suggests that lowering the voting age to 18 has the effect of enfranchising precisely that group within society which is the most atomized socially – the least well integrated into established social networks and, as a consequence, the least rich in social capital. As a consequence, he suggests, it is the most likely to behave in an atomistic way. Atomized voters are, in turn, less likely to vote, since, he suggests, they are less likely to perceive themselves as members of potentially winning coalitions of like-minded voters.

Each of these theses can draw support from some aspects of the empirical evidence summarized in the previous section. Yet none is easily reconciled with it all; indeed, each draws rather selectively on certain aspects of the evidential base to the exclusion of others. Consequently, before considering each thesis in turn, it is perhaps useful to remind ourselves of the stylized facts about contemporary political disaffection and disengagement. These are summarized in the list below. They provide a benchmark against which to judge the contending theories of political participation described in this section.

1 Turnout levels in established democracies have seen a near universal long-term decline since the 1960s, with some acceleration since the 1990s.
2 Turnout levels vary considerably between established democracies, being invariably highest in co-ordinated market economies and lowest in liberal market economies; there is no evidence of convergence between turnout levels.
3 Generational cohorts of voters display a remarkable consistency in their propensity to vote over time; newly enfranchised voters display a lower propensity to vote than any other age cohort.
4 Educational attainment is positively correlated with all forms of political participation, including voting, yet it is negatively correlated with deference to political authority.
5 Voter cynicism is growing, and is most prevalent amongst the young, the more educated and the affluent ('critical citizens').
6 Party membership has suffered a precipitous long-term decline in all established democracies since the 1960s, the pace of which is accelerating.
7 Formal politics is less able than ever before to mobilize the most politically engaged to political activism and the least politically engaged to electoral participation.
8 Party membership levels are so low in most established democracies as to threaten the capacity to engage in local/constituency campaigning.
9 There has been a decline in all indices of conventional political participation.
10 There has been a parallel increase in levels of unconventional political participation which bypass government, political parties and other formal channels of political expression and protest.

11 Non-voters are often the most active in such unconventional forms of political participation; such activists are likely to see their electoral non-participation as a political statement.

12 Levels of political trust in almost all established democracies have suffered a significant long-term decline that is ongoing, and in many cases accelerating.

13 High levels of support for the ideals and institutions of democracy persist, though there has been some decline in support for the idea that democracy is an innately good form of government.

14 Contempt for politicians and political institutions is high, and has been relatively stable since at least the 1980s; it is significantly higher, however, than it was in the 1950s and 1960s.

15 Attitudinal surveys in the US and the UK indicate that a majority of respondents see politicians as motivated primarily by self-interest, and government as serving a handful of corporate interests and as wasting a significant proportion of taxpayers' money.

The social capital thesis: a problem of supply or demand?

For Putnam, alarmingly low levels of electoral participation are part of a much broader societal malaise. Extrapolating from the US experience, he diagnoses in the advanced liberal democracies more generally a profound disintegration of the social bonds which previously knit society together. A society which once 'bowled together' in extensive networks of community leagues now 'bowls alone' if it can summon the energy to put down the remote control and lift its bloated carcase from the sofa. Social capital, civic engagement and respect for the obligations and duties of citizens in a democratic polity are all largely gone, casualties of the pervasive atomism that comes with the disintegration of community (1993, 1995; see also 2000, 2002).

This exceptionally bleak depiction of the contemporary condition of civic and moral decay has proved either extremely resonant or extremely persuasive. For it has rapidly established itself as the primary lens through which the *problem* of political disengagement is viewed (for, seen through this lens, that is precisely what it is – a problem). Nonetheless, there may well be something of a generational divide in the reception of Putnam's thesis. It is perhaps unremarkable that it has proved quite so attractive to the contemporary generation of political leaders and their peers, who were socialized politically in the era of heightened civic and political participation to which the thesis refers. Indeed, part of its appeal surely lies in the nostalgic reconstruction of a mythic past of pristine social cohesion and extensive civic, social and political engagement. Yet nostalgia does not necessarily make for good political analysis. In particular, we might note that levels of political participation in Putnam's privileged case, the US, have always been low in comparative terms. Indeed, as we saw in figure 1.1, minimum post-war levels of electoral turnout in the majority of advanced liberal democracies were significantly higher than the maximum attained in the US over the same period. It may well be that civic and political engagement in the US has tracked parallel trajectories of decline. Yet it is wrong to counterpose a historical state of near total participation to the present condition of societal and political decay. Furthermore, as is now well documented, there is little evidence of a decline in *civic* engagement in advanced liberal democracies other than the US. Again, it would seem, Putnam's acolytes are in danger of extrapolating too readily from the US experience. If anything, the more general trend runs in the other direction – with levels of social capital in countries as diverse as Japan, the UK, Germany and Sweden proving either stable or even increasing whilst political participation has declined (see for instance Dalton 2004: 69–71; Hall 1999, 2002; Inoguchi 2002; Offe and Fuchs 2002; Rothstein 2002).[13] The key point is that, at least as it applies to political participation, the core proposition of the social capital thesis – namely, the co-variance of social capital and political engagement – does not seem to hold beyond the US case.[14]

Though Putnam is philosophical in conceding the point (see, especially, Putnam 2002), he is less clear about the consequences of so doing for the social capital thesis more generally. What is clear, however, is that its rather shaky empirical foundations do not seem to have weakened its hold over contemporary political elites. Nor do they exhaust the problems with the social capital thesis. A number of additional points might here be noted.

First, Putnam's disposition, it would seem, is to consider the problem from the demand side – examining in detail the receptiveness of citizens to political appeals and their responsiveness to invitations to civic and political participation. This is most definitely an important part of the picture; *but it is only part of the picture*. The problem is that Putnam's demand-side emphasis is an exclusive one.[15] As a consequence, he simply fails to consider the possibility that it is not the receptiveness and responsiveness of citizens that have changed so much as the character of the appeals and invitations to participate that they receive. To extend the economic analogy, it may well be that consumers' preferences have changed rather less than the quality of the goods on offer. It is perhaps more likely to be some combination of the two. The point is, though, that Putnam's demand-side emphasis has tended to preclude a consideration of the supply side. And, as we shall see in the next section, there are a number of plausible supply-side factors which might be considered. Moreover, as we shall see even more immediately, this blindness to the supply side has proved contagious – shaping decisively the development of the literature on political participation even amongst critics of the social capital orthodoxy.

Second, much of the literature inspired by the social capital thesis is dangerously tautological in character. Presented as an explanation of declining political participation, it is in fact little more than a (partial) re-description of the phenomenon. To account for an exhibited decline in political participation by reference to a broader decline in civic virtue or respect for the duties and obligations of citizens in a democratic polity is rather like blaming the seasonal cull of turkeys on the latter's tendency to put on weight in the run-up to Christmas. As this would further suggest, it is potentially to confuse correlation and causation. For even if it could be shown definitively that levels of social capital and political trust were correlated – and, as we have seen, that may be more difficult to demonstrate than is conventionally assumed – why should we see the relationship as causal, and why should we see the lines of causation running one way rather than the other? Put slightly differently, to settle for an explanation of changing patterns in political participation in terms of variations in the level of social capital begs as many questions as it answers – most notably how we might account for the latter. And in the absence of a clear and definitive answer to this question, to what extent can we really claim to have explained patterns in political participation?

To explain changes in political participation in terms of variations in levels of social capital is, then, as much as anything else, to re-describe the phenomenon to be explained. Yet this is not a neutral or innocent re-description. For, to consider declining electoral participation as an index of declining civic virtue, for instance, is to engage in a normative judgement (in this case, a condemnation) of that conduct. It is, moreover, to attribute certain characteristics (here passivity, even apathy) to those exhibiting such conduct. This is an important point. For to appeal to the existence of such characteristics amongst non-voters is to make an empirical claim of sorts – one on which the normative judgement of their conduct rests. If non-voters are active politically, then they cannot be so easily seen as lacking in civic virtue, and if they cannot be seen as lacking in civic virtue, they may not be so deserving of condemnation for their conduct. The point is that the available empirical evidence, as discussed in the previous section, does not substantiate the assumption that non-voters are politically passive or apathetic. As is now well demonstrated, those who are the most disaffected and disengaged from formal politics are amongst the most active in alternative/extra-parliamentary political arenas. They are also extremely likely to view their electoral non-participation as an acutely political decision. They are politically aware and politically engaged; moreover, their electoral non-participation is a key facet of that political engagement (see e.g. O'Toole et al. 2003a, 2003b).

As the above paragraphs perhaps suggest, unassailable though it may well be amongst the political elites whose (short-term) interest (in displacing responsibility for declining voter participation) it serves rather well, the social capital thesis is far from unproblematic theoretically or empirically.

The 'critical citizens' thesis

Rather better supported by the empirical evidence is the 'critical citizens' thesis developed by Pippa Norris (1999a, 2002) and the related 'dissatisfied democrats' thesis associated with the work of Hans-Dieter Klingemann (1999). Though these theses take a variety of different forms, some purely analytical, others more unapologetically normative, they share a common optimism – certainly in comparison with the social capital thesis – about the sources and consequences of contemporary political disaffection.

At their most normative, proponents of such views detect in contemporary disaffection and disengagement with formal politics a welcome antidote to what are seen as the worrying levels of deference to political authority exhibited throughout much of the post-war period (e.g. Citrin 1974). The argument has an unmistakably North American ring to it; indeed, it would seem very much in keeping with the Madisonian and Jeffersonian tradition of the US Constitution. It goes something like this. Animated, as we must presume them to be, by ulterior and self-interested motives, we cannot afford to trust politicians too much. Thus, in so far as the naïve idealism of the post-war period has been replaced by a rather more sanguine, realistic and cynical political culture, this is a tendency that we should welcome. It is, just as much as institutional/constitutional checks and balances, a guarantor of our political freedoms.

Yet it is in its rather more dispassionate and empirical incarnations that the thesis has proved most influential. In the work of Pippa Norris, in particular, it provides a persuasively argued alternative to the social capital thesis drawing on similar sources of data. The thesis acknowledges that democratic polities draw legitimacy from political participation and that, as a consequence, there are levels of participation below which it is dangerous to fall. Yet, beyond this, it does not regard participation as a necessary good in itself. Indeed, reassured by attitudinal data which seem to suggest continued confidence, if not in the political system itself, then in the democratic values on which it is predicated, it discerns in contemporary trends the growth of a healthy critical orientation amongst citizens towards the political goods they are offered. Such critical citizens are more difficult to please than their parents' or grandparents' generations, and are more ready to display that dissatisfaction, through either electoral non-participation or alternative channels of political protest. They are found in the greatest concentration in younger cohorts of voters, and tend to be better educated and better informed politically. Finally, they pose an additional challenge to political parties, in that their political preferences are more nuanced, more differentiated, more ephemeral and correspondingly more difficult to satisfy. They are, moreover, increasingly *post-material* in their political values and orientations, motivated more by 'quality of life' concerns and individual freedoms than by traditional *materialist* concerns such as financial well-being and economic security (Inglehart 1990, 1997, 1999; Dalton 2000, 2004: 97–110).

This is clearly a very different picture of the contemporary condition of political disaffection and disengagement from that offered by Putnam and his followers. Indeed, it is one that, at times, challenges the very description of the present in terms of disaffection and disengagement (see, most notably, Norris 2002). It is supported by a considerable body of corroborating evidence; indeed, this is hardly surprising, since, in contrast to Putnam's rather more deductive approach, it emerges inductively from an analysis of such evidence. Yet it is arguably no less problematic for this. Again, a number of points might be made.

First, this is once again a largely demand-side perspective. Understandably perhaps, given its behaviouralist methodology (its preference for the inductive analysis of quantitative data), it is also one which tends to focus narrowly on those variables that are readily quantified. As a consequence, it too fails to consider the many plausible supply-side factors which might account for the greater propensity of citizens to express themselves critically. This is nowhere clearer than in its treatment of post-materialism. For, rather than trace the origins of post-material values and the role of politics itself in establishing or reinforcing such trends, authors from this perspective content themselves with mapping such values and calculating their statistical correlates. Having established, in so doing, the complexity of the post-material value set, they then infer the increased difficulty that political parties are likely to face in galvanizing support for themselves. The result is, in effect, to excuse political parties for their failure to find and construct resonant political appeals. No consideration is given to the nature of the political appeals to the electorate they actually present. Nor is there any acknowledgement that the proliferation of voters' preferences may reflect the prior failure of political parties to engage citizens politically, thereby shaping the very preferences they might seek to satisfy.

Second, as in the social capital thesis, there is a related tendency to tautology. To point to the rise of 'disaffected democrats' or 'critical citizens' – groups defined to a significant extent in terms of their lower propensity to vote – is hardly to explain declining voter participation. It is, at best, to re-describe the phenomenon in terms which might make it easier to explain. The same applies to the ascription of post-material values to critical citizens. Such labels may well help us to achieve a better understanding, in the form of a richer description, of the contemporary condition of voter disaffection, but they should not be mistaken for an explanation. If it can be demonstrated that rising voter disaffection and disengagement are a product of a younger, better-educated cohort of politically astute citizens with post-material values, then we now know what needs to be explained if we are to account, say, for aggregate trends in electoral participation. But being one step closer to an explanation is not the same thing as having explained the exhibited outcome.[16]

Finally, there is perhaps a certain complacency about this approach to the question of declining formal political participation and engagement. Understood as a corrective to the apocalyptic pronouncements of the death of civic community associated with the social capital thesis, this may be fair enough – though there is clearly a danger in tilting the stick too far in the opposite direction. Yet, seen less as a corrective to the social capital thesis and more as a theory in its own right, as perhaps it should be, this is a more significant point. Consider the US, for instance. As we have seen, turnout levels in Presidential elections are currently little over 50 per cent (those in all other elections far less); those who distrust political parties outnumber those who trust political parties by ten to one; 98 per cent of citizens of voting age believe that government wastes a significant proportion of taxpayers' money; more than 50 per cent believe that government serves merely a handful of large (generally corporate) interests; over 60 per cent believe that politicians do not care what people think; and over 50 per cent that government cannot generally be trusted to do the right thing. Yes, citizens may well be more critical than they once were; but should we not also consider the possibility that they may have more to be critical about? The attitudinal data in particular show unprecedented levels of contempt for politics, politicians and political institutions – and not just in the US. Surely this suggests something altogether more significant and altogether less benign than the development of a healthy dose of realism amongst a previously all too deferential electorate. Either there is something terribly wrong with contemporary politics – in which case we need a diagnosis of this affliction – or an unprecedentedly vast chasm has opened up between public perceptions and contemporary political realities – in which case we need an explanation. Either way, demand-side theses which concentrate on the changing receptiveness and responsiveness of the electorate to political appeals will not suffice.

The consequences of lowering the voting age

A third, and altogether more technical, solution to the problem of declining voter turnout is offered by Mark N. Franklin (2004). His thesis is perhaps the most compelling empirically, though, as we shall see, it is also by far the most limited, in that it concentrates solely and exclusively on declining electoral participation.

Franklin starts with the so-called rational voter paradox, about which we will have more to say in chapter 3. The paradox is relatively simply stated. If we assume, as rational choice theory does, that political subjects are instrumental actors seeking to maximize personal benefits net of the costs they incur in so doing, it is not difficult to see that it is irrational in almost all situations for them to vote. For, even if they believe themselves to have a significant stake in the outcome of an election, the probability of their vote proving decisive in determining that outcome is very close to zero. For instance, since the abolition of 'rotten boroughs' in 1867, no seat in a British general election has been decided by a single vote. As a consequence, even the cost in shoe leather in walking to the polling station is sufficient to ensure that the benefits net of cost to the voter are negative.

Put in algebraic terms, a rational voter will vote if her stake in the outcome of the election multiplied by the probability of her vote proving decisive (ρ) is greater than the costs she incurs in voting (C_{voting}). Her stake in the outcome of a two-party contest is equal to the anticipated utility she will receive if her chosen party wins (U_{chosen}) minus that if the other party wins (U_{other}). In other words, she will vote if, and only if, the following condition pertains:

$$[U_{chosen} - U_{other}]\, \rho > C_{voting}$$

But since we know that ρ and hence the term ($[U_{chosen} - U_{other}]\, \rho$), both approximate to zero, C_{voting} will always be larger than ($[U_{chosen} - U_{other}]\, \rho$). Our voter will stay at home (Riker and Ordeshook 1968; Ordeshook 1996). Of course, if all voters did as the model predicted, there would be no paradox. The paradox is that, however more inclined potential voters may now be to stay at home, a significant proportion of them (in many cases the majority) do not do as the model would predict.

The rational voter paradox has plagued rational choice theory for decades, prompting a series of often highly imaginative, if ultimately unconvincing, solutions (for useful reviews of the literature, see Dowding 2005; Geys 2006). Moreover, as turnout has declined, so interest in the paradox has grown. Indeed, it is presumably the somewhat closer correspondence between the predictions of the rational voter model and exhibited electoral trends that has led Franklin to revisit the question once more. His solution is in fact compelling, but arguably it violates the core tenets of rational choice itself.

Franklin suggests that the problem with the rational voter model is that it looks at the tendency or otherwise of political subjects to vote in narrowly individualistic terms. As he explains, the paradox arises from misperceiving 'the potential voter as an individual divorced from any social context that would give her vote meaning other than its unitary contribution to the pool of votes needed to elect a party or candidate'. If, instead, we perceive individuals as members of potentially winning coalitions of like-minded voters,[17] then the circumstances under which it may be rational for them to vote are greatly increased. Indeed, as Franklin continues, 'for the member of a potentially winning coalition who believes that her coalition could win if every member voted, uncertainty about the true balance of political forces leaves her with no excuse for not voting' (2004: 202). This is an elegant solution to the problem, but it is true only to the extent that the collective rationality of the group as a whole replaces individual rationality as the primary motivation for electoral participation or non-participation. It is certainly rational, from the vantage point of the potentially winning coalition, for each and every member of that group to vote. Yet that hardly guarantees such an outcome. Indeed, such a scenario is instantly recognizable by a rational choice theorist as a classic collective action problem. For it remains the case that individuals within the group can free-ride on the actions of others. From the vantage point of the individual, whether the coalition is successful or not depends not on her actions but on those of other members of the group. This makes an individually rational, yet collectively irrational, decision not to vote all the more likely, since (a) it is most unlikely that her non-voting will be detected, and (b) she will know that the probability that her vote will itself prove decisive is negligible. In other words, the problem is resolved only if we abandon rational choice theory's (defining) commitment to individual rationality and substitute in its place collective rationality.

Yet for present purposes, whether this is a genuine solution to the rational voter paradox, or not, is not the issue. Far more important is the theory of voter participation and non-participation to which it gives rise. Before developing such a theory, and testing it, Franklin adds one further assumption drawn from exhibited regularities in voting behaviour. The assumption is that of inertia.[18] As Franklin himself puts it, 'turnout changes only gradually because most people have adopted a "standing decision" to vote or not to vote, based on their early experiences of elections in their country' (2004: 22–3).

These assumptions together form the basis of Franklin's highly distinctive explanation for declining levels of voter turnout in recent decades. His work draws attention to a factor mentioned nowhere in the pre-existing literature – namely, the lowering of the voting age (to 18) in most established democracies. Franklin effectively divides the voting population into a succession of generational cohorts on the basis of the national parliamentary election at which they were first eligible to vote. Such generational cohorts, he suggests, will develop a propensity to electoral participation or non-participation that will last their entire political lives. It will, moreover, be shaped to a significant extent by their initial decision whether to vote or not at the election at which they first receive the mandate. That decision will, in turn, reflect the extensiveness of the social networks to which they belong at the time (their levels of social capital in Putnam's terms). For it is this that will determine the likelihood that they will conceive of themselves as members of a potentially winning coalition, with a correspondingly higher propensity to vote.

Lowering the voting age to 18 has had the effect of enfranchising, one election earlier than would otherwise have been the case, all subsequent generational cohorts. It has also had the effect, Franklin argues, of lowering the propensity of first-time voters to exercise their democratic mandate, since it has served to enfranchise that age group within society

which is the most atomized socially. It has served, in other words, to enfranchise those most likely to correspond to the assumptions, and hence also
the predictions, of the rational voter model. As a consequence, it has
reduced aggregate levels of voter turnout. Yet that immediate effect is not
as significant as its longer-term cumulative impact. For electoral participation and non-participation are inertial or habit forming. Consequently,
enfranchising voters at the point at which they have yet to acquire an extensive network of social contacts may inadvertently serve to suppress their
propensity to vote throughout their entire political lives. With each new
generational cohort to acquire the vote, the problem is compounded, until
some fifty years or so later on, the full impact of lowering the voting age on
turnout is eventually realized. As this would suggest, we are at present in
the midst of a decline in turnout anticipated to last several decades.

Franklin does not, of course, see the differential propensity of generational cohorts to vote as the only factor determining aggregate levels of electoral participation. His model contains a range of other, more ostensibly
political variables, such as the closeness of the contest between the principal parties. Yet these are invariably election-specific, and are, as a
consequence, incapable of accounting for any secular trend in levels of
turnout. The lowering of the voting age is thus the principal explanatory
variable.

Franklin's thesis is innovative, compelling and persuasive in equal
measure. It has also been rigorously tested empirically. Perhaps most
impressive of all is his ability to use the statistical model he constructs to
predict, albeit retrospectively, turnout levels to within a few percentage
points for most of the countries he considers.[19] Yet none of this makes his
attempt to explain away the problem of turnout decline in terms of the
lowering of the voting age unproblematic.

As already suggested, Franklin's remit is, quite consciously and explicitly,
a limited one. His concern is to explain – and *only* to explain – declining
voter turnout. As a consequence, he does not consider the wider condition
of political disaffection and disenchantment of which, arguably, declining
voter turnout is a symptom. That is, of course, a perfectly legitimate analytical choice on his part. But it is one with significant consequences for the
ease with which we might incorporate the findings of his research within
the broader picture of political disenchantment that we are seeking to
develop in this chapter.

For if declining electoral participation is seen as part of a wider condition
of political disaffection and disengagement, as I have argued that it should
be, then there is a danger of inferring too much from the statistical corre-

lates of one symptom alone. It would, for instance, be decidedly strange to see the lowering of the voting age to 18 as responsible in any way for the wider condition of political disaffection and disenchantment that now seems to pervade the established democracies. Indeed, it seems inherently unlikely that changes in the formal rules by which the electorate's preferences are aggregated (such as the lowering of the voting age) can account for any long-term decline in levels of political trust. Yet we know that levels of political trust display precisely such a trend. Of course, one could argue that precisely because declining voter participation can seemingly be explained without reference to political disaffection and disengagement, we should cease regarding it as a symptom of the latter condition. But that, too, is an invalid inference, since levels of political disaffection and electoral non-participation are very strongly correlated until generational cohort effects are taken into consideration. What Franklin's data do draw our attention to is the importance of youth political participation in shaping long-term aggregate trends. They reinforce the point that if we are to understand political disaffection and disengagement, we must account for the particularly low levels of formal political participation amongst the young.

This brings us to a second point. Franklin's explanation for declining voter participation rests on one undisputed fact – the lowering of the voting age to 18 in most established democracies – and three core claims: (1) the inertial character of each generational cohorts' propensity to vote; (2) the importance of social capital to initial voter participation; and (3) the comparative lack of social capital of those enfranchised by the lowering of the voting age. Of these claims, only the first is adequately defended by Franklin. The second and third are in fact core analytical assumptions on which the abstract model of voting behaviour that he constructs is predicated; yet they are never in fact tested directly. And although the model itself it both plausible and largely consistent with his empirical findings, there are grounds in the broader literature on participation to question both assumptions. First, as we have seen, with the exception of the US, there is no consistent correlation between levels of social capital and levels of political participation. The absence of such a correlation certainly doesn't refute Franklin's assumption – it may well be, for instance, that social capital does influence *initial* voter participation but not *subsequent* levels of participation.[20] But it does suggest that the burden of proof still rests with the author. More problematic still is the third assumption, on which much of the persuasive power of the thesis rests. It may well be that those newly enfranchised by the lowering of the voting age are, indeed, amongst the most atomistic within society.[21] Yet, as research on youth

political participation has made very clear, it is wrong to see this generational cohort as politically apathetic. Indeed, though the least engaged in
formal politics, they are amongst the most active in informal/extra-parlia-
mentary politics (e.g. O'Toole et al. 2003a, 2003b). This suggests either that
this generational cohort is rather richer in social capital than we have
tended to assume, but is still characterized by the lowest propensity to
vote, or that it is able to overcome its comparative lack of social capital to
engage in alternative/non-conventional political activism, but not to participate in formal politics. Either way, there is a conundrum still to be
solved.

Finally, there is a certain fatalism in Franklin's view of the determinants
of voter participation. In emphasizing the 'stickiness' of generational
cohorts' differential propensities to vote, he seems to imply that little or
nothing can be done on the supply side to raise aggregate levels of participation. Indeed, his proposed solution to the problem of declining voter participation is, in effect, a technical fix – namely, to lower the voting age to 15,
and to enlist the support of the educational system in socializing first-time
voters into the habit (or civic duty) of voting. This is certainly ingenious,
but arguably it is a rather cosmetic strategy of alleviating the systems rather
than addressing their origins. For the problem surely lies in the propensity
of those voters who do not feel themselves to be part of a potentially
winning coalition to conceive of their decision to participate electorally in
narrowly instrumental terms. Democratic political participation could, and
perhaps should, be about more than rational self-interest; and as the rational voter model demonstrates all too well, citizens (if we can call them that)
animated solely by considerations of self-interest will rationally absent
themselves from the electoral process altogether. Moreover, in concentrating on constitutional change, Franklin effectively gives up all hope for those
who are set to suffer, in his own terms, 'a lifetime of disenfranchisement'
as an unintended consequence of the previous lowering of the voting age
(2004: 213). Given his own stated view that 'there is nothing inevitable
about declining turnout' (2004: 212), this seems both unnecessarily fatalis-
tic and somewhat premature.

Bringing politics back in: towards a supply-side alternative

In the previous section we considered three influential accounts of the contemporary condition of political disaffection and disengagement. What
these perspectives share is a perhaps surprising tendency to depoliticize the

question of political participation. The social capital thesis looks at the problem of political disengagement in terms of the growing atomism of citizens and the associated diminution in their sense of civic and political obligation. The critical citizens thesis attributes a very similar set of outcomes to the increasingly questioning and post-material orientation of the voting age public towards politics. And Franklin's thesis of 'generational replacement' attributes declining electoral turnout to the enfranchisement of a particularly atomistic, and correspondingly self-interested, cohort of young potential voters. In so doing, it endorses significant elements of the social capital thesis.

Each provides, in effect, a sociological explanation for exhibited trends in political participation, highlighting the socio-economic and demographic determinants of behavioural change over time. Such sociological explanations are also *demand-side* explanations, in that the principal explanatory work that they do is in accounting for (or often simply in documenting and mapping) changes in the receptiveness of political constituents to political appeals. Virtually no consideration is given to a range of potential *supply-side factors* – changes in the content of the appeals that the parties make to potential voters, changes in the character of electoral competition, changes in the substantive content of the 'goods' that politics offers to political 'consumers', and changes in the capacity of national-level governments to deliver genuine political choice to voters.

The demand-side bias of the existing literature is very clearly demonstrated in table 1.11, in which a variety of potentially significant supply- and demand-side factors are identified. Those largely absent from the existing literature are italicized. Each of these appears on the supply-side of the balance sheet; each forms a core part of the alternative explanation for the contemporary condition of political disaffection and disengagement that I seek to develop in the chapters that follow.

So what are these potential supply-side factors?

The first is what I have termed the 'marketization' of electoral competition in the advanced liberal democracies. This is by no means a new phenomenon, or one confined to the advanced liberal democracies, though it has reached unprecedented levels in recent years in these polities. The competition between parties for votes has long been considered analogous to that between businesses for market share (see Downs 1957 for a classic exposition). But it is only recently that this has been taken to its logical conclusion – the direct deployment of marketing and advertising techniques in strategies of electoral competition and engagement (see Lees-Marshment 2001). The consequences of this are multiple, and are explored more

Table 1.11 Potential demand-side and supply-side factors responsible for declining political participation

Demand-side factors	Supply-side factors
Changing public sense of civic and political duty as levels of social capital are eroded (Putnam)	*The 'marketization' of inter-party electoral and the competition individuation of electoral appeals*
Changing public receptiveness to political appeals/the supply of political goods (Norris)	*Policy convergence between the principal parties increasing the electoral salience of more ephemeral 'brand' issues and considerations of*
Decline in the culture of political deference that emerged in the post-war years (Citrin, Inglehart)	*trust and competence*
Difficulty of accommodating electorally post-material values and greater value diversity (Inglehart, Norris)	*The internalization by political elites of public choice theoretic assumptions about the inefficiency of the public sector when compared to the market and the incapacity of politics to deliver public goods*
Changing balance of societal preferences pooled in elections due to the enfranchisement of younger, more atomistic voters (Franklin)	*The tendency towards depoliticization associated with the displacement of responsibility for policy making or implementation to independent public authorities*
	A growing awareness (*or perception*)* of the diminished capacity of national-level government in an era of complex economic interdependence to deliver public goods (Franklin, Katzenstein)
	Higher levels of financial and sexual impropriety on the part of political elites may have served to discredit politics in the public imagination (Norris)

* Although some of the existing literature does consider the potential salience of globalization as an explanatory variable, none of which I am aware looks at perceptions of globalization – amongst either political elites or the public more generally.

systematically, and in greater detail, in chapter 3. Amongst these, the most significant is the effective downgrading of electoral competition. Today it has become little more than another exercise in brand marketing, brand management and product placement, the aim of which is to mould the party cosmetically to appease what are perceived to be the preferences of the target voter. Unremarkably, perhaps, what is lost in this process is all that previously distinguished political competition from competition for market share – such as the principled advocacy and defence of consistently articulated policy platforms by political parties. As a consequence, elections are fought over an increasingly narrow range of the policy spectrum, to the extent to which they are fought over policy content at all. Moreover, to differentiate themselves electorally, parties increasingly compete on the basis of more ephemeral differences in branding and on the images of trust and competence they seek to construct for themselves. Assessments of party leaders' character traits, credibility and trustworthiness, which arguably the electorate are singularly ill-placed to judge, tend to replace those of policy substance. Finally, often facilitated by new digital technologies, individuated appeals to the electorate as atomistic consumers tend to replace strategies of mass political persuasion. The result of each process is to replicate ever more closely the assumptions of the rational voter model, reducing the stakes of the contest (the difference in the expected utility associated with the election of the principal parties) and contributing to the atomism of the voter. Parties appeal to voters as individual rational consumers; and, as the rational voter model predicts, rational consumers will rationally disengage.

Changes in the marketing of political goods to the consumer are not the only relevant changes on the supply side of the political marketplace, however. For, since the 1980s, political elites throughout the advanced liberal democracies (and beyond) have increasingly come to embrace and internalize a very distinctive set of academic and quasi-academic theories. These are associated with public choice theory, and have arguably led to something of a crisis of self-confidence amongst political elites. Public choice theory is predicated on the projection on to politicians, political elites and public officials more generally of narrowly instrumental assumptions. It shows, in effect, that if we assume politicians and public officials to be rational, calculating and self-interested, then we cannot trust them to deliver public or collective goods. Public choice theory came to prominence through its seeming ability to account for the widely identified crises of the 1970s. These it described as crises of political 'overload', in which a bloated state had simply taken on too much by sanctioning ever spiralling expectations and siphoning off an ever growing share of national output through taxation receipts in the attempt to satisfy such expectations (see for instance Crozier et al. 1975). It argued that what we needed was rather less 'politics' (for which read the instrumental self-interest of politicians and those whose sectional interests they really served) and rather less 'public sector' (for which read the inefficiencies of mass public bureaucracy protected by the vested interest of 'public servants'). It may seem rather perverse that political elites should come to embrace such assumptions about themselves. There is certainly something of the self-denying ordinance about the influence of public choice theory on contemporary public policy. But this does not make it any less influential. The widespread current tendency to 'depoliticize' public policy by displacing responsibility for policy making and/or implementation to independent public bodies, such as operationally independent central banks, is but the latest illustration of that influence. The point is that it is hardly surprising that in a context in which even politicians concede that 'politics' is something we need rather less of, public political disaffection and disengagement is rife.

A final factor is the impact – real or imagined – of globalization on public policy-making capacity and autonomy. This forms the focus of chapter 4. Once again, whether they are right to do so or not, political elites have increasingly come to accept that their ability to offer genuine choice to the electorate is significantly restricted by virtue of globalization. In an era in which flows of information, people, pollutants and, most significantly, goods, services, investment and finance are global, it is argued, domestic policy cannot afford to answer solely, or perhaps even primarily, to the wishes of the electorate. In such a context domestic policy-making autonomy and, indeed, democratic responsiveness need to be curbed such that they do not interfere with ultimately more pressing considerations – most notably, economic competitiveness. The extent to which this is an accurate representation of the contemporary domestic political landscape, indeed, the extent to which it is perceived as such, is the extent to which democratic processes at the national level matter less than they once did. As such, it is also likely to be an index of disaffection and disengagement with formal politics.

These supply-side factors provide the basis of the alternative account of political participation and non-participation that I offer in this volume. They are largely absent from the existing literature. Yet, as table 1.11 shows, that literature does not completely overlook supply-side factors and does at times acknowledge the possibility that the changing content of politics might have something to do with contemporary levels of disaffection and disengagement. Yet, however important it is to acknowledge this, a number of qualifications must be made immediately.

First, when they are considered at all, supply-side factors are invariably grafted on to predominantly demand-side accounts, as at best secondary considerations (see for instance Franklin 2004: 179–81; Newton and Norris 2000: 53–4; Norris 2000: 250; Scharpf 2000: 101–8). Second, to suggest that such factors are actively considered may be something of an exaggeration. In many cases it would be more accurate to state that they are mentioned in passing, and not actively dismissed as potentially significant. Pippa Norris, for instance, concludes her excellent analysis of the (exaggerated) impact of television viewing on civic malaise by stating: 'if leaders in high office are increasingly rocked by financial sleaze and sexual shenanigans, if the public is increasingly disillusioned with government institutions, we should look more directly at the functioning of representative democracy and stop blaming the messenger' (2000: 250). Yet these are her last words on the subject. Similarly, Mark N. Franklin notes the potential salience of globalization as a factor which might account for declining electoral turnout (2004: 179). But, pointing to its relatively late onset in the time-series data with which he is working (an assumption we will have reason to question later on), he does not pursue the suggestion empirically. Third, the most frequently cited (indeed, often the only cited) supply-side factor – the decline in domestic policy-making competence and/or autonomy in an era of globalization – is treated as a simple and unproblematic structural constraint (e.g. Franklin 2004: 179–8; Katzenstein 2000). As a consequence it, too, is depoliticized. Finally, Peter J. Katzenstein, who is the only author to examine the question in any empirical depth, dismisses the role of globalization in declining electoral participation on the grounds that small open economies (like the Nordic countries) are characterized by high levels of political trust, whilst large closed economies (like the US) are characterized by low levels of political trust (Katzenstein 2000: 136). This is a very peculiar inference to draw. At best, these data suggest that the extent of economic integration itself cannot account for a high proportion of the variance between cases in aggregate turnout levels. But who would suggest that it could? Globalization, and the perception of globalization (be it accurate or otherwise), may well have contributed to turnout decline, in small open economies and large closed economies alike. But it is unlikely to be able to explain the difference in turnout levels between such cases.

As this suggests, even the literature most sensitive to supply-side factors either (i) notes, but then fails to consider in any detail, such factors; or (ii) serves to absolve elite political actors from responsibility for such factors by attributing them to processes beyond their control; or (iii) dismisses the salience of such factors on the basis of dubious statistical inferences. Either way, supply-side factors have yet to receive adequate consideration. But before we turn to these factors directly in chapters 3 and 4, it is first important to problematize the simple demand-side/supply-side analogy we have adopted thus far.

The clear separation of demand- and supply-side factors is certainly neat; but arguably it is too neat, and perhaps serves to do a certain injustice to the existing literature on political participation. For, in a sense, a focus on the demand side is inevitable. The reason for this is simple. Ultimately it is the electorate, not those whom they elect, who must choose whether or not to participate, and whom to vote for, should they choose to participate. As a consequence, if we are to explain trends in electoral participation – or, indeed, any other form of political participation – we must consider the attitudes, perceptions and motivations of potential participants. In considering the determinants of electoral participation, this takes us immediately to the *demand* of potential voters for the political goods with which the parties seek to *supply* them. As this suggests, it is much easier to ignore the supply side than the demand side, for the former is always at one remove. The point, however, is that in seeking to account for any trend in levels of participation, we can choose to emphasize either dispositional factors in the character of the electorate or factors associated with the provision of political goods by the parties and the political system more generally. Up until this point we have labelled the former demand-side explanations, the latter supply-side explanations. But that is not, strictly speaking, accurate. For supply-side factors are only important in so far as they come to influence voters' disposition to participate or not. In other words, they are only important in so far as they influence demand. And in order to influence demand, they must be *perceived* by potential participants as salient. Moreover, it is the perception rather than the reality of the supply-side factor that is important here. Thus, the US may remain an essentially closed economy in comparative terms, but if it is perceived to have undergone a process of globalization, if globalization is perceived to have led to a loss in governmental capacity and autonomy, and if this is perceived to be electorally salient, then it may well influence a citizen's disposition to vote.

This, of course, makes the task of demonstrating empirically the existence of such supply-side factors rather more difficult than it is for their demand-side counterparts. That, in part, must surely explain the comparative silence of the existing literature on such factors. But it cannot entirely excuse such a significant oversight. It is to the task of rectifying that omission that the rest of this book is principally devoted. Before proceeding, however, it is first important to reflect on the concept of politics itself. For it has already been deployed in a variety of different ways, and it is important that we inject some clarity and precision into our usage of the term.

2

Politics, Participation and Politicization

In the previous chapter we sought to map empirically the contemporary condition of political disaffection and disengagement, contextualizing it historically and locating it in terms of the changing popular associations and connotations of the term 'politics'. In the process we appealed to a number of different conceptions and senses of politics – of what it is, where it takes place, and its distinctive traits and characteristics. We did so without seeking formally either to define the term or to impose restrictions on how it might be deployed. In a sense, we concentrated more on how the term is used practically by those engaged in (or disengaged from) activities they regard as political, focusing rather less on how the term might appropriately be used to frame or provide a focus for a political analysis of political participation. As a consequence, whilst noting in passing the potential incommensurability of alternative lay conceptions of politics and 'the political', we did not explore systematically such tensions; nor did we consider their consequences for political analysis and the analysis of political participation. That is the task to which we now turn.

In so doing it is useful to start by reflecting on the contents of the previous chapter. For in examining the variety of forms that political participation may take, we may inadvertently have drawn attention to the various respects in and by which activities might be regarded as political or non-political – at least to those who engage in such activities. This may give us clues as to those factors which discriminate or differentiate, and those which are conserved between, different conceptions of the political. In reviewing the preceding chapter, at least twelve different, if sometimes closely related, senses of the term 'politics' are appealed to. These are summarized in the following list.

1 Politics as any and all social interaction occurring within the sphere of government.
2 Politics as government, where government is understood as a formal decision-making process the outcomes of which are binding upon members of the community in question.

3 Politics as a public and formal set of processes and rituals through which the citizens of a state may participate, often at arm's length, in the process of government.

4 Politics as the noble art of preserving a community of citizens (the 'republic') through the construction, pursuit and defence of the common or public interest.

5 Politics as the art of stabilizing and insulating the power and authority of those with access to and control over public institutions through the use of the resources that they thereby possess.

6 Politics as a process of public deliberation and scrutiny of matters of collective concern or interest to a community.

7 Politics as a process for holding to account those charged with responsibility for collective decision making within the community.

8 Politics as a perverse set of influences upon society, associated with deception, duplicity and the promotion in the name of the collective good of singular or sectional interests.

9 Politics as a descriptive noun for a range of collective and public, yet informal and extra-governmental/parliamentary, activities designed to draw attention to issues of contention.

10 Politics as concerned with the distribution, exercise and consequences of power.

11 'Political' as an adjective to describe the motivations of participants and non-participants in a range of both formal and informal, public and private, processes – where such motivations are political to the extent to which they reflect or express a view as to the legitimacy of the process.

12 'Political' as an adjective to describe the motivations of participants in matters of public governance or social interaction – where such motivations are political to the extent to which they reflect or express the narrow self-interest of the participant.

This list is by no means exhaustive – as we shall see, there are a variety of significant alternative definitions of politics and the political that it does not include. Yet it certainly serves to indicate the rather disparate and, in many cases, incompatible senses in and through which activities might either be seen as political or be seen to be motivated by political considerations.

If we start by considering what divides these various conceptions, we can see that some are narrow and formal in their understanding of politics, whilst others are broad and more inclusive. The first, second and third conceptions are perhaps the most formal and institutional. They have often served to delineate a separate realm of politics, distinct from the economy and the private sphere, that has formed the traditional subject matter of political science. Here politics is synonymous with government and the formal processes of accountability and representation with which it is associated in democratic polities; political science, by extension, is the rigorous and dispassionate science of government. Towards the bottom of the list we see a range of rather broader and more inclusive conceptions. Typically, these refer not to 'politics' as a noun, but to the 'political' as an adjective, describing the motivations of actors wherever such motivations might be displayed. Such definitions take politics beyond the sphere of government into all social contexts, thereby broadening the focus of political analysis. Yet we need to be careful here. For the final sense (in which politics is synonymous with the pursuit of self-interest), though broad and inclusive in one sense, is narrow and restrictive in another. It is certainly inclusive in terms of the settings or contexts within which politics might be seen to occur, but in restricting politics to conduct driven solely by considerations of material self-interest, it may serve to exclude much of that conventionally labelled political.[1] As this suggests, it is important to differentiate between two rather different respects whereby which definitions might be seen as inclusive or exclusive. The first of these relates to the range of social spheres within which politics might be identified, the second to the prevalence of such conduct within each sphere. The final definition is inclusive in terms of the former, but exclusive in terms of the latter. Contrast this with the very first definition. Here politics is synonymous with government, and is defined simply as whatever goes on within the sphere of government. This is entirely exclusive in terms of the context in which politics occurs, yet entirely inclusive in terms of the content of politics itself. These differences are summarized in table 2.1. This shows the degree of inclusivity / exclusivity in the appeal to political content and context of the various definitions listed above.

Table 2.1 serves to draw attention to a second difference between conceptions of politics. Some identify politics as a *function*, others see it as a *process*, and still others define politics in terms of the site, locus or *arena* within which it occurs, rather than by reference to anything distinctive about it as an activity. Definitions 4 and 5 both see politics as a function – whether benevolent or malevolent. In the former the function that politics performs is that of ensuring the common or collective interest of the community; in the latter, it is that of insulating and protecting the power and authority of a governing elite. Definitions 3, 6, 7 and 9, by contrast, see politics as a more open-ended process – whether of participation in public governance, of public deliberation, of holding power to account, or of drawing attention to matters of conflict and contention. These definitions have a

Table 2.1 Politics as context, politics as conduct – narrow and inclusive definitions

		Context	
		Narrow – politics occurs only in the sphere of government	*Inclusive* – politics may occur in all social settings
Content	*Narrow* – politics as a distinct type of conduct	2, 3, 4, 5	8, 11, 12
	Inclusive – no distinctly political modes of conduct	1	6, 7, 9, 10

particular appeal, since they each see politics as dynamic and fluid, rather than static. They do not define politics in terms of the successful delivery of a particular function or outcome, but see it instead as open-ended and as subject to the vagaries of social conflict and human agency. They serve to open up a field of possibilities and, indeed, a field of inquiry, prompting such questions as the extent to which existing institutions facilitate a genuine process of public deliberation or democratic participation.

Both function and process definitions serve to define politics in terms of its content. Yet there are definitions – notably the very first in the list – which seek to define politics independently of content. Here politics is simply an arena – that of government – and issues are regarded as political only in so far as they acquire significance within that arena. Such definitions of politics are generally seen as the most traditional and restrictive (see for instance Leftwich 2004). They have the appeal of identifying unambiguously a set of political issues and a set of non-political issues, bringing some analytical precision to the frequently rather blurred distinction between the two. They have also proved extremely influential in defining a field of scientific inquiry – political science – separate from the other social sciences. Yet in recent years they have increasingly lost favour. The reason for this is relatively simple – they serve, in effect, to denote a range of issues which many protagonists see as innately political, but which have yet to register on legislative agendas. An obvious example is the feminist concern with the patriarchal character of the nuclear family. In an attempt to rectify its prior exclusion of such issues as non-political, political scientists and political analysts now tend to favour process definitions over arena definitions. The former take a variety of forms, but invariably they serve to re-politicize such issues as the domestic division of labour and the power relations inscribed in the architecture of the nuclear family.

Again, however, we need to proceed with caution. For there is a certain danger here that in our well-intentioned desire to stretch the definition of politics to include issues that are not formally recognized as such, we may define away something very important. For whether or not a particular issue or set of concerns has been incorporated into the formal political process is phenomenally significant in its own terms. Feminists will, no doubt, take little comfort from finding their concerns being elevated to the status of 'political' by political analysts if such concerns remain marginal to the agenda of government. This suggests that we need a conception of politics sufficiently broad to acknowledge, as political, struggles like those that feminists are engaged in, but at the same time sufficiently nuanced and multi-layered to be able to acknowledge the salience of the distinction between issues that are formally political and those that are not. This may be a tall order, but it is the task we set ourselves in the next section.

Towards a differentiated yet inclusive conception of politics

Before turning to this task directly, it is important that we consider what the above list of definitions share – for it is out of such common factors that we might start to build a broad and inclusive conception of politics. There are four features here to which I wish to draw particular attention: *choice*, the *capacity for agency*, (public) *deliberation*, and a *social context*.

Politics as choice

Despite their many differences in locating politics within the social sphere, in identifying its characteristic or defining features, and in attributing to it positive, neutral or pejorative connotations, each definition sees politics as occurring – and as occurring only – in situations of *choice*. This is perhaps most obvious in those definitions which either associate politics directly with decision making or which see the political as residing in the motivations which actors bring to situations of choice. Yet it is true also of definitions which conceive of politics, say, as a process of holding power to account. For it is only in so far as those exercising power face genuine choices that their conduct can be held to account. If all actors similarly placed would have done the same – if there was, as it were, no alternative – then there is no decision for which they can be made to answer. Similarly, the understanding of politics as the attempt to draw to public attention issues of contention relies on the capacity for things to be different, and hence on the importance of (political) choice. As well as the definitions listed above, this focus on choice also characterizes the broader literature on politics. Perhaps the three most influential definitions of politics that we have not yet considered are:

1. Politics as collective choice (Weale 2004).
2. Politics as the allocation of scarce resources (Lasswell 1958).
3. Politics as the public exercise of force (Nicholson 2004).

The first of these, which renders politics and collective choice interchangeable, is clearly the most explicit in placing choice at the heart of politics. Yet it is not difficult to see that the other two definitions also emphasize choice, if somewhat less directly. To define politics in terms of the distribution of assets within society is to point, in so doing, to the almost inherently conflictual nature of decisions about resource allocation, and hence to the contested character of political choice. Similarly, to associate politics with the public and authoritative deployment of force is to draw attention both to the conflict which almost invariably accompanies public decision making and to the need to manage that conflict. As John Dunn suggests, politics arises from 'collisions of human purposes'. Moreover, 'anything about which human beings have come to care is apt to become part of politics' (2002: 133). Such conflict would not arise were it not for the existence of choice and, indeed, the high (perceived) stakes, for the parties to the conflict, of that choice.

Politics as the capacity for agency

A second key feature of politics follows logically from the first. It is also present, at least implicitly, in each definition we have considered thus far. It is the capacity for agency. Whether understood as the art of government, statecraft, or deception, as participation in a set of more or less formalized rituals, as a process of deliberation, as the exercise of influence or power, or as a distinct set of (benign or malevolent) motivations, politics and the political involves actors doing things with consequences.[2]

Politics occurs, and can only occur, in situations in which actors can make a difference. In a way this is but a logical extension of associating politics with choice, yet it serves to draw attention to some potentially rather different and distinct aspects of the political. For we may be aware of our capacity to influence events without necessarily conceiving of this in terms of obvious and discrete choices presenting themselves to us. Indeed, politics is often about recognizing that we do not *yet* have the capacity to make a difference, but that if we come to act differently – perhaps by pooling our resources, perhaps by being less intransigent in the position we take up, perhaps by striving to find more persuasive arguments for our cause – we may acquire that capacity. Emphasizing agency in this way serves to bring out the strategic dimension of politics. Politics may well be intuitive or habitual, but in so far as it involves reflexive actors, it is, or has the capacity at any point to become, strategic.

Associating politics with situations in which actors possess and display the capacity for agency serves also to counterpose politics and fate (see also Gamble 2000). Fatalism and resignation are the antithesis of politics. The extent to which our destiny is determined by processes beyond our control is the extent to which it is non-political. If we allow environmental degradation to proceed to the point from which there is no return, the political moment will have gone. Similarly, the extent to which we entrust our destiny to fate is the extent to which we deny ourselves the capacity to shape outcomes. If we throw up our hands at the prospect of environmental degradation, trusting to divine or natural intervention, we merely foreclose the political prematurely. In so doing, we disavow politics and we depoliticize environmental degradation. Yet, by the same token, when we question the inevitability of processes previously left to the benign stewardship of fate, and bring them once more under human influence and design, we expand the realm of politics, engaging thereby in a process of politicization.

Of course, this may or may not be a good thing. Arguably, the environmental degradation we now face is a consequence to a significant extent of the misplaced confidence we had in the benefits of taking nature into the realm of human design and politics in the first place. That earlier politicization we may now regret. Yet that cannot be an argument for a contemporary depoliticization. Returning the environment to the realm of fate today would surely only compound our earlier sins. Politics is a realm of contingency; fate, one of inevitability and necessity. We can only hope that the trajectory of environmental change does indeed prove contingent, and that viewing the problem of environmental degradation as a political issue – belonging to the realm of contingency rather than necessity – does not prove naïvely optimistic.

Politics as deliberation

This emphasis on politics as occurring, and as only having the potential to occur, in contexts in which there is a genuine capacity for agency serves to draw attention to a third and, again, closely related aspect of the political.

Though this is certainly not emphasized in all of the definitions we have considered, it may serve to draw many of them together.[3] It is politics as deliberation. Conceiving of politics as arising in situations in which there is both choice and the capacity for agency arguably captures some necessary, but not in themselves sufficient, conditions for the existence of politics. That an issue be seen as political would seem to entail, in addition, the capacity to highlight, to focus on, and draw attention to that issue, and to dissect the choices available to those charged with or claiming authority to fashion a response. This would tend to associate politics with deliberation, public deliberation in particular.

There are, of course, a range of arenas within which deliberation may occur, from the private and informal to the public and formal. This implies that politics is an activity or a set of activities that is made what it is not by virtue of the context in which it arises. Yet that is not to suggest that context is irrelevant here. As I shall argue in the next section, whilst recognizing that all deliberation is political, it is possible to point to a variety of levels of politicization. This offers us the capacity to reconcile a common, broad and inclusive definition of politics (as deliberation in contexts of choice) with a differentiated conception of the arenas within which such deliberation might occur. This, in turn, allows us to track the politicization and depoliticization of particular issues and concerns over time, and indeed, to map political participation in a differentiated manner.

Thus far the attempt to identify defining features of politics is unlikely to have ruffled too many feathers – few commentators would, I think, dissent from the view that choice and the capacity for agency are necessary, even logical, preconditions for politics to exist. Yet, as we move from necessary to sufficient conditions, from contextual factors which make politics possible to defining traits and characteristics, our definition becomes more discriminating, and correspondingly more controversial. There are undoubtedly those for whom the notion that politics necessarily entails deliberation, or even the capacity for deliberation, is a dangerous move. Indeed, to conceive of politics in this way is, implicitly, to reject at least some of the potential definitions of politics offered above. The most obvious casualties here would be definitions 5, 8 and 12. Proponents of such definitions would no doubt protest that to define politics in terms of (public) deliberation is to present an idealized and distorted depiction of politics, is to move from the analytical to the normative, and is in fact to offer an endorsement of politics in place of a definition.

This kind of exchange takes us into some interesting and difficult terrain, which we have touched on, albeit briefly, at various stages in the development of the argument to this point. Whether politics – as deliberation or, indeed, as a means to deliver collective or public goods – is conceivable or not depends largely on our assumptions about human nature. Assume, as in definitions 5, 8 and 12, that political arenas are populated by actors who are narrowly instrumental and self-serving, and deliberation and public goods are likely to be in short supply. But soften or allow variation in such assumptions, and the potential space for public deliberation and the provision of public goods opens up again. If we assume the worst of human nature, then we are likely to be deeply cynical about politics and politicians. The language of deliberation, accountability and the delivery of public goods is likely to be dismissed as part of the duplicity that we are much more likely to discern as politics' defining characteristic.

Yet we can perhaps be too cynical for our own good. If we assume the worst of human nature, and appeal only to individuals' baser instincts, we are in danger of confining our modes of expression to those consistent with our most pessimistic of assumptions. Moreover, to define politics in terms of deliberation need not entail attributing benign or altruistic motives to the protagonists of such deliberation; nor does it prevent us from exposing the language of public scrutiny and deliberation where it would seem only to serve a legitimating function. All things being equal, deliberation is likely to be better than the absence of deliberation. To define politics in terms of deliberation may entail something of a value-judgement – and a positive one at that. But there are a great variety of forms that such deliberation may take, some more inclusive and egalitarian, some more exclusive and authoritarian, than others. To associate politics with deliberation is neither to endorse all activity which falls under that rubric, nor to commit ourselves to taking the legitimating rhetoric of formal politics at face value. It is, however, to look at matters of collective interest, concern and potential conflict in such a way as to seek to identify opportunities for public debate, reflection and deliberation. It is, in short, to look for ways in which processes of collective decision making might be held to account.

Politics as social interaction

A final, and almost certainly less contentious, feature of politics is that it is a social activity. This, at least in the sense referred to here, is entailed by all of the definitions that we have considered thus far. Yet we need to be careful. For the kind of decisions that we are accustomed to calling 'political' can, of course, be made by individuals acting alone. They often are. And I want to suggest that such decisions are not necessarily any less political as a consequence. This may at first appear somewhat paradoxical. If that is so, it is because I rely on a rather unusual conception of the social. Activities, choices and decisions are social, I argue, if they have, or are likely to have, direct or indirect consequences for others. The edict of a monarch, considered and issued in isolation, yet binding on a population is, by this token, both social and political. By contrast, the deliberations and decisions of a ship-wrecked sailor alone on a desert island are unlikely to prove social or political – that is, unless they serve to attract the attentions of her potential rescuers.

The example of the ship-wrecked sailor is perhaps a good one, and worth pursuing a little further, for it serves to indicate the various respects in and by which activities might be regarded as political. Consider her decisions about the use of environmental resources on the island. These might be judged political only in so far as (i) they have consequences for future generations (by, for instance, making the island more or less habitable for a later group of settlers); or (ii) they are taken collectively (if, as and when the sailor finds that she is not alone); or (iii) they have immediate consequences for others (fellow ship-wrecked sailors or islanders who have yet to discover her presence on their island). Decisions which are taken by her alone and affect only her are neither social nor political. In other words, actions might be deemed political only in so far as they either arise out of situations of collective choice or are likely to have collective consequences, at whatever point those consequences arise. We could extend this further, to suggest that the sailor's decisions about the use of environmental resources are also political in so far as they have, or may have, consequences for current and/or future inhabitants of the island, regardless of their species. This obviously entails stretching the concept of the social still further – some might argue, dangerously so. Although it is perfectly compatible with the conception of politics that I have thus far developed, it is not a conception I choose to defend. Yet the point is that, regardless of whether the consequences of our choices and actions for species other than our own are regarded as political, the ship-wrecked sailor on a desert island may well act politically.

Political participation and non-participation

Having set out a relatively inclusive conception of politics in the previous section, we are now in a position to consider some of its consequences for our understanding of political participation and, indeed, for the processes of politicization and depoliticization that will form the subject of much of the next section and much of the rest of this volume. Concepts such as political participation, politicization and depoliticization are, in the absence of a clear definition of politics, likely to obscure more than they illuminate. Indeed, much of the controversy that surrounds these terms in the existing literature derives simply from semantic confusion. Those with a narrow and formal understanding of politics are likely to detect in current trends a decline in *levels* of political participation, whilst those with a broader and more inclusive conception of politics are more likely to detect a change in the *form* of political participation. Both have important points to make, but in their often heated exchanges over aggregate levels of participation, there is a danger that they simply talk past one another. It is wrong to infer political apathy on the part of those who fail in increasing numbers to participate in formal politics when there is plenty of evidence that they are engaged in other activities which they regard as political. But it is no less wrong to infer from such alternative forms of participation that all in the political garden is rosy. What we need, as already noted, is a conception of politics that is both broad and inclusive and yet capable both of acknowledging, and of differentiating between, the range of social arenas within which politics can occur.

The simplest solution to this problem is to insist on a distinction between formal public/governmental political arenas on the one hand and informal private/non-governmental political arenas on the other – though we will have reason to build further on this basic schema presently. If we consider that actors may be motivated to engage politically in response to issues and concerns arising in either domain, and we recognize that either domain can provide the locus for their political engagement, we can construct a simple two-by-two table (see table 2.2.). This serves to generate a fourfold typology of political participation.

Type 1 political participation has attracted by far the greatest attention from political analysts. It is both motivated by, and oriented towards, the formal and governmental sphere. Examples of such participation include voting in local elections, national elections and referenda, membership of and more active involvement in political parties, and communication with

Table 2.2 Forms of political participation

What motivates political participation?		Response to formal/ governmental concerns	Response to non-governmental concerns
Locus of political participation	Formal/governmental	Type 1	Type 2
	Non-governmental	Type 3	Type 4

elected representatives. Common to all of these forms of participation is that they are sanctioned by the state. And they take place (largely) on its terms. It is, after all, invariably the calling of an election or the decision to hold a referendum by the incumbent administration that presents the opportunity for the electorate to vote.[4] Such forms of participation are governed by, and in part serve to define and codify, the formal relationship between the state and the citizen – in effect they constitute a contract. Indeed, understood in such contractual terms, the calling of an election presents less a discrete invitation to political participation issued by the state to each (eligible) citizen than the instantiation of a political right (the right to be so invited under such circumstances). Indeed, for many, the calling of an election is misconceived if it is viewed simply as an *invitation* to participate. It is better understood in terms of an *obligation* or *duty* on the part of the citizen towards the state. As such, the issuing to a citizen of a ballot paper may have more in common with the issuing of a tax demand than it does with the sending of a wedding invitation.[5] This is likely to be more obvious to citizens of Australia and Belgium, where voting is obligatory, electoral non-participation a misdemeanour punishable (in theory at least) with a fine. Yet the notion of voting as both a right and an obligation is by no means confined to states that impose penalties for non-compliance. Indeed, this contractual view of the relationship between the voter as citizen and the state also clearly underpins the tendency in the existing literature (both popular and academic) to attribute declining voter participation to the lack of a sense of civic duty on the part of citizens, rather than the failure of politics to animate potential participants.

Type 1 political participation also includes those forms of lobbying of government, political representatives and/or political parties which seek to influence decision making rather than agenda setting – in other words, lobbying which seeks not to add new issues to the political agenda but to persuade those lobbied to take up different positions on issues that have already been incorporated into the agenda of government. The petitioning of government either in support of, or in opposition to, proposals to extend licensing hours or to restrict smoking in public settings are obvious examples.

In an attempt to avoid public conflict over potentially contentious issues, routinized lobbying is often formalized. Here particular interests and/or associations are brought into an ongoing relationship with government through the establishment of so-called policy networks (Marsh and Rhodes 1992; Marsh 1998). Typical network participants include representatives of the business community, the voluntary sector, trade unions, and a range of public and professional bodies. This is advantageous both to network participants, who gain, as it were, privileged access to the ear of government, and to government itself, which acquires a greater capacity to anticipate, stave off and / or accommodate opposition in advance of 'going public' with legislative proposals.

Type 2 political participation is somewhat less discussed in the existing literature. Here political participants seek, in effect, to expand the realm of formal politics by mobilizing for the incorporation within the legislative agenda of issues not currently politicized in this way. In so doing, they seek to politicize formally issues which may well be of general public concern, but which are not presently subject to legislative consideration. All lobbying whose aim is agenda setting as opposed to decision making belongs in this category. Similarly, the petitioning of government by pressure groups and non-governmental organizations of all types to legislate on issues to which parliamentary time is not currently devoted is political participation of this type. A current example is the co-ordinated public campaigning and petitioning of government in a number of European countries to issue regulations setting minimal nutritional standards for school meals.

Other forms of political participation which fall into this category are public protests – or, conceivably, public outpourings of support for – formal political processes or decisions. The anti-globalization demonstrations in Seattle in 1999 are but one example (S. Gill 2000; Kaldor 2000; Scholte 2000).[6] Though clearly expressing broader concerns about the process of globalization more generally, they targeted and sought a symbolic focus in the meeting of the World Trade Organisation in Seattle. As such, though quite clearly external to the formal political context constituted by the meeting, such protests were motivated by opposition to this institutionalized political process and the politics with which it was symbolically linked by the protestors. Such protest may or may not be deemed illegal. What most definitely is illegal is political terrorism – another, however unconventional, form of political participation. This, too, falls into type 2 in so far as it is either motivated by, or targets explicitly, the institutions of the state or the formal process of government.

Types 1 and 2 participation are widely recognized as political in the existing literature. Indeed, they form the principal subject matter of mainstream political science. Yet, as table 2.2 suggests, they by no means exhaust potential forms of political participation.

Type 3 political participation is motivated invariably (if not exclusively) by opposition to, or contempt for, formal governmental processes, practices and outcomes. This leads participants to express themselves politically in non-governmental arenas either about (the state of) formal politics itself or about issues which are currently subject to formal political scrutiny and deliberation. As such, type 3 political participation is motivated by, but not oriented to, formal political institutions, and takes place within the non-governmental sphere.

Such participation may take a variety of forms, perhaps the most obvious of which is what has been termed 'political non-participation' (O'Toole et al. 2003a, 2003b). This is the self-consciously political decision not to participate in formal political processes – by choosing either not to register to vote or, having registered, choosing not to cast a vote. Provided that the potential voter does not go to the polling booth to cast an invalid vote by spoiling or failing to complete her ballot paper (a form of political participation of type 1, since it occurs in a formally political arena), this is a form of type 3 political participation – for it occurs in the non-governmental realm. Yet there is some potential for confusion here. For it is important to distinguish political non-participation from simply forgetting to vote or being so disinterested in politics as to decide not to participate. Both might, in some sense, be seen as political (in so far as they might be seen to have collective societal consequences).[7] Yet it is difficult to see a failure to remember to vote as a political *decision*. Moreover, it is surely more appropriate to see this as a form of non-participation, albeit with potential political consequences. Similarly, to be so disinterested in formal politics as to choose not to vote is surely better characterized as a non-political form of non-participation, since it is not seen as a political decision by those who take it. To complete this developing schema and for the sake of completeness, we might also identify those who participate in electoral politics (by voting) but who do so almost entirely out of habit and without consciously making a political choice. This might be labelled 'non-political participation'. These various forms of political and non-political participation and non-participation are distinguished in table 2.3.

It is, of course, an empirical question as to what proportion of non-voters fail to vote because they fail to remember to vote, what proportion are so disinterested as not to bother to vote, and what proportion choose not to vote in order to express their contempt for electoral/formal politics.[8] In the absence of clear evidence, we should resist any temptation to assume that all non-participants are apathetic or disinterested.

A variety of other forms of type 3 political participation can be identified. Many of these effectively seek to bypass formal political channels and processes whilst concerning themselves with matters which are

Table 2.3 Political and non-political participation and non-participation

Is the decision to participate or not seen as a political one?		Yes	No
Does the citizen participate?	Yes	Political participation (identification with party or candidate)	Non-political participation (habit)
	No	Political non-participation (protest)	Non-political non-participation (apathy / disinterest)

nonetheless subject to formal political scrutiny and debate. The flagrant and public violation of legislation of which one does not approve, such as the continued hunting of foxes in Britain following the passing of legislation banning such activitiy, is an example. Many forms of consumer politics also fall into this category. Examples might include boycotting pubs and restaurants which allow smoking in exasperation at the government's failure to impose a ban in all such premises, or boycotting goods from countries which violate widely accepted environmental and/or human rights standards in the absence of international sanctions or trade embargoes. Such forms of political participation take place outside of the governmental arena, yet respond to concerns which are formally recognized politically and on which there may well be active legislative or diplomatic agendas.

Yet type 3 political participation need not necessarily be so public. Though many would dismiss them as either of little interest, or as decidedly non-political, or both, private yet vocal expressions of exasperation, frustration, irritation or, indeed, approval directed at formal political processes, practices or outcomes in a social (say, domestic) setting also fall into this category. Conversations in a bar, pub, coffee shop or whilst loading the dishwasher, or expletives directed at the latest news bulletin or an interview with a politician are obvious examples. However cathartic they may be, the vocalization of such immediate gut reactions may not prove especially consequential. Yet, given the barrage of media coverage of formal political processes to which we are now exposed, it probably constitutes our most frequent and perhaps also our most intuitive mode of engagement with formal politics.

This brings us to type 4 political participation. This is largely ignored in the existing literature on the subject, even that which concerns itself with stretching conventional conceptions of political participation beyond electoral and party-political arenas. It is distinguished by being animated by concerns that are external to the sphere of government and by being oriented towards non-governmental arenas. This, for most mainstream political science, identifies it as doubly non-political. Again, it may take a variety of different forms. Indeed, it may take such a diverse array of forms that it is impossible to map it in any detail in the space of a couple of paragraphs.

Such participation includes all forms of consumer politics which respond to issues which are not (yet) politicized formally and which do so by effectively bypassing formal political processes (Bryant and Goodman 2004). Examples might include the boycotting of suppliers of powdered milk (such as Nestlé) in the developing world by many Western consumers, the co-ordinated campaign of anti-globalization protestors against McDonald's restaurants, and the ultimately successful pressure exerted by Greenpeace and international protestors on Shell Oil not to dispose of the Brent Spar drilling platform at sea. Such political participation need not always be oppositional, however. Ethical consumption and investment might be seen as more positive forms of political participation of this type, rewarding what consumers and investors regard to be good corporate practices rather than penalizing poor ones. Such activity is clearly on the increase, with the Trade Directorate of the OECD, for instance, reporting that the annual value of the world market for 'fairly traded' commodities had risen to $700 million by 2003 (Vihinen and Lee 2004: 4, cited in Maloney, R. 2006).

Type 4 political participation may also refer to attempts to draw public, if not formal political, attention to issues previously regarded as private, domestic or personal matters. The attempt publicly to expose unethical corporate practices or, indeed, the private lives of celebrities, by publicizing information previously confined to the private domain might be seen as both politicizing the conduct it seeks to expose and as a form of political participation. Similarly, attempts publicly to highlight, say, systematic gender inequalities in workplace practices or discrimination against individuals on the basis of their gender, sexual orientation, religious identification or ethnicity might be seen to fall into this category – at least in so far as their aim is to politicize such issues within the public realm but not, in the first instance at least, to seek a legislative response. Finally, the negotiation domestically of such issues as the gendered division of labour within the home might be seen as a form of political participation, as might any collective deliberation over the distribution, investment and expenditure of household resources.

Arguably this does not leave much that might not be classified as some form of political participation. And herein lies a potential problem. Is there not a risk that we have stretched the definition of politics so far as to have emptied the political/non-political distinction of any meaning, subsuming everything within the former category? Andrew Heywood states this objection as clearly as anyone when he writes: 'one danger of expanding "the political" to include all social institutions . . . is that it comes close to defining everything as politics, thus rendering the term almost meaningless' (1994: 25–6). Whilst Heywood is right to suggest a certain trade-off between the inclusiveness of a concept and its ability to discriminate analytically, there are at least three important respects in which his legitimate objection does not apply here.

First, it is simply not the case that the definition of politics that I have sought to develop in this chapter renders everything political. Indeed, if anything, the political and the non-political are more starkly contrasted than they are in more traditional/formal understandings of the distinction. For in the latter, the distinction is both arbitrary and conventional rather than analytical – politics is what politicians do, political issues are those which happen to make it on to the agenda of government. By contrast, my aim in this chapter has been to define politics in terms of its content, rather than to see it as a domain. Politics, I suggest, is the capacity for agency and deliberation in situations of genuine collective or social choice. However broad and inclusive this definition is, it is not undiscriminating. For politics does not, and cannot, arise in situations in which human purpose can exert no influence. Politics is synonymous with contingency; its antonyms are fate and necessity (see also Gamble 2000).

Second, that politics may occur in contexts not conventionally understood in such terms and may be more prevalent, as a consequence, than we often assume does not commit us to analysing all that we might now label 'political' in an exclusively political way. As I have argued elsewhere, 'to suggest that politics . . . has the potential to exist in all social locations . . . is neither to insist that we must see politics everywhere, nor that such social relations are exhausted by their description and analysis in political terms' (2002: 74). The labels 'social', 'economic', 'cultural' and 'political' are not mutually exclusive, and expanding the range of potential referents of one is not to impose limits on the relevance of the others. Indeed, an inclusive conception of the political might even be seen to entail a similarly inclusive conception of the social, the economic and the cultural. Moreover, to suggest the potential value of examining situations of social choice beyond the formal political realm in terms of the opportunities for agency and deliberation that they present is not to imply that such considerations will always prove illuminating. They may do, they may not. But limiting the scope of political analysis to formal political arenas prevents us from finding out.

Third, and perhaps most importantly, that such a diverse range of activities might be identified as forms of political conduct or participation does not imply that they have a political equivalence by virtue of that common designation. Quite simply, some arenas and modes of political expression matter more than others. That is a crucial, but separate, consideration. To suggest that the domestic negotiation of the division of labour is political is not to diminish the relative significance of more conventionally political processes; nor is it to argue that it is not important that matters of domestic political deliberation become politicized more formally. As this suggests, as well as defining politics in a broad and inclusive manner, we need to be able to differentiate very clearly between the contexts within which it may occur. Moreover, it is crucial to note the very different degrees to which such contexts are politicized publicly. That the division of labour may be politicized within the private and domestic sphere is, of course, no guarantee that it is also politicized within the public sphere, far less that it is a focus for formal political deliberation and legislative activity.

This is a crucial point. It suggests that in addition to offering a content-oriented understanding of politics, we need: (i) to differentiate between the contexts within which political processes might be seen to occur; (ii) to see such contexts or arenas for potential political deliberation as politicized publicly to differing degrees; (iii) to order, and identify a hierarchy amongst, such arenas of potential public politicization; and (iv) to consider the processes of politicization and depoliticization by which issues of contention are 'promoted' or 'relegated' from one arena to another. This is the task to which we turn in the following section.

Politicization and depoliticization

Of these four tasks, it is only really the first and second that we have already begun to tackle in any systematic way. Consistent with the first of these, the previous section sought to differentiate between formal/governmental and informal/non-governmental arenas. Yet this distinction is ultimately too crude if we are to identify, map and explore processes of politicization and depoliticization. In particular, to identify a single informal/non-governmental arena is to conflate at least two important and distinguishable domains of politicization. In what follows, then, the non-governmental sphere is further subdivided into the private sphere and the public sphere. The resulting schema is depicted in figure 2.1.

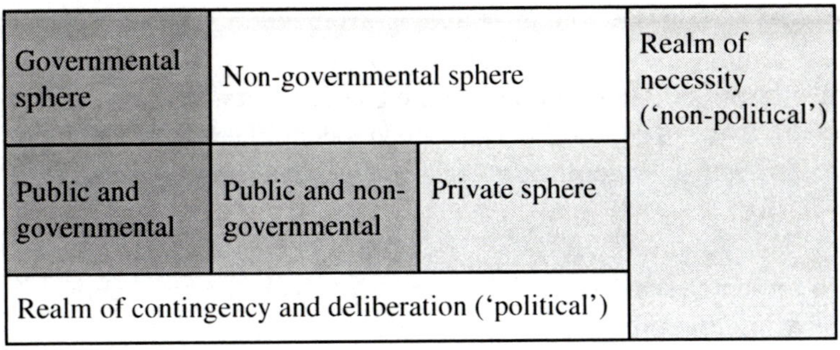

Governmental sphere	Non-governmental sphere		Realm of necessity ('non-political')
Public and governmental	Public and non-governmental	Private sphere	
Realm of contingency and deliberation ('political')			

Figure 2.1 Mapping the political realm
Note: Shaded areas indicate categories used later in the analysis

The apparent complexity of this schema reveals something of the conceptual mire into which all reflection on the semantics of the political seems almost inexorably to be drawn. Politics, conventionally understood, is invariably seen as synonymous with both government and the public sphere. Yet, what this figure shows is that two rather different conceptions of the boundaries of the political follow from viewing politics as a synonym for government and as a synonym for the public sphere. These two concepts are not coextensive, far less interchangeable.

Such confusion is avoided if we define politics more inclusively to refer to what I have termed the realm of contingency and deliberation. This distinguishes it from the realm of necessity in which, in the absence of the capacity for human agency, it is fate and nature that fight it out for supremacy. Understood in this way, the political realm is inclusive of both governmental and public spheres. Yet that still leaves us with the question of how to departmentalize the political realm. To maximize our ability to discriminate between potential spheres of the political, I differentiate between three arenas: (i) the public and governmental sphere, (ii) the public but non-governmental sphere, and (iii) the private sphere. For simplicity, I will refer to the first as the governmental sphere and the second as the private sphere. Each of these three spheres is seen to be politicized to a lesser extent that the preceding one. Consequently, issues can be politicized in one of three ways:

- *Politicization* 1: promotion from the realm of necessity to the private sphere.
- *Politicization* 2: promotion from the private to the public sphere.
- *Politicization* 3: promotion from the public to the governmental sphere.

Issues may be depoliticized in an analogous manner:

- *Depoliticization* 1: demotion from the governmental to the public sphere.
- *Depoliticization* 2: demotion from the public to the private sphere.
- *Depoliticization* 3: demotion from the private sphere to the realm of necessity.

This is presented schematically in figure 2.2, which shows the three spheres which define the political and within which deliberation may occur and,

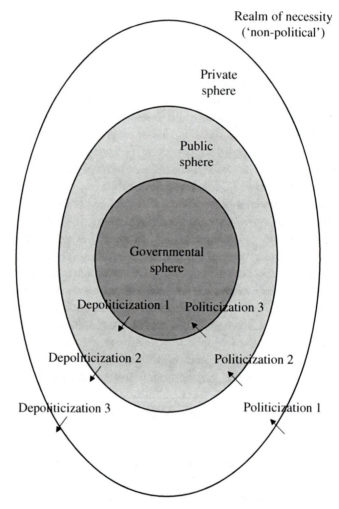

Figure 2.2 Politicization(s) and depoliticization(s)

beyond that, the realm of necessity. It also displays the three types of politicization and the three types of depoliticization that operate between them. It is important briefly to discuss each.

Politicization

It is depoliticization rather than politicization that has received the most sustained and considered attention in recent years (see for instance Buller and Flinders 2005; Burnham 2001; Pettit 2004); and it is depoliticization rather than politicization which will form much of the subject matter of the following chapters. Yet it is important that we do not overlook the concept of politicization.

In the most simple terms, issues are politicized when they become the subject of deliberation, decision making and human agency where previously they were not. Accordingly, the most basic form of politicization (type 1) is associated with the extension of the capacity for human influence and deliberation which comes with disavowing the prior assignment of an issue – or issue domain – to the realm of fate or necessity. This may, in turn, be associated with the questioning of religious taboos and of religious authority more generally,[9] the extension of the capacity for human influence arising from scientific or technical advancement, or the recognition of the impact of human agency on matters previously seen as the preserve of natural processes (such as eco-systemic and environmental change). The development of the modern state as a secular authority or, indeed, the secularization of a state which previously claimed a religious license for its authority, are thus both forms of politicization.[10] For they tend to result in the transfer of issues from the realm of fate to that of deliberation. Similarly, in increasing the capacity for human agency or interference (depending on one's perspective) in matters previously the preserve of nature, the development of modern science has proved politicizing.[11]

In addition to this initial politicization, we may refer to issues as becoming further politicized when they become subject to *public* processes of deliberation, where previously such deliberation was confined to the private sphere. This is politicization of type 2. It, too, may take a variety of different forms. The 'consciousness-raising' activities of new social movements such as feminism in drawing public attention to issues of domestic violence and discrimination provides an example. Similarly, a private business which becomes a public limited company, and in so doing takes on a far greater requirement to disclose publicly its internal affairs, has undergone a politicization of type 2. Finally, the dubious investment behaviour of a private firm exploiting sweatshop wages in the developing world becomes subject to a politicization of type 2 at precisely the point at which its behaviour is exposed publicly – whether by an undercover journalist or by a tip-off from a guilt-ridden employee.

A further and final process of politicization might be seen to promote issues from the public (but non-governmental) sphere into the arena of direct governmental deliberation. Here, either through the successful lobbying of government, the replacement of one administration by another, or the attempt by an incumbent administration to expand its political reach, issues that may already have considerable salience within broader public discourse are taken up and incorporated within formal legislative processes. Examples might include the development and passing of new legislation outlawing altogether the smacking of children (an issue not previously politicized separately from other forms of domestic violence) or the imposition of a carbon tax levy directly on businesses proportionate to emission levels. In both of these hypothetical examples, issues of considerable public concern and, indeed, contention become newly politicized, or politicized in new ways, within the sphere of government as they become part of the formal political agenda.

As examples like these suggest, despite the considerable attention now devoted to processes of depoliticization, it is not at all difficult to identify real and/or plausible examples of politicizing dynamics. Whatever the balance between them, then, politicization and depoliticization both remain ongoing processes. As such, if we discern in contemporary trends a net tendency to depoliticization, as many have, it is important not to close our eyes to the many processes of politicization that are also under way.

Depoliticization

Unremarkably, depoliticization operates in an analogous fashion to politicization – only in reverse.

The first type of depoliticization we might identify (type 1) is the effective demotion of issues previously subject to formal political scrutiny, deliberation and accountability to the public yet non-governmental sphere. This may take one of two general forms: the displacement of responsibility from governmental to public or quasi-public authorities and the offloading of areas of formal political responsibility to the market (through privatization).

The first of these is particularly interesting for the argument of this volume – and we shall return to it at greater length in the next chapter.

What distinguishes this process of depoliticization is that, often with little or no substantive change in policy content, issues previously subject to formal political deliberation and accountability are displaced to less obviously politicized arenas (Strøm, Müller and Bergman 2003). The potential advantages of this to government are considerable – in that responsibility for contentious issues can now effectively be passed to public or quasi-public bodies and to officials who can present them as purely technical matters. Politicians are thus insulated from having to answer for the consequences of policies that may continue unchanged and for which they would previously have both claimed and borne responsibility.

The immediate downside for politicians is the potential loss of policy-making capacity that displacement of responsibility may entail. Yet where, as is so often the case, responsibility is in fact displaced only to a quasi-public body such as a newly independent central bank, and where the power of appointment to such a body remains with the government, that loss of capacity is unlikely to be considerable. Where it threatens to become so, retained reserve powers may be invoked. If the governor of one's central bank, for instance, starts making decisions which provoke consternation in the Treasury or Finance Ministry, then she or he can be replaced. Any resulting re-politicization of monetary policy is likely to prove temporary. Moreover, for as long as that need does not arise, depoliticization does not interfere with governmental autonomy at all. It is presumably for precisely this reason that depoliticization of this kind is proving so politically attractive to governments across the world – especially in high-consequence areas of policy with significant distributional consequences and where a policy consensus has been established. Monetary policy is but one example.

If the displacement of responsibility to quasi-public bodies like independent central banks has become something of a contemporary fashion in the depoliticization of public policy, then the previous fashion was for a slightly different mode of depoliticization. This sought not so much to transfer responsibility for policy from one domain (the political) to another (the public), as to replace formal political governance outright with that by the market. This was not a disavowal of responsibility for policy, but a rejection of the very need for policy, and hence public deliberation, in the first place. Informed by ideas that we shall consider in some detail in the next chapter, political elites from the late 1970s in the advanced liberal democracies increasingly came to contrast the perceived inefficiency of political governance to the allocative efficiency of the market. The result was an initial wave of privatization, in which state assets were sold to the highest bidder (Feigenbaum, Henig and Hamnett 1998; Vickers and Yarrow 1988). This was followed by a more protracted process of commodification and internal marketization, in which new incentive structures resembling those of the market were constructed within public sector institutions like hospitals, schools and public bureaucracies (Hughes 2003; McLaughlin, Osborne and Ferlie 2001). In this way the boundaries of the state were decisively reconfigured. Whole areas of what was previously the public sector were formally depoliticized and reassigned to the realm of market governance, whilst others were restructured to more closely approximate market rationality.

Not all depoliticizations of type 1 are so systematic, however. As noted above, the processes of politicization and depoliticization are ongoing and dynamic – some issues join or return to the agenda of government, whilst others are dropped, displaced or simply resolved. The future of the Falkland Islands (the subject of a war between Britain and Argentina in 1983) is no longer politicized formally to anything like the extent it once was. Similarly, with the democratic election of the African National Congress (the ANC) and the ending of apartheid, the future of South Africa has been significantly depoliticized in formal international political arenas. Yet the future of other African nations – the Democratic Republic of Congo (formerly Zaire) and Zimbabwe, for instance – continues to give international cause for concern, and remain highly politicized as a consequence.

Depoliticization of type 1 is also manifest in the attempt by government to present environmental degradation as an issue of corporate or collective societal responsibility. If government chooses not to legislate directly to regulate carbon emissions, for instance, but rather 'facilitates' and 'encourages' corporations and consumers to behave in a more environmentally conscious manner, it displaces responsibility from the formal political realm to the public sphere. Indeed, if it publicizes environmentally sustainable corporate practices it may thereby simultaneously divest itself of policy responsibility whilst politicizing consumption. Depoliticization in the formal governmental arena here translates into politicization in the public realm and the marketplace. Of course, whether government can successfully divest itself of policy responsibility in this way depends largely on societal and corporate attitudes to such a strategy. Government can try all it likes to displace responsibility for issues, but its ability to control the political agenda is far from absolute. There is nothing better designed to politicize an issue than the perception that government is seeking inappropriately to wash its hands of responsibility. There is a danger that the strategy of depoliticization might itself become politicized.

A final form of depoliticization of type 1 is the transfer of responsibility for particular issues from political institutions at the national level to those operating at the trans-national level. The transfer of monetary policy autonomy from a number of European national capitals to the European Central Bank in Frankfurt in the development of a European Single Currency Area (the 'Eurozone') is perhaps the most extreme example to date (on which see Dyson 2002). Yet a similar process is at work in the development of any common regional policy – on security, competitiveness or agriculture. Yet, in one sense at least, such transfers of political responsibility are not depoliticizing in so far as the transfer occurs between institutions that are formally political. The point is, however, that the attentiveness of still essentially nationally oriented political audiences to trans-national political processes is, at best, sporadic and limited. Moreover, even were this not the case, the channels of accountability running from such trans-national institutions to national publics are both considerably longer and far less developed than they are at the national level. As a consequence, the displacement of responsibility for contentious domestic issues to trans-national bodies is, if successful, quite an effective form of depoliticization. This line of reasoning has obviously not been lost on governments themselves (Moravcsik 1998).[12]

This brings us to depoliticization of type 2. Here issues previously politicized within the public sphere but not currently the subject of formal political deliberation are displaced to the private realm – becoming matters for domestic deliberation or consumer choice. To extend an earlier example, the representation of the issue of environmental degradation in such a way that responsibility is seen to lie neither with government nor with business, but with the consumer is, if successful, a form of depoliticization of type 2. Here environmental degradation, and action to address this, becomes purely a matter of consumer choice. If consumers desire a more environmentally sustainable capitalism, it is argued, then their choices in the marketplace will reveal this. The laws of supply and demand will ensure that such preferences are reflected in the greater provision of environmentally sustainable commodities, without the need for either the interference of government or the taming of the profit motive of business with an environmental ethic.

Attitudinal changes in civil society may also serve to depoliticize issues in the public sphere. Though we have clearly yet to reach this point, one might hope that at some time in the future the sexual orientation of public officials, politicians and celebrities will no longer be seen as an issue of public interest *per se*.[13] In so far as this proves to be the case, sexual orientation will have undergone a depoliticization of type 2. By the same token, however, the careless and undifferentiated association in much of the

Western media of 'the terrorist threat', fundamentalism and the Islamic faith may have served to politicize within the public realm Islamic religious identity.

Issues of corporate governance may also be more or less politicized. In general, any reduction in levels of public disclosure of information about decision making, whether in response to legislative change or to decisions internal to the firm, involves a depoliticization of type 2. The demutualization of a building society, the change in legal status of a firm from a public limited company to a private concern, and, more specifically, any decision not to disclose agents' fees in the transfer of professional sportsmen from one club to another are all examples of this type of depoliticization. Similarly, any legislative change in liability and accountability of public companies that reduces the requirement to disclose publicly potentially sensitive information – perhaps in the name of preserving competitiveness – is a form of depoliticization.

Finally, depoliticization of type 1 is often accompanied by depoliticization of type 2. Consider the privatization of health care. This involves a transfer of responsibility for the provision of a range of services from the public to the private sector and for the co-ordination of such provision from the realm of government to that of the market. This is a depoliticization of type 1. Yet it also involves a depoliticization of type 2 in so far as the newly constituted 'consumers' of health care services must now make for themselves choices about the services they consume – decisions which were previously made for them. The locus of decision making now shifts from public sector health providers to the domestic sphere, and hence from the public sphere to the private realm.

The final, the most easily overlooked, yet, in many respects, one of the most important forms that depoliticization may take is type 3. This involves the transfer of responsibility from the realm of deliberation (the 'political' realm) to that of necessity and fate (the 'non-political' realm). Though, for simplicity, figure 2.2 presents this in terms of the displacement of issues from the private realm to the realm of necessity, issues can be displaced to the realm of necessity from any politicized sphere (the governmental, the public or the private). Depoliticization of this type involves a disavowal of the capacity for deliberation, decision making and human agency. This, too, may take a variety of different forms.

First, though extremely rare in the advanced liberal democracies, any process of de-secularization which serves to reassign to a divine authority matters which were previously the subject of human deliberation is a depoliticization of this type. Where a divine authority is invoked for the imposition or reimposition of gender inequalities, for instance, and where that authority comes to be widely accepted, issues politicized by the process of secularization are again depoliticized. Such a de-secularization has been widely and influentially associated with a fundamentalist response to a cultural globalization seen to threaten traditional (often religious) identities (see for instance Giddens 1994). It is an unusually depoliticizing form of anti-globalization.

A second depoliticization of type 3 is rather more prevalent in advanced liberal democracies. This is associated with the identification and appeal to processes, often of our own making, that we no longer have the capacity to manage or steer. In effect, it disavows and denies the very possibility of deliberation, choice and human agency, and entails a certain fatalism – be it optimistic or pessimistic. The appeal to the perceived imperatives of globalization often takes this form. Politicians, for instance, often invoke globalization as a non-negotiable external economic constraint from which follows a series of policy necessities – typically those associated with retaining or securing a competitive advantage in an interdependent world.[14] Such appeals, whether warranted or not, are depoliticizing in the sense that they effectively deny political responsibility for policy choices.

Some of the more apocalyptic pronouncements about the extent and trajectory of global environmental degradation are similarly depoliticizing. They, too, deny the possibility of politics, suggesting that the point beyond which human intervention can no longer prevent the slide to environmental catastrophe has now been reached. Such fatalism need not be pessimistic, however. Equally depoliticizing is perhaps the most optimistic view of the process of environmental degradation. This suggests either that the slide to environmental catastrophe will be averted by the planet's capacity for self-correction (the mechanism, of course, remaining unspecified) or that (again in some unspecified manner) our unbounded capacity for scientific and technological innovation will avert, presumably just in time, global environmental meltdown. Again, whether these prove to be accurate predictions or merely comforting delusions, they are deeply depoliticizing.

Not all depoliticizations of type 3 need be so profoundly consequential. The resolution of issues of broad societal or more parochially domestic concern also entails a depoliticization of this type in so far as such matters cease to be a cause for deliberation and/or collective choice. The repeal of a piece of legislation, the ending of a relationship, and the final execution of the terms of a will may each bring to an end periods of intense politicization; they are, as a consequence, depoliticizing.

Conclusions

In this chapter my aim has been to reflect in a more systematic and sustained manner on the concepts of politics and the political. I have argued, uncontroversially I think, that how we understand politics has a considerable bearing on what we mean by, and how we approach questions of, political participation, politicization and depoliticization. In so doing, I have sought to differentiate clearly between narrow and formal definitions of the political on the one hand and broad and inclusive definitions of the political on the other. The former tend to treat politics as synonymous with government, defining the political in terms of the *context* in which it occurs rather than its content. By contrast, the latter definitions are rather more varied. They tend to appeal to politics as a process and define 'the political' in terms of its *content* rather than by specifying a site (or context) in which it occurs.

I went on to show how these two rather different definitional strategies inform two rather different approaches to the question of political participation. I argued that although each brings a range of important insights, neither is unproblematic. The former's overly restrictive conception of the political leads it, as in much of the literature discussed in the first chapter, falsely to attribute apathy and disinterest to those it labels political non-participants. By contrast, the latter's conception of politics is so inclusive as to render almost all social interaction political, with the effect that worrying trends in levels of formal political participation may be overlooked.

In the section that followed I sought to outline a conception of the political prone to neither problem. This is inclusive in its conception of the political, yet both sufficiently exacting as to discriminate clearly between political and non-political processes, and sufficiently differentiated to acknowledge the diverse contexts within which participation may occur and their relative significance.

In the second half of the chapter I sought to explore the implications of this differentiated conception of the political, first for our understanding of political participation and then for the processes of politicization and depoliticization to which we turn more directly in chapters 3 and 4. I argued that a differentiated conception of political participation and non-participation, such as that set out in tables 2.2 and 2.3, focuses our attention on the contexts within which, and the processes in and through which, issues come to be politicized and depoliticized. This, in turn, is suggestive of a potential relationship between levels and forms of political participation on the one hand and the manner in which issues are politicized and depoliticized on the other.

It is to this intriguing proposition that we now turn more directly. The central concern of the next two chapters is to assess the extent to which the contemporary condition of formal political disaffection and disengagement that we mapped in chapter 1 is connected to a range of contemporary processes of depoliticization. If it is, and if we can show that it is, then we will have demonstrated that there is a supply-side alternative to the pervasive demand-side explanations for formal political disengagement and disaffection.

3

The Domestic Sources of Depoliticization

In the preceding chapters I have made much of the argument that what we expect from politics is dependent to a considerable extent on the assumptions about human nature that we project on to politicians and other public officials. If we assume the worst of political actors, then politics – understood either as a process of deliberation or as a mechanism for the provision of collective or public goods – is likely to be in short supply. This is not, of course, an argument for assuming the best of political actors regardless of their conduct. But it is to suggest that if we are to understand contemporary levels of formal political disengagement and disaffection, we might do well to reflect upon the assumptions we project on to political actors and our reasons for so doing. That is the task of this chapter.

Its argument is relatively simple and can be summarized in six core claims:

1. We do indeed tend to assume the worse of political actors.
2. Although this is by no means unprecedented historically (as we saw in chapter 1), the prevalence of such assumptions does serve to characterize the period since the 1980s in the advanced liberal democracies.
3. Crucially, yet ironically, such assumptions also seem to be shared by political elites themselves, informing much contemporary public policy.
4. Whether in the minds of political elites or the citizens who return them to office, such assumptions have a series of unfortunate, unintended and often perverse consequences.
5. Our reasons for holding such assumptions are not especially good ones, and reflect less changes in the character traits of those we elect than changes in intellectual fashion.
6. The prevalence of such assumptions is in fact an index of the hold that a particular body of theory – public choice theory – has come to exert over public policy since the 1980s.

None of these claims is likely to prove uncontroversial. Indeed, as we go down the list, the controversy that each is likely to provoke intensifies. Yet, if the argument that these six propositions map out is correct, it has considerable potential consequences. For it suggests that, tragically and inadvertently, and whether as citizens, political actors or, indeed, theorists of politics, we have conspired to demonize and discredit politics and the political – arguably at precisely the time that we need them the most.

Either by projecting the worst of assumptions on to political actors or, as political actors, internalizing precisely the same assumptions about ourselves, we have discounted prematurely our ability collectively to deliver the public goods which are now in such short supply. The result is that, rationally protecting ourselves from irrational fears about politicians' self-interested motivations, we have come to entrust less and less to formal political deliberation, to expect less and less from formal politics, and to disengage in increasing numbers from the increasingly unedifying spectacle that is left.

If that, in essence, is the contemporary political affliction that I have sought to diagnose and describe in this volume, then the aim of this chapter and the next is to explain how this might have come to pass. I begin with what might, at first, seem like a rather unlikely target – an academic theory: namely, public choice theory. But before turning to it directly, it is first important to return to the theme of depoliticization with which I concluded the previous chapter.

The public politics of depoliticization

The politics of depoliticization, as already alluded to, has had a significant role to play in all of this. And as well as attracting considerable and growing academic interest, it has also increasingly come to feature in policy-makers' own discussions of public policy. For our present concerns that discussion is extremely illuminating. For, in marked contrast to almost all of the existing academic literature on the topic, the practitioners' discourse of depoliticization presents it in a very positive light. Depoliticization is a good thing. It is seen to provide, in particular, a solution to a range of often difficult, even otherwise intractable, political problems. There is potentially much that could usefully be said about this. But for present purposes I will concentrate solely on the stark contrast in the assumptions about politics in the practitioners' and academic discourses of depoliticization.

Consider first the academic discourse. The consensus here is considerable. Those discerning in contemporary trends depoliticizing tendencies are engaged in a critical exposition of a normatively dubious practice or process (e.g. Boggs 2000; Buller and Flinders 2005; Burnham 2001;

Crouch 2004; Flinders 2004; Pettit 2004; Rancière 1995). Peter Burnham, for instance, defines depoliticization as 'the process of placing at one remove the political character of decision-making' (2001: 128). In so doing he is effectively suggesting that in a democratic polity, the political character of decision making should *not* be placed at one remove. In this he is by no means alone. Depoliticization, in the academic literature, serves to insulate politicians and their choices, immunizing them from responsibility, accountability and critique. It is a disavowal of the democratic obligations of a government to its citizens in a democratic polity. It is a convenient mechanism for disarming opposition, sweeping under the carpet potentially contentious issues. And it is a technique that is likely to prove both especially useful and particularly insidious where the chosen reform trajectory is certain to prove unpopular. None of this commends itself to academic commentators. Depoliticized and presented as a purely technical solution to a complex problem, almost any policy proposal is likely to appear more palatable. Moreover, with any luck, it won't matter whether it appears palatable or not since, to the extent that it is depoliticized, the policy proposal will simply not register with the electorate, at least until such time as it is being, or has already been, implemented. Here depoliticization is a bad thing, because it disavows politics, and politics is a good thing. The conception of politics that underpins this simple equation, though very rarely stated explicitly, is not so very different from that defended in the previous chapter. Politics is about deliberation and collective choice, and whilst it can occur in a variety of more or less public arenas (including, presumably, those into which it is displaced when it is formally depoliticized), the more public, open and inclusive the process of deliberation, the better.

The practitioners' discourse on depoliticization could scarcely be more different.[1] The influential London-based European Policy Forum, for instance, describes 'the depoliticisation of many government decisions' in glowing terms. Indeed, it refers to this process as 'one of the most promising developments since the last war' (2000: 11). The World Bank (2000) is scarcely less effusive, conceiving of the process of depoliticization as central to the building of state capacity and market confidence in new or fledgling democracies. Similarly, the European Commission's (2001) White Paper on the future of European governance is built around the principle of depoliticization. Finally, the extension of depoliticization from monetary policy to fiscal policy and beyond has come to feature increasingly prominently in discussions of economic policy reform. Thus, Alan S. Blinder, former vice-chairman of the Board of Governors of the US Federal

Reserve – someone who knows a fair bit about depoliticization – has argued:

> Those who say that big government is the problem have got it wrong. The real problem is that government is pushed and pulled by interest groups and partisan politicking, often at the public's expense . . . Shift responsibility for things like tax from the politicians to the experts; besides knowing more, they work in a politics-free zone. Tossing the ball to the technocrats won't weaken democracy . . . but it will produce better policy. (1997: 115)

Yet nowhere are the assumptions which underpin this practitioners' discourse more clearly spelt out than in a speech to the Institute for Public Policy Research delivered by the British Secretary of State for Constitutional Affairs, Lord Falconer. His comments are worth quoting at some length.

> What governs our approach is a clear desire to place power where it should be: increasingly not with politicians, but with those best fitted in different ways to deploy it. Interest rates are not set by politicians in the Treasury, but by the Bank of England. Minimum wages are not determined by the Department of Trade and Industry, but by the Low Pay Commission. Membership of the House of Lords will be determined not in Downing Street but in an independent Appointments Commission. This depoliticis-ing of key decision-making is a vital element in bringing power closer to the people. (<www.dca.gov.uk/speeches/2003/lc031203.htm>p. 5)

This is a most illuminating extract from a fascinating speech. When set alongside the above comments of Alan S. Blinder, it serves to delineate very clearly the assumptions about politics which inform the increasingly warm embrace of depoliticization that practitioners now seem to be giving. Politics, here, is at best an unhelpful interference, at worst a malevolent force. It is prone to 'capture' by powerful interest groups; it can only prevent the adoption of the technically most proficient policy solution to any given challenge; it is aloof and distant from 'the people'; its respon-siveness to societal demands leads it to inappropriate policy choices; it lacks the technical proficiency and specialist knowledge required to select the optimal policy choice; it is costly, inefficient, bureaucratic and self-referential to the point of becoming tiresome; and it has an inexorable ten-dency that needs to be curbed to expand into areas where it has no legitimate business. Politics is a pathogen; depoliticization an antidote.

A number of points might usefully be made here. First, is it really that surprising that citizens should be disengaging in their droves from electoral and other forms of formal political participation when those they might elect are quite so dismissive of their own capacity to do good – and so ready to use the power conferred upon them at the ballot box to discharge their responsibilities to some independent authority or commission? There is a very real sense in which formal politics is diminished both by the admission (if that is what it is) of political incapacity on the part of politicians and the institutional depoliticization that follows from this. Electoral politics, it would seem, is supplying rather less – to be reduced, in effect, to the selection of mere functionaries responsible for allocating and assigning policy-making duties to more technically proficient and politically insulated technocrats. In such a context, formal political disengagement may seem like a perfectly rational response. Yet we need to be careful here. For whilst elected officials may make much of their proclivity to displace policy-making responsibility to those better placed to adjudicate technically the implications of such choices, considerable policy-making autonomy continues to reside with government. Elections continue to matter, whatever the practitioners' discourse might imply. Yet in one sense it is not whether elections matter or not that is the significant issue here – but whether they are *perceived* to matter. And politicians' public disavowals of their own credibility and competence to adjudicate policy choices is hardly conducive to maintaining the impression that they do.

This brings us to a further point. There is something strangely perverse about politicians, like Lord Falconer in the above extract, effectively pronouncing themselves unfit to govern and declaring enthusiastically their commitment to depoliticization. Again, the contrast between the practitioners' and the academics' discourse is potentially suggestive. The latter would seem to expect depoliticization to be, at best, something of a guilty secret on the part of politicians – not something to be proudly proclaimed as a strategy for delivering better government. Seen as a disavowal of the office they sought and won, and an illegitimate discharging of a democratic mandate and the obligations with which it is associated, depoliticization is a technique that works only to the extent that one can get away with it; and the best way to get away with it is not to draw too much attention to it.

So what is going on here? Possibly, two things. First, that politicians should be so brazen about depoliticization suggests that they do genuinely believe that it is likely to ensure better government. That, in turn, suggests that, for whatever reason, they have imbibed and internalized a rather negative view of politics, to which depoliticization is in some sense a logical precautionary response. If this is true, then it also reveals a certain tendency for the academic literature to be overly cynical in the motivations for depoliticization that it projects on to political actors. There is, of course, a delicious irony to this. If politicians are cynical and duplicitous, they will seek to depoliticize contentious issues as much as they can, discharging in so doing their responsibility to others. Yet the last thing they will do is admit to this. That depoliticization has become a subject of public political discourse shows either that politicians are incompetent rogues (they are duplicitous and self-serving, but not very good at it) or that their motivations are rather less cynical, self-serving and duplicitous. Yet, by the same token, depoliticization is likely to improve the quality of government only to the extent to which politicians are, indeed, cynical, self-serving and duplicitous. And we have seen that their conduct (not least in discharging their responsibilities to others) suggests that they are not. The argument is a complex one, but it leads clearly in one direction. Politicians are rather less instrumental, self-serving and duplicitous than both the assumptions they project on to themselves and the assumptions projected on to them in the academic literature. This is a crucial point. It suggests that if we are to understand depoliticization and its role in the process of political disaffection and disengagement, then what we really need to explain is why it is that both politicians and their academic critics should have come to project such pessimistic assumptions about human behaviour on to political elites.

The practitioners' discourse of depoliticization gives us an important clue. For the assumptions of politicians about politics that I sought to isolate from the practitioners' discourse – of politics as interfering, prone to capture by powerful interests, prone to exponential growth and encroachment, prone to inefficiencies, technically incompetent and so forth – are precisely those of public choice theory. Indeed, they read like a potted summary of that theory. What is more, that theory rose to prominence and became highly influential in the neoliberal reform of the state at precisely the point at which such assumptions also rose to prominence. It is to this body of theory, its relationship to neoliberalism, and its influence that we must then turn.

Public choice theory

Public choice theory is a variant of rational choice theory (for useful introductions, see Dunleavy 1991; Hindmoor 2006; Mueller 2003). It developed, initially, in the US in the 1960s as a response to the then influential tradition of welfare economics. The latter had sought, in effect, to derive the need for a state which might intervene within and regulate the market, correcting its natural tendency to failure. Such a state would, in particular, be charged with correcting the innate tendency of the market to under-supply public or collective goods – such as security, health and welfare more generally.[2] Countering this, public choice theorists sought to develop, in Nobel laureate James Buchanen's terms, a 'science of political failure' (1988: 3) in place of welfare economics' science of market failure. As Andrew Hindmoor explains, 'whilst welfare economists had shown how and why the market might sometimes fail they had simply asserted rather than demonstrated the ability and willingness of the state to correct those failures' (2006: 85). At best they had demonstrated the need for a function to be performed (that of market regulation and the correction of market failure), not the capacity of the state to perform that function. Indeed, in challenging the conventional fiction of the perfect market that had tended to dominate professional economics, they had constructed a similarly idealized depiction of the state. A rather more sanguine and realistic view of the similarly imperfect state, it was argued, would lead to a rather safer set of inferences about the need for state intervention. Public choice theory sought to provide that assessment. From the start, then, public choice theory was not favourably predisposed towards the state and, in its preference for the market over the state, had something of a natural affinity with neoliberalism (on which see Dunleavy and O'Leary 1987: 72–135; D. S. King 1987; Self 1993).

Public choice theory approaches the question of state failure using fairly standard rational choice theoretical techniques and assumptions. In short, it models political behaviour on the simplifying premise that political actors are instrumental, self-serving and efficient in maximizing those benefits (net of cost) that they seek to achieve (their 'utility function'). Its aim is the construction of a series of stylized (often, algebraic) models of political conduct. What make this possible is the assumption that political actors and public officials are rational and behave *as if* they engage in a cost–benefit analysis of each and every choice available to them before plumping for the option most likely to maximize their given 'utility function' (generally, an expression of their material self-interest).[3] They behave rationally, maximizing personal utility net of cost whilst giving little or no consideration to the consequences, for others, of their behaviour.[4]

The product of all of this is a series of stylized models (many algebraic in form) which explore logically the consequences of assuming the worst of elected officials on the one hand and 'public servants' on the other.[5] In the sections that follow we turn in some detail to these models, considering the extent to which they have informed public policy since the 1980s and the consequences, for the supply of collective or public goods, of modelling the redesign of the state on such assumptions. Before doing so, however, we turn more directly to the relationship between neoliberalism and public choice theory.

The natural affinity between neoliberalism and public choice theory

The above paragraphs are suggestive of a potential connection between political disaffection on the one hand and the projection of public choice theoretical assumptions on to public officials and politicians on the other. But, in so doing, they perhaps serve to draw our attention away from the role of neoliberalism in this process. For although public choice theory and neoliberalism have, as suggested, something of a natural affinity, they are by no means synonymous. Each, potentially, has a significant role to play in the explanation of depoliticization and the process of political disaffection and disengagement. But before addressing this issue directly it is important that we define our terms. In what follows I deploy a composite definition of neoliberalism, which identifies a series of core tenets:

1. A confidence in the market as an efficient mechanism for the allocation of scarce resources.
2. A belief in the desirability of a global regime of free trade and free capital mobility.
3. A belief in the desirability, all things being equal, of a limited and non-interventionist role for the state.
4. A conception of the state as a facilitator and custodian, rather than a substitute for market mechanisms.
5. A defence of individual liberty.
6. A commitment to the removal of those welfare benefits which might be seen to act as disincentives to market participation (in short, a subordination of the principles of social justice to those of perceived economic imperatives).
7. A defence of labour market flexibility and the promotion and nurturing of cost competitiveness.
8. A confidence in the use of private finance in public projects and, more generally, in the allocative efficiency of market and quasi-market mechanisms in the provision of public goods.

Having defined neoliberalism, it is important to note that its relationships to public choice theory and to political disenchantment and disengagement are not simple. Three important points might here be noted.

1 In mapping these relationships, it is important that we periodize the development of neoliberalism. In particular, we must differentiate between the rise of neoliberalism in the late 1970s and 1980s in the Anglophone democracies (Britain, the US, Canada, Australia and New Zealand) and its subsequent and more general diffusion and consolidation in the 1990s and beyond. The highly politicized nature of the former process contrasts markedly with the latter – a process of institutionalization, normalization and depoliticization. I will refer to the first as the phase of *normative neoliberalism*, the second the phase of *normalized neoliberalism* (see also Hay 2005b).

2 Public choice theory has played a crucial but decisively different role in legitimating, intellectually and in broader public discourse, both phases of neoliberalism's development. In the earlier, normative phase, public choice theory – in the form of the theories of political and bureaucratic overload – came to provide a powerful, public and highly politicized dramatization of the 'crisis' afflicting the advanced liberal democracies – a crisis to which neoliberalism was presented as the solution. In the latter phase of normalization and institutionalization, public choice theory, allied now to new public management theory, rational expectations microeconomics and open economy macroeconomics, served to pronounce neoliberalism the only feasible economic paradigm in an era of globalization. In so doing, it served effectively to depoliticize neoliberalism and to render it non-negotiable.

3 Not all advanced liberal democracies that have since come to embrace neoliberalism as a governing economic paradigm went through a period of normative neoliberalism.

A number of implications follow from this. Arguably, by significantly raising the stakes of electoral competition in the late 1970s and throughout the 1980s, the highly politicized and distinctly normative neoliberalism of Reagan and Thatcher in particular may well have served to promote political identification and participation.[6] Yet, since the 1990s things have changed. Thus, whether ostensibly chosen domestically or at the instigation of international institutions (such as the World Bank, the World Trade Organisation or the International Monetary Fund), the international diffusion of neoliberalism as a largely technical set of devices for managing a national economy in a context of globalization has served to depoliticize economic policy-making. This, I shall argue, has contributed to a process of disengagement and disenfranchisement. Yet, as we shall see, this has as much to do with the projection on to public officials, by international and domestic opinion-formers of public choice theoretical assumptions as it does the more direct accommodation to neoliberal orthodoxies.

Moreover, as this suggests, the rise and consolidation of neoliberalism may in fact have served to mask a rather deeper, and arguably more significant, transformation in our collective assumptions about politics itself. As I sought to show in chapter 1, conventional conceptions of politics are less about holding power to account publicly than they are about the subversion of the public interest. What I aim to show in this chapter is that the intellectual antecedents of such a view lie in public choice theory.

Finally, it is important to note that neoliberalism and public choice theory are depoliticizing in two rather different respects. First, animated as they are by a rather pessimistic conception of the human subject, they are deeply cynical about the motivations of public officials (elected or otherwise) and their capacity to satisfy the over-inflated expectations of the electorate that they are (rationally) predisposed to stimulate. Consequently, they have considerable trouble in conceiving of the state as either an effective or an honest guarantor of the public good. Thus, although as many have noted, they require a (presumably temporary) activation and empowerment of the state to do so, their central goal is the scaling back of political deliberation and the rolling forward of the purview and influence of the market.[7] This is, in a most obvious way, depoliticizing. Indeed, it is as clear a case as one might imagine of depoliticization of type 1 (as in figure 2.2).

Yet no less significant is the peculiarly depoliticizing manner of neoliberalism's consolidation and legitimation in recent years – as not so much desirable as necessary. This might almost be seen as a depoliticization of type 3 (as in figure 2.2). The necessitarian character of neoliberalism's legitimation as the only game in town has served to insulate it from critique. As I aim to show, it also has much to do with that legitimation having been constructed on rational/public choice theoretical terms.[8] In other words, neoliberalism's normalization has been achieved through a process of rationalization which is itself powerfully depoliticizing.

Politicizing neoliberalism, depoliticizing neoliberalism

The above paragraphs suggest that public choice theory has played two separate and rather different roles in the development of the contemporary condition of political disaffection and disengagement. The first was to demonize politics and the political in the process of narrating the crisis of the 1970s – a crisis to which neoliberalism was presented as the logical solution. As we shall see, public choice theory – in the form of the political and bureaucratic overload theses in particular – sought to expose the naïvety of the unduly optimistic assumptions about politics that had developed in the post-war years. Politics, in this conception was, above all else, *capable* – capable of supplying public or collective goods, capable of correcting market failure, and capable of distributing resources fairly and equitably without compromising economic efficiency. It was this conception of politics that public choice theory set out to expose as not only naïve, but dangerously so. Indeed, it was this naïvety that it ultimately held responsible for the crisis that had come to afflict the state by the mid-to-late 1970s – a crisis born of political and bureaucratic overload; a crisis precipitated by over-inflated expectations about what politics could deliver; and a crisis whose ultimate origins lay in the blithe and unrealistic optimism of assuming the best of political actors. In short, public choice theory sought to inject a long-overdue dose of political realism into proceedings. This came in the form of a healthy cynicism about both the motivations and the capabilities of politicians and public officials; it was to prove highly contagious.

The role of public choice theory in the phase of normalized neoliberalism is entirely different. Here, allied not to overload theory, but to rational expectations microeconomics, new public management theory and open economy macroeconomics, public choice assumptions are used to derive stylized models which demonstrate the necessity of the neoliberal economic paradigm. Each theory serves to rationalize neoliberalism as the necessary and only feasible strategy for managing the collectively sub-optimal consequences of instrumentally rational behaviour – on the part of elected officials, bureaucrats and bureau chiefs, political parties, the electorate and, in an open economy, finance and investment capital. In this way neoliberalism has been logically necessitated by the projection on to political and economic actors of stylized rational/public choice assumptions. Neoliberalism is defended not as normatively superior to the alternatives, but as the only option – there simply are no alternatives. It is the very condition of economic credibility and competence in an era of globalization. As we shall see, the necessitarian defence of neoliberalism is predicated entirely on the projection of precisely the same narrow and instrumental assumptions on to political actors. From these assumptions is logically derived the need to normalize and embed the neoliberal economic order in a series of institutions (such as independent central banks) charged with responsibility for the technical details of its delivery. In this process neoliberalism is both normalized and depoliticized, the space for formal political deliberation and accountability radically circumscribed.

In the remaining sections of this chapter it is to the details of these distinct, but cumulatively significant, processes that we turn. The central thrust of the argument is summarized in table 3.1. This describes the various contributions of the political and bureaucratic overload theses, new public management theory, rational expectations economics, and open economy macroeconomics (to which we turn in chapter 4) in this two-step process.[9] I begin, however, with some more general comments about the origins of public choice theory in the work of Kenneth Arrow in particular and the conception of democracy which it draws from his seminal influence.

Arrow's impossibility theorem

Kenneth Arrow's *Social Choice and Individual Values*, published in 1951 and in no small part responsible for the Nobel Prize he was awarded twenty-one years later, is invariably credited as the founding work of public choice theory (Amadae 2003; Green and Shapiro 1994: 7–8; Hauptmann 1996; Mueller 2003: 2–5). In it Arrow set out his now rightly famous '(im)possibility theorem', often now simply abbreviated to the 'Arrow paradox'. The question Arrow posed himself is disarmingly simple: can the preferences of a society of rational actors be aggregated fairly and in a manner which does not violate the principles of democracy to arrive at a rational collective choice preferred by the majority?[10] His answer is that they cannot, without infringing at least one of the minimal technical conditions he specifies for the just aggregation of preferences or the 'condition of non-dictatorship'. As Emily Hauptmann usefully puts it, Arrow shows that 'if we grant all individuals' preferences equal weight in making social [or other] policy, and if individuals have at least three alternatives from which to choose, it is logically impossible to construct a procedure that allows us to move from individual preferences to a rational collective choice' (1996: 13–14). Though this is not quite the inference that Arrow himself draws, the impossibility theorem is usually taken to imply that democracy, understood as the just aggregation of all (unconstrained) societal preferences, is impossible. Consequently, collective decisions claiming democratic legitimacy are likely to include choices that are either arbitrary, dictatorial, or both.[11]

The Arrow paradox has proved phenomenally influential. Indeed, were we to insist on tracing the logical antecedents of the contemporary condition of political disaffection and disengagement to a single point, the publication of *Social Choice and Individual Values* would undoubtedly prove a very strong candidate. For perhaps more than any other single intervention it served to puncture the confidence that had come to surround the concept

Table 3.1 Rationalizing neoliberalism

	Political overload thesis	Bureaucratic overload theory/new public management theory	Rational expectations economics	Globalization thesis (open economy macroeconomics)
Assumptions	instrumental rationality of sectional interests lobbying the state	instrumental rationality of bureaucrats	instrumental rationality of elected politicians	existence of an open and perfectly integrated world market
	instrumental rationality of the electorate – pocket-book voting	bureaucrats' monopoly of information about necessary bureau and budget size	time-inconsistent inflationary preferences of elected officials	instrumental rationality of (profit-maximizing) capital
	instrumental rationality of political parties in accommodating the self-interest of interest groups and the electorate		electorate's lack of information about conditions of optimal management of the economy	(near) perfect mobility of capital
Diagnosis or prediction	political overload and ungovernability	bureaucratic oversupply and public inefficiency	inflationary expectations where politicians control monetary policy	competitive arbitrage
	crisis of democracy		politicians can't be trusted to deliver price stability (or any declared anti-inflation target)	anticipated 'exit' of capital and mobile investors from high taxation and highly regulated economies
			political business cycle	unsustainability of social democratic policies in an era of globalization
			higher inflation and unemployment than would otherwise be the case	

Table 3.1 Rationalizing neoliberalism (*continued*)

	Political overload thesis	Bureaucratic overload theory/new public management theory	Rational expectations economics	Globalization thesis (open economy macroeconomics)
Policy stance	Disciplinary neoliberalism'	new public management internal marketization privatization incentivization of published targets	institutionalized monetarism or neo-monetarism central bank independence.	accommodation of the preferences of capital and mobile investors deregulation and marketization enforced neoliberalism
Political consequences	re-scaling of democratic expectations 'post-democratic politics decline in political confidence	the movement towards a post-'public service ethos' 'decline of the public' (Marquand)	technicization of monetary policy depoliticization of monetary policy	technicization of economic and social policy (answerable to the imperative of competitiveness) accommodation of the preferences of capital rather than the electorate

of democracy in the early post-war years. Moreover, it very rapidly became a focus of academic attention. This was predominantly of two kinds. First there were those who sought (largely in vain) to rehabilitate democracy from the early grave seen by many to have been dug for it by Arrow's exegesis in set theory. Second were those who sought to deploy algebraic modelling rather than set theory to explore and develop further the implications of the 'impossibility theorem'. Public choice theory is the fruit of the latter's individual and collective labour.

There are many problems with Arrow's statement of the 'impossibility theorem' – or, perhaps more accurately, with the inferences which have been drawn from it – and it is important that we consider these briefly. Yet it is equally important that we do not lose sight of its central significance in so doing. The 'impossibility theorem' is important not for any devastating blow to democracy that it poses logically. For, as I hope to show, it is far from self-evident that it describes at all well the democratic predicament, far less that it demonstrates the impossibility of democracy itself. Its importance lies elsewhere – in the challenge to the spirit of post-war confidence and optimism in the capacity of the state for democratic governance that it was *seen* to pose, and for the literature to which it would ultimately give rise (see also Amadae 2003).

The 'impossibility theorem' is problematic in at least five central and, in many cases, closely related respects. These can be summarized as follows:

1 The elucidation of the paradox simply assumes, like much of the public choice theory to which it would later give rise, that the preferences of individuals are fixed, given and immutable. This is a most unrealistic assumption in an open and democratic society characterized by public debate and deliberation. Indeed, in many respects, all that Arrow shows is that the random assignment of preferences to individuals is likely to generate scenarios in which those preferences cannot simply and consistently be aggregated into a collective choice. But preferences are not randomly distributed in a democratic society – indeed, arguably what characterizes such a society is less its procedures for aggregating preferences than those for resolving differences amongst them and for deciding what to do in situations in which this does not prove easy.

2 As this suggests, Arrow reduces democracy to a procedure for the aggregation of preferences alone. Consequently, he fails to allow for the consequences of processes of public deliberation and persuasion – which many would see as defining features of democratic governance – on the distribution of the preferences to be aggregated. As Emily Hauptmann puts it,

'precisely because his paradox cannot capture the range of democratic solutions to political differences, Arrow's work indirectly demonstrates the impossibility of proposing a formal, choice-driven definition of democracy' (1996: 15). In effect, what Arrow shows is not the impossibility of democracy, but the impossibility of capturing its complexity in rational choice-theoretic terms.

3 Arrow is wrong to assume that democracy is predicated on the aggregation of unconstrained choices. As we saw in the previous chapter, the realm of formal democratic deliberation in any polity is, in fact, quite limited. It is invariably circumscribed by a tightly delineated governmental agenda which changes over time as issues become politicized and depoliticized, but which at any given point in time renders some issues and preferences admissible, others inadmissible. Moreover, there is no democracy in the world, contemporary or historic, which has not excluded certain preferences from being articulated. As this suggests, democracy is, as much as anything else, a system for selecting preferences to be aggregated. This Arrow does not and cannot consider.

4 As a number of commentators have pointed out, and as already noted, Arrow does not demonstrate that the pretence to the democratic aggregation of preferences can never be realized, but merely that *under certain conditions* it is impossible. What he shows, in effect, is that there are certain conceivable societal preference distributions from which no rational collective choice can logically be derived. This is as true for the market, as a mechanism for aggregating preferences, as it is for democracy – raising the question of what might be done in such scenarios. This Arrow does not really address, concluding simply that ostensibly democratic systems of governance must rely on the arbitrary or dictatorial imposition of collective choice where no rational aggregation is possible. Yet that is both a dangerous inference and an uncharacteristically sloppy appeal to the concept of dictatorship. To show that preference distributions can be imagined which cannot rationally be aggregated and to conclude from this that, if a choice is to be made in such a scenario, it must be imposed, is not to reveal the dictatorial wolf from under the democratic fleece. For democratically elected leaders are answerable for their decisions in a way that dictators are not. Moreover, no liberal democratic polity has ever claimed that every decision made in the name of its citizens is a fair, just and rational expression of the collective will. Leaders in democratic polities enjoy prerogative powers – yet they are answerable for what they choose to do with them.

5 As this in turn suggests, democracy is as much as anything else a set of procedures for selecting those who must adjudicate between the available

options in situations in which societal preferences are either unclear or do not resolve themselves into an unambiguous collective choice. Its legitimacy resides in the perceived appropriateness of those procedures, the public accountability of elected officials, and the extent to which such decision-makers might credibly claim to have acted in the collective interest in discharging their duties. Demonstrating that there are situations in which elected officials themselves make choices for which they will ultimately have to answer is hardly a devastating critique of the democratic system of government.

Political overload theory

Problematic though it may well be, Arrow's 'impossibility theorem' was to prove extraordinarily influential. In questioning the very possibility of democratic governance itself, and in exposing the necessarily arbitrary character of political power, even in ostensibly democratic political systems, it sowed the seeds of academic political cynicism, especially in the US. It gave rise to a vast secondary literature, exposing the proneness of the state to failure where welfare economics had sought to expose the proneness of the market to failure. Consequently, when the economic and political crises of the 1970s hit, this new body of literature – public choice theory – was ready to supply a powerful diagnosis of the condition of state failure that it saw as afflicting the advanced liberal democracies. Indeed, the crisis was, for it, a powerful confirmation of the veracity of public choice theory.

No individual thesis was more influential in the public dramatization of the crisis than the overload thesis (see for instance Buchanen and Wagner 1977, 1978; Crozier, Huntingdon and Watanuki 1975; A. King 1975). Indeed, though initially formulated in the academic literature, it was soon enthusiastically adopted by an international network of New Right think tanks, eventually coming to inform both the editorial commentary and the very framing of the tabloid and broadsheet news media's coverage of events as they unfolded (see Hay 1996, 2001; D. S. King 1987).

The overload thesis came in two variants – the political overload thesis and the bureaucratic overload thesis. The former was arguably more influential in Europe, the latter in the US.

The immediate condition to which the political overload thesis sought to provide a diagnosis was one of 'stagflation' – a situation of high and rising inflation (associated with the steep rise in oil prices following the Yom Kippur War) combined with high and rising unemployment. This posed seemingly insurmountable problems for the then ascendant Keynesian economic paradigm.[12] For the Keynesian inclination in conditions of rising unemployment was to engage in deficit-financed public expenditure to inject demand into the economy. Yet, in all likelihood, this would prove inflationary, merely compounding the initial problem. By the same token, an increase in interest rates sufficient to bring inflationary pressures under control would almost certainly result in a steep rise in unemployment. In short, this was a lose–lose situation.

Enter the political overload thesis. Its diagnosis was elegant in its simplicity, and in its simplicity lay its persuasive capacity. It was premised upon the crudest of public choice theoretical assumptions – the narrow instrumental rationality of politicians (in maximizing votes irrespective of the economic consequences of so doing) and electors (whose soul motivation for voting was assumed to be the blind pursuit of material self-interest). Given these assumptions, the rest was merely a matter of logical deduction. Accept the assumptions, and a simple diagnosis of a simple condition followed.

Thinking merely of narrow electoral advantage, politicians would seek to accommodate themselves to the (rational/instrumental) preferences of the electorate for immediate material gain. In so doing, they would sanction ever spiralling and ever more costly electoral expectations. Consequently, in the run-up to an election the parties (rationally maximizing their electoral prospects) would seek to outbid one another in terms of the promises they made to the electorate and sectional interests (like the trade unions) therein. This served to establish a political competition for votes, yet one lacking the disciplining price mechanism of a genuine market – in which consumers are forced to bear the costs of their choices. Since the cost of each vote could effectively be discounted by politicians motivated only by short-term electoral advantage, and voters themselves would discount the long-term cumulative consequences of the parties' budgetary indiscipline that their greed encouraged, the effective price of a vote would spiral from one election to the next. Eventually demand would increase to the point of political 'overload'. The result was a fiscal crisis of the state – a situation in which taxation receipts could no longer offset expenditure commitments, a situation of spiralling debt. The point of political overload had now been reached.

The image was a simple one – a vicious political whirlpool from whose centripetal clutches parties could escape only at considerable cost to their electoral prospects. The solution was simple: a severe bout of fiscal austerity, tight monetary control, and the programmatic withdrawal of an overloaded, overburdened yet beleaguered state. In other words, the state needed temporarily to reassert its authority and then unburden itself of the excessive commitments it had taken on.

The overload thesis provided a populist narration of the crisis that resonated powerfully with public opinion. It attributed responsibility for the crisis exceptionally clearly, it promised a relatively simple solution, and it gave Reagan and Thatcher in particular the opportunity to show what that solution might look like in practice. Yet, perhaps more significantly still, it served to generalize a completely different set of assumptions about politics and politicians from those which had dominated the post-war period. Politics was synonymous with the blind pursuit of individual self-interest. As such, it could not, and should not, be trusted to deliver public goods. It was, at best, a necessary evil; at worst, a sinister force that needed to be kept in check. It had a natural tendency to expansion, was inefficient, prone to corruption, and an impediment to the proper functioning of the market. In short, its purview needed to be rained back, its reach and influence radically curbed.

Like the Arrow 'impossibility theorem' before it, the political overload thesis is crucial, not for its accuracy or intellectual coherence, but for its influence. It is nonetheless important to establish the numerous inconsistencies and obvious distortions on which it relied. Four, in particular, might be noted.

1 The thesis is, like all public choice theory, predicated on assumptions which are neither justified in themselves nor tested empirically. Individuals, be they politicians or electors, are assumed to be efficient and self-interested utility-maximizers, interested only in the benefits to themselves (as individuals) of any given choice. In a sense, then, the thesis is less a theory than an exploration of the logical implications of adopting such assumptions. What it shows, in effect, is that if we assume the worst of both the electorate and those they elect, then politics is prone to perverse and self-reinforcing dynamics, and incapable of the efficient supply of public goods. That is hardly surprising. The overload thesis shows that a more or less compelling account of the crisis of the 1970s can be constructed on the basis of the assumption of rational self-interest on the part of all political actors. It does not show that this account is accurate.

2 Yet even were this not deemed a problem, there is a further issue with the overload thesis's appeal to the assumption of instrumental rationality. It is uneven and self-contradictory. In diagnosing the 'crisis of democracy', the electorate is assumed to be so narrowly self-interested as to fail to consider the cumulative consequences of its actions (fiscal irresponsibility and ultimately overload). Yet, when it comes to providing a solution, this assumption is conveniently overlooked. Indeed, if electors were as narrowly self-interested as the model implies, there would presumably be little

point in appealing to them for a decisive break with the practices responsible for overload. Here the thesis's proponents appeal to precisely the ability of the electorate to exhibit an alternative rationality that they earlier denied. Similarly, if it is rational for political parties to be fiscally irresponsible in making electoral commitments, and political parties are rational, then presumably there is little point in suggesting that things might be better for us all if they stopped behaving in such a way. In diagnosing the problem, political actors are rational utility-maximizers. Yet, when it comes to fashioning solutions, they are not. Indeed, if it is rational for parties to play 'the overload game', then the election of a governing party committed publicly to breaking the cycle of overload is a compelling refutation of the most central assumption of the thesis – that political parties are rational.

3 The thesis is incompatible with the evidence. The model assumes that the electorate simply discounts fiscal irresponsibility on the part of the political parties vying for their votes. Yet the available empirical evidence clearly points to the significance, in determining success at the polls, of the perceived health of the economy (e.g. Pissarides 1980; Price and Sanders 1993).

4 Finally, the thesis does not in fact explain the emergence of a condition of 'stagflation' at all. At best, it provides an explanation for rising inflation and escalating levels of public debt in the 1970s. It does not explain the simultaneous presence of both inflationary pressures and high levels of unemployment. Indeed, this is crucial to understanding the monetarist and supply-side economics pursued by Reagan and Thatcher in office. For both policy responses to the crisis targeted inflation alone, rather than unemployment or the combination of the two, resolving the crisis of 'stagflation' by pursuing a range of policies designed to bring inflation under control. The result was to drive up levels of unemployment further – to previously unprecedented levels.

Yet, to concentrate on the internal inconsistencies of the overload thesis, and to assess its contribution in terms of intellectual cogency, is to miss the point. For the thesis, as diluted and refracted by the think tanks of the New Right and as it appeared in the pages of the tabloid and broadsheet papers alike offered a spectacular, rhetorically rich and ultimately persuasive narration of the events of the crisis as it was to unfold in the mid to late 1970s. It would not only mould perceptions of the nature of the condition afflicting the advanced liberal democracies, the culprits and the villains, but it would also contribute to a reassessment of the meaning, associations and connotations of politics itself.

Bureaucratic overload theory

If the political overload thesis served to demonize politics and politicians, then it did not do so alone. An equivalent role was played in the demonization of public officials, and the state more generally, by the bureaucratic overload thesis.

This latter body of theory sought to explore the collectively irrational consequences of budget-maximizing bureaucratic behaviour. In a manner almost directly analogous to the political overload thesis, a range of authors, from Anthony Downs, William Niskanen and Gordon Tullock onwards, have sought to demonstrate the tendency of the state, in ostensibly seeking to correct market failure, to over-supply public goods (see e.g. Downs 1967; Niskanen 1971; Tullock 1965; and for useful reviews Dunleavy 1991; Hindmoor 2006; Mueller 2003).

The central logic of the argument is instantly recognizable from the political overload thesis, even if its details are subtly different. In place of a political world populated by narrowly self-interested political parties, politicians and electors, we must now imagine a bureaucratic world populated by similarly self-interested bureaucrats. Such functionaries are assumed to exist in a complex, yet privileged, relationship with their political sponsors in that, although reliant on the former for their budget, they control the flow of information, they are monopoly providers, and they retain a fair degree of budgetary autonomy. They are, furthermore, assumed to be motivated not, as is the then contemporary mythology, by some vague and benign 'public service ethos' but by a rather baser and more familiar set of concerns. Though these vary from one public choice theorist to the next, typically they include (i) a desire to increase their salary; (ii) a desire to increase whatever tax-discountable, non-financial benefits they can get their hands on; (iii) a desire for promotion; (iv) a desire to maximize the size of the bureau budget for which they are responsible; (v) a desire to maintain their position as monopoly providers of a given (public) service; (vi) a desire, all things being equal, to do as little work as they can get away with; (vii) a desire to protect the budgetary and managerial autonomy of their bureau; (viii) a desire to expand their areas of competence and responsibility and the kudos that this is likely to bring; (ix) a desire to maximize their workplace security; and (x) a desire to ensure that they are well catered for in retirement. This is, of course, not a terribly edifying image of public servants. And it is hardly surprising that, building from such initial assumptions, the models of public bureaucracy that result do not see such bodies as efficient guarantors of the public interest.

Nor is it difficult to imagine how such assumptions might inform a stylized model of the tendency for public goods to be over-supplied by a bureaucratic state. For if bureau chiefs are motivated by pecuniary gain, if that in turn is a reflection of the size of the bureaux and bureau budgets for which they are responsible, and if they are in a position to control information about the budget required to deliver a given level of public service, then the delivery costs of any public service will be artificially inflated. Add to that the privileged position enjoyed by bureau chiefs in their budgetary negotiations by virtue of their position as monopoly providers, and then extrapolate to all bureaux, and there is a natural built-in tendency for bureau creep, bureaucratization, and for the public sector to consume an ever greater share of national output. That, in its simplest form, is the bureaucratic overload thesis.

It, too, has exerted an immensely powerful influence. Like the political overload thesis, it played a crucial role in the dramatization of the crisis of the 1970s – proposing a further mechanism for the over-burdening of the state, a series of clearly identified villains of the piece, and a simple remedy. Indeed, it provided a powerful focus for entirely legitimate complaints and concerns about the character and quality of the provision of public goods in the advanced liberal democracies in the late 1960s and early 1970s. In so doing, it served to puncture the deference to public officials which had previously characterized societal attitudes towards the state, demystifying the 'public service ethos' in the process. Just as the political overload thesis shattered societal illusions about politicians, so the bureaucratic overload thesis bred a pervasive cynicism about all other guardians of the public interest and, more significantly still, the capacity of the state to deliver collective goods.

Its consequences have been enduring. Since the 1980s and in a great variety of guises, its assumptions have come decisively to reshape the public sector in the advanced liberal democracies. Indeed, it is difficult to think of a significant public sector reform since that time which has not been predicated on the projection of instrumental assumptions on to public servants. Initially, this was through privatization and the unburdening of the state of the responsibilities it had swelled to encompass during the early post-war years. Later on, in the form of new public management theory, precisely the same assumptions came to inform the commodification, marketization and incentivization of both the provision of public goods and public sector performance (for useful reviews of the vast literature, both theoretical and applied, see Dunleavy and Hood 1994; Hood 1991; Hughes 2003; McLaughlin, Osborne and Ferlie 2002; Walsh 1995).

As this suggests, the theory of bureaucratic overload, rather more than the political overload thesis, has come to play a key role in both the normative and the normalized phases of neoliberal development. As a consequence, it has served to influence not only the public narration of the crisis of the 1970s but also the often iterative yet cumulatively significant reform of the state and its responsibilities that has followed over the last three decades.

This is a particularly important point, since, in the form of new public management theory in particular, public choice theoretical assumptions have been embedded in the reform of public institutions. This is nowhere clearer than in the development of the contracting-out of services (such as hospital cleaning) to the private sector, the development of internal markets within the public sector itself, and the incentivization of highly publicized targets for public sector performance (such as performance league tables in schools or hospitals). All of these reforms rely on the notion that, in the absence of market or quasi-market competition, public sector workers, thinking only of themselves, will free-ride on the labour of others, with the net effect that public funds will be wasted. It is only if quantifiable outcomes are identified, closely and independently monitored, and their attainment incentivized that rational utility-maximizing public officials can be trusted to deliver public goods. Contemporary public sector reform, it would seem, is based on the precautionary principle. If there is any doubt at all about the extent to which public sector employees are likely to exhibit a 'public sector ethos', taking pride in their contribution to the public good, we should assume the worst of them. Consequently, we should incentivize their behaviour, rewarding them only for those outcomes that we are seeking to maximize. For this is the only way that we can ensure the efficient allocation of resources for the delivery of public goods.

Yet there is a clear danger in all of this. In assuming (if only in a precautionary manner) the total absence of a 'public service ethos' and incentivizing public servants' behaviour accordingly – appealing, as it were, to their baser instincts – we merely encourage such actors to orient themselves towards the delivery of public goods in a purely instrumental fashion. Is there not a significant risk here that in assuming the absence of a public sector ethos we conspire to turn such a fear into a self-fulfilling prophecy? For it leads us to destroy the very contexts in which such an ethos might be exhibited.

In a very real sense, this may also undermine the capacity of the state to deliver public goods. For being treated (successfully) for a medical condition by a doctor who regards one as a potential performance indicator (an instance of an ailment cured) is, arguably, to receive rather less of a public good than to be treated by the same doctor as a patient. Moreover, are there not likely to be significant spillover effects from such a process of incentivization and rationalization? If we spend our entire working lives chasing public sector performance targets, since the state does not trust us to do what is right for those whose welfare it charges us with delivering, is that not also likely to influence our interactions in other domains? Is there not a similarly grave danger that contractual relationships increasingly replace those once built on trust? And is not trust simultaneously the most fragile and the most valuable public good of all?

Finally, the marketization, commodification, incentivization and rationalization of the provision of public goods is also a process of depoliticization – in at least two rather different respects. First, and rather obviously, in so far as such techniques displace responsibility for the provision of public goods (or, indeed, merely aspects of their delivery) from the public to the private sector, this is depoliticizing. Indeed, in so far as private and/or 'consumer' choice replaces public choice, this is a depoliticization of type 2. Yet, a rather more complex process of depoliticization is also discernible in such trends. For in so far as a collective good like health care is reduced to a set of quantifiable and measurable indices, much of its public political character is lost.

Political business cycle theory: the need for depoliticization

A further spin-off of public choice theory that has proved increasingly influential in recent years – in both the institutionalization of neoliberalism and in the more general depoliticization of public policy – is 'political business cycle theory'. Formalized by William D. Nordhaus (1975) and others (e.g. Alesina 1989), this suggests that the capacity of political actors to manage the economy will lead them artificially to seek to align the natural cycle of the economy (the business cycle) with the electoral cycle to maximize their chances of re-election (for a useful review, see Paldam 1997). The result is a 'political business cycle'. In its most contemporary form, and aligned with rational expectations economics, political business cycle theory lies behind the current fashion for central bank independence. It provides a powerful case-study of the way in which public choice theoretical assumptions may serve to depoliticize whole areas of public policy – here monetary policy.

Central bank independence is widely promoted by a range of international institutions, such as the World Bank, the International Monetary Fund and the European Commission, as the most effective guarantor of sound monetary policy. The public rationale for the ceding of operational independence to central banks is the same in each case, and draws directly on public choice theory. It is couched in terms of the (supposedly) 'time-inconsistent inflationary preferences' of public authorities and the 'rational expectations' of market actors. Despite the specialist terminology, the rationale, given the assumption of rational expectations, is very simple. It is summarized schematically in figure 3.1.

Given (the perception of) a short-term trade-off between inflation and unemployment – that in the short term allowing inflationary pressures to remain unchecked will provide a boost to levels of employment – rational politicians will seek to orchestrate a 'political business cycle', trading inflation in the immediate aftermath of their anticipated re-election for growth and employment in the run-up to that election. Yet this, it is argued, can serve only to dampen the aggregate long-term growth potential of the economy whilst, at the same time, driving up the natural or equilibrium rate of unemployment. In other words, rational political actors will interfere with the natural business cycle of the economy to the detriment of its long-term performance.

Moreover, in order to encourage investment, rational politicians will be keen to signal to market actors their desire to keep inflation to a minimum. They are likely, in so doing, to commit themselves to a target level of inflation. Yet, as rational actors seeing the advantage of a political business cycle, they will, again quite rationally, flagrantly violate any such commitment in the run-up to an election they are seeking to win. In short, it is rational for politicians to set for themselves inflation targets that they have no intention of keeping, since their preferences for inflation are dependent on the phase of the political business cycle – they are 'time-inconsistent'.

Yet this is likely to have consequences. Indeed, in a world of 'rational expectations', market actors will anticipate such defection, (rationally) adapting their investment behaviour accordingly. In other words, their rational expectations will lead them to expect politicians to claim a higher sensitivity to inflation than they are actually likely to exhibit; they will adjust (downwards) their propensity to invest as a consequence. In such a scenario, the effects of *anticipated* inflation for the investment behaviour of market actors are just as severe as if that inflation were real. Accordingly, so long as control of monetary policy rests in the hands of public officials, unemployment, the aggregate rate of inflation and interest rates averaged over the economic cycle will all be higher than they would otherwise need to be whilst levels of investment will be suppressed (Alesina 1989; Kydland and Prescott 1977).

If anti-inflationary credibility and the good economic performance with which it is associated by neo-monetarist economists are to be restored, the public authorities need to be able to make a credible pre-commitment to a given inflation target. There is only one way in which they can do this – by assigning responsibility for monetary policy to a body that is not only independent, but seen to be independent, of political influence. In other words,

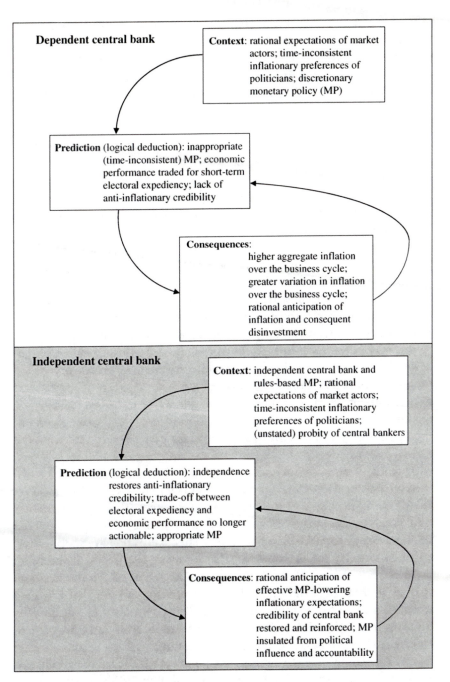

Figure 3.1 The rationale for central bank independence

what is required is an institutionally guaranteed depoliticization of monetary policy (an independent central bank mandated constitutionally to deliver a specific inflation target – typically in low- to mid-single digits). In such a scenario (rational) inflationary expectations are diminished, with consequent beneficial effects upon the cost of borrowing, the equilibrium rate of unemployment and the level in investment in the economy.

This rationalization of monetary orthodoxy is interesting in a number of respects. First, it follows logically from the internalization of (now conventional) rational expectations assumptions. The time-inconsistency problem is presented as a non-negotiable bind on elected officials, necessitating the institutionalization of an independently accountable new monetarist macroeconomic regime. This must, in turn, guarantee the privileged status of the control of inflation as macroeconomic objective number one. That status is seen to be inviolable and beyond political contestation – indeed, it is only because it is inviolable and beyond political contestation that any credible commitment to its delivery can be made.

Second, this new monetarist macroeconomics is justified, not principally in its own terms, but as the only possible (and hence purely technical) solution to the time-inconsistency problem in a world of rational expectations. In this way rationalist assumptions normalize and institutionalize neoliberal policy such that no alternative is conceivable. Macroeconomic policy (certainly monetary policy) is thus relegated to a purely technical and entirely apolitical matter beyond the sphere of effective democratic scrutiny or accountability. The perpetuation of neoliberal macroeconomics is guaranteed institutionally, and monetary policy is removed from the formal political agenda.

This, of course, immediately raises the question of political actors' motivations for depoliticizing monetary policy in this way. Three answers to that question almost naturally present themselves: (i) that policy-makers have come to accept the time-inconsistency thesis, conceding in so doing their incapacity to make monetary policy effectively, and have simply internalized its policy implications; (ii) that an expressed belief in the time-inconsistency thesis is seen as an appropriate signal to the markets and market analysts of economic policy competence; and (iii) that invoking the time-inconsistency thesis and internalizing its policy implications is a means to a rather different end – the insulation, from critique, of neo-monetarist economics. The last of these options perhaps requires a little more explanation than the others. The point is that central bank independence translates potential public and political disputes about appropriate policy instruments and settings into purely private and technical matters, to be adjudicated by competent professionals. Moreover, it diverts attention from the (neo-monetarist) content of (orthodox) monetary policy choices, allowing them to be presented as a simple consequence of sound economic management. As such, it both institutionalizes and insulates from public scrutiny a neo-monetarist macroeconomic regime.

It is, of course, impossible to generalize from one case to the next. Yet it is nonetheless interesting to consider the British case in a little more detail. A Labour government, under the leadership of Tony Blair, was returned to power in 1997 after eighteen years in opposition. Within a week, the new Chancellor of the Exchequer, Gordon Brown, had announced that operational independence would be granted to the Bank of England. No hint of this had been given in the party's election manifesto.

As I have already argued, we should be cautious in attributing sinister, self-interested and duplicitous motivations to politicians engaged in processes of depoliticization from which they might benefit. Yet, of the three potential explanations outlined above, it is the first that is the easiest to discount in the British case. For, were New Labour policy-makers genuinely wedded to the non-negotiable bind implied by the time-inconsistency thesis, they would not at any point have been able to contemplate British membership of the single European currency. Though technical, the reason is relatively simple. Were Britain to join the Eurozone, the likely disparity in interest rates between that set by the European Central Bank and that which would have been set by the Bank of England would effectively restore political responsibility for anti-inflationary policy. For it would require compensating action by the Treasury to offset the consequences of a sub-optimal monetary policy set in Frankfurt.

In all likelihood, then, the Blair government's adoption of a time-inconsistency rationale for its new monetarist macroeconomics arose from a combination of the second and third factors. It is both a marker of credibility and competence and, at the same time, an effective guarantor of the kind of monetary policy discretion that the New Labour Treasury clearly wishes to deny itself. As such, it would seem to be part of a fairly conscious strategy of depoliticization (see also Burnham 2001).

In this context it is interesting to note that the empirical evidence on the effects of central bank independence is hardly unambiguously supportive of the case for depoliticization. There is no statistically significant correlation between the granting of independence and improved anti-inflationary performance (Posen 1993, 1998).[13] When it is considered that central bank independence tends to be seen as an institutional solution for administrations anxious to enhance their anti-inflationary credibility (who might, as a consequence, be expected to exhibit more hawkish attitudes than they had previously exhibited towards inflation), this is all the more telling. If the suggestion is that the ability to control inflation is, and must be, the principal objective of macroeconomic policy, that this rests on anti-inflationary credibility, and that such credibility can be maintained only through operational independence, then the absence of compelling evidence that independence improves anti-inflationary performance is somewhat damaging. It suggests that the necessitarian logic underpinning the global depoliticization of monetary policy is somewhat misplaced. We return to a now consistent theme – the ability of stylized public choice theoretical assumptions to deliver a spurious necessity to economic policy choices, rendering them purely technical, and further eroding the realm of formal political deliberation.

Downs and the marketization of electoral competition

There is one final body of literature and, indeed, source of professional advice to politicians, that we need to consider in this section. This concerns itself with the marketization of electoral competition. The literature here does not, in fact, tend to draw directly on public choice theory for the assumptions on which it is predicated. But, as we shall see, these assumptions are essentially identical to those first set out in Anthony Downs's classic *An Economic Theory of Democracy* (1957) – the founding work of public choice theory in the analysis of electoral politics.

Like the public choice theory which, in many respects, it replicates, the literature and self-styled 'science' of political marketing is predicated on an economic analogy (Lees-Marshment 2001). The competition between parties for votes is assumed to be directly equivalent to that between rival businesses for market share. Without acknowledging it, this directly reproduces Downs's own initial premise – that 'parties in democratic polities are analogous to entrepreneurs in a profit-seeking economy' (1957: 295). Indeed, it is precisely this assumption that allows Downs to develop an 'economic' theory of democracy and the political marketing literature to apply the techniques of marketing to the political realm. From this initial assumption a series of core premises follow. Like market actors, political parties (as entrepreneurial businesses) and voters (as consumers) can be assumed to be rational and self-interested utility-maximizers. Parties seek to maximize votes or, perhaps more realistically, the chances of their election/re-election;[14] voters seek to maximize their (largely economic) well-being.

In a simple two-party electoral system in which voters' preferences are normally distributed about the mean, it is not difficult to show that it is rational for the parties to squabble over the centre ground in a race towards the median voter (for a detailed elaboration of this logic, see Hay 1999: 76–104; see also Downs 1957). The result, *ceteris paribus*, is bipartisan convergence, the party best accommodating the preferences of the median voter proving the victor. In fact, if we assume that parties seek not to maximize their share of the vote *per se*, but their chances of being returned to office, it is likely that the voter on whose preferences the parties converge is not in fact the median voter for the electorate at large, but the median voter in the constituency most likely to prove decisive. Yet, either way, the powerful centripetal pull of rational utility-maximizing behaviour draws both parties towards the centre. The problem with this, as in many public choice theoretical models, is the collective irrationality of individually rational behaviour.[15] A number of points might be made here – notably about the consequences of the marketization of political competition and median voter convergence on levels of formal political participation.

The first and most obvious is that any race towards the preferences of the median voter is likely to dilute the policy content and hence the salience of the contest. It is, as a consequence, profoundly depoliticizing, in the sense that it effectively serves to insulate policy choices from public scrutiny, deliberation and contestation. Yet, at the same time, it also serves to politicize a series of more ephemeral and non-policy matters – as personality contests replace the clash of competing policy trajectories in the determination of electoral outcomes.

This has two important consequences. First, it increases the salience in electoral contests of issues that the electorate are singularly ill-placed to adjudicate. Chief amongst these is the issue of trust. Contemporary elections, it seems, are increasingly competitions for the electorate's trust. Party leaders present themselves as credible and competent administrators, not, for the most part, as principled advocates of a set of policy preferences. Once again, it is personality rather than policy content that the electorate is increasingly asked to adjudicate – and it has very little to go on in making such an assessment.

The declining policy salience of electoral competition, and the extent to which issues like trust and credibility have replaced substantive differences in policy content as the focus of electoral competition, have surely both contributed towards the disengagement of potential voters. Even in public choice theoretical terms it is easy to see why. For, as we saw in chapter 1, the extent to which it is rational to vote is an index of the difference in anticipated personal utility associated with the election of each party. If that difference falls, or even if it becomes more difficult to assess (as the content of the contest shifts from matters of policy substance to those of credibility and competence), it becomes less and less rational to vote.

Moreover, committed as most political parties now are to an essentially economic view of the voter-as-consumer (a conception clearly reinforced by the growing influence of political marketing techniques in electoral contests), parties increasingly appeal to the electorate in narrowly instrumental terms. In so doing, they are in danger of replicating precisely the assumptions in rational choice theory that lead to the so-called rational voter paradox. As we saw in chapter 1, it is simply not rational for atomistic and individuated potential voter-cum-consumers to cast a vote. Consequently, the extent to which political parties appeal to potential voters in such terms is the extent to which they are in danger of turning the rational voter paradox into a self-fulfilling prophecy. In short, the marketization of electoral competition is in danger of reducing the electorate to a series of atomistic rational consumers who, as atomistic rational consumers, will rationally disengage.

Closely related to this are the consequences of a further assumption which characterizes the political marketing literature – the essential fixity of voter preferences. If we assume that the distribution of voter preferences is given and immutable, then political parties have no option if they are genuinely committed to winning an election but to accommodate themselves to that preference distribution (by, for instance, appealing to the median voter). Persuasive or preference-shaping strategies of electoral competition are eliminated at a stroke. Consequently, the language of electoral competition today is less emotive, less ideological, less impassioned, and the resulting contest less engaging politically.

Finally, as already noted, rational political parties seeking to maximize their chances of election or re-election will tend not to target the electorate as a whole, but only those key sections of the electorate (invariably, swing voters in marginal constituencies) most likely to determine the overall outcome. Armed with the political marketeers' battery of techniques for targeted electoral appeals, they will turn their back on a substantial share of the electorate (typically, core voters in safe seats). This is merely likely to exacerbate any tendency on the part of the latter to non-participation.

Taken together, these observations suggest the pervasive and perverse effects on contemporary electoral competition and turnout of the economic analogy which underpins both public choice theory and the political marketing literature. If political parties behave like rival businesses competing for market share, and they appeal to voters as atomistic consumers, they may well maximize their electoral utility, but they are in danger in so doing of turning the rational voter paradox into a self-fulfilling prophecy.

Conclusions

In this chapter my aim has been to consider the domestic sources of the contemporary condition of political disaffection and disengagement mapped out in chapter 1. Building from the notion that we are unlikely to get more from politicians than we project on to them, I sought to trace the origins of contemporary political discontent in our tendency to assume the worst of political actors and public officials. For clues, I turned first to the seemingly paradoxical phenomenon of the public advocacy of depoliticization by professional politicians, revealing the profoundly pessimistic assumptions about politics on which this discourse is publicly predicated. I contrasted these assumptions with the rather more optimistic conception of politics – as a field of potential public deliberation – that underpins the critical academic literature on depoliticization. More significantly, perhaps, I also showed that the conception of politics animating the practitioners' discourse – of politics as interfering, prone to capture by powerful interests, prone to exponential growth and encroachment, and prone to inefficiency – was precisely that of public choice theory.

This suggested the potential significance of the latter in the transformation and downgrading of expectations about formal politics – a notion merely reinforced by noting its rise to prominence and its role in providing the principal theoretical inspiration for the reform of the state and public policy since the 1980s. In the remaining sections of the chapter I sought further to explore the potential role of public choice theory in sowing the seeds of the contemporary condition of political disaffection and disengagement. In so doing, I demonstrated its profound intellectual affinity with neoliberalism and its two-stage role – first, in serving to demonize the political in the normative phase of neoliberalism and, second, in serving to rationalize and depoliticize neoliberalism in its phase of normalization and institutionalization.

Finally, I showed how, drawing not on public choice theory directly, but on almost identical assumptions, the literature and practice of political marketing have served further to narrow the field of domestic political/electoral contestation. In each case I showed how public choice theory's antipathy to 'politics' is a direct correlate of its projection of the assumption of instrumental rationality on to politicians, voters and public officials.

The central message of this chapter is brutally simple. Seemingly innocent assumptions may have alarmingly cumulative consequences. Indeed,
as I have sought to demonstrate in the final sections of this chapter, the intuitive notion of electoral competition as analogous to that between rival
businesses for market share and the associated instrumentalization of the
appeal to voters-as-consumers may well have served to render the so-called
rational voter paradox a self-fulfilling prophecy. The rational voter
paradox – that in a democratic polity in which parties behave in a 'rational'
manner, it is irrational for citizens to vote (since the chances of the vote they
cast proving decisive are negligible) – has always been deemed a central
weakness of rational choice theory as a set of analytical devices for
exploring electoral competition. Yet, as the above analysis suggests, in a
world constructed in the image of such assumptions, it may become
depressingly accurate. Political parties behaving in a narrowly rational
manner, assuming voters to behave in a similarly rational fashion, will contribute to a dynamic which sees real electors (rational or otherwise) disengage in increasing numbers from the façade of electoral competition.

That this is so is only reinforced by a final factor. The institutionalization
and normalization of neoliberalism in many advanced liberal democracies
in recent years have been defended in largely technical terms, and in a
manner almost entirely inaccessible to public political scrutiny, contestation
and debate. The electorate, in recent years, has not been invited to choose
between competing programmatic mandates to be delivered in office, but
to pass a judgement on the credibility and competence of the respective
candidates for high office to behave in the appropriate (technical) manner
in response to contingent external stimuli. Is it any wonder that they have
chosen, in increasing numbers, not to exercise any such judgement at all at
the ballot box?

4

The Global Sources of Depoliticization

It is in many respects remarkable that we have got to this point in a book on the nature, character and content of contemporary politics without a sustained discussion of the concept of globalization. To be fair, we have had plenty of opportunity for that discussion – the term has cropped up at various points in the analysis thus far and, indeed, in each chapter. Indeed, you might almost think that I have been putting it off – and in a sense I have. In seeking a supply-side alternative to the prevailing demand-side explanations for contemporary political disaffection and disengagement, it is all too tempting to turn first and last to globalization. That is a temptation that I have sought to resist. My task in this chapter is, as much as anything else, to explain why.

In brief, and at the risk of distorting just a little the argument I will go on to make at greater length in what follows, I want to suggest that the domestic sources of depoliticization and disaffection have rather more to do with it, and what might be termed the global sources of depoliticization and disaffection rather less to do with it than is conventionally assumed. This is not to argue that globalization has nothing to do with it; nor is it to suggest that there is not a powerful prima facie case for seeing globalization and the capacity for public deliberation as profoundly antagonistic. It is, however, to suggest that we cannot afford to supply politicians too readily with the convenient alibi that they will no doubt claim for themselves anyway – namely, that in an era of globalization their hands are so tied by processes beyond their control that it is naïve of us to project our political frustrations on to them.

I also want to suggest that we need to be extremely cautious in implying that the domestic and global sources of depoliticization, disenchantment and disaffection can be readily distinguished and easily disentangled. I have already been careful to speak not of the global sources of depoliticization but 'what might be termed' the global sources of depoliticization. This is for a very good reason. As will become clear presently, I simply do not think that many of the phenomena casually associated with the term 'globalization' are the product of genuinely globalizing tendencies. Indeed, I will argue that although the contemporary political and economic world is traversed by an ever denser web of complex interdependencies, it continues to be poorly characterized in terms of globalization.

As this perhaps already serves to indicate, the argument of this chapter is an involved one. Nonetheless, its core contentions can be summarized relatively simply as follows.

1. Whether or not globalization is happening and whether the consequences often attributed to it should be attributed to it depend, unremarkably, on what globalization is taken to imply.
2. If we are to assess the implications of the complex economic and political interdependence that many would see as synonymous with globalization, then it is important that we adopt a relatively exacting defining of the latter. In particular, it is important that we retain the capacity to differentiate between globalization and regionalization, acknowledging that one does not necessarily entail the other.
3. If we do so, we see that much of what is conventionally labelled globalization is in fact more accurately described in terms of regionalization.
4. The influential hyper-globalization thesis, like much of the neoclassical open economy macroeconomic modelling on which it relies, is predicated on the assumption of perfect global market integration.
5. That assumption cannot be reconciled with the available empirical evidence, calling into question its apocalyptic pronouncements about the capacity for policy-making autonomy at the domestic level.
6. Consequently, there may well be considerably more room for domestic political autonomy and effective democratic deliberation at the domestic level than is conventionally assumed.
7. Perversely, however, if policy-making autonomy is not perceived to exist, policy choices will continue to be dictated by the perceived imperatives of globalization (however false these may be).
8. This may, in turn, contribute to the perceived obsolescence of domestic political processes and, hence, to political disaffection and disengagement.

It is to the details of this argument that we turn in the central sections of this chapter. Before doing so, however, it is first important to lay out the prima facie case that we have already alluded to for seeing globalization and democratic political deliberation as antagonistic.

Globalization *versus* democratic political deliberation?

Whether triumphalist or critical, radical or sceptical, the existing literature invariably casts globalization and democratic political deliberation as antagonistic. A variety of more or less plausible mechanisms for this tension can be pointed to. Perhaps most frequently, globalization is seen to challenge the public nature of (domestic) political deliberation by summoning a series of non-negotiable, external and largely economic imperatives that must be appeased in a technically proficient manner if good economic performance is to be maintained. Similarly, globalization is seen as the enemy of political deliberation in the sense that it is seen to dictate policy choices whilst itself being beyond the capacity of domestic political actors to control. In such accounts, globalization is seen to intensify the competitive struggle amongst nations for global market share, driving states to subordinate public policy considerations to economic imperatives, thereby exposing their expenditure commitments to an exacting 'competitive audit'. Yet, however familiar, this is by no means the only mechanism by which globalization might be seen as in tension with political deliberation. Indeed, at least three rather different sources of such tension might be identified.

First, globalization is often held to necessitate a certain privatization and depoliticization of public policy, rendering it less publicly accountable. Here it is the distinctly 'public' character of political deliberation that is challenged by globalization. The condition of complex interdependence to which it gives rise is seen to render policy deliberations so technical and so involved as to necessitate significant changes in the conduct – and notably the legitimation – of public policy. To reduce the risk of co-ordinated speculative dynamics being unleashed against one's currency by global financial markets, for instance, it is argued that monetary policy must be removed from political control and rendered both predictable and rules-bounded rather than discretionary.[1] Here globalization is cast as a powerful agent of depoliticization (see also Berman and McNamara 1999). If the inference is valid, this is a very important, and potentially troubling, development. For it implies that in a context of globalization policy choices cannot be held to account publicly to the extent to which we have become accustomed. Globalization and public deliberation are indeed antagonistic, since there are potentially significant trade-offs between the effectiveness of policy on the one hand and its democratic accountability on the other. If this is indeed the case, it would suggest yet another source of (rational) discontent and disengagement with formal politics.

Second, globalization is seen to necessitate an internalization by the state of the preferences of capital and an associated squeezing of the fiscal resources from which public policy is funded. This is perhaps the most conventional sense in which globalization is depoliticizing. As will be discussed in more detail in later sections, the mechanism invoked here is relatively simple. Globalization is treated as synonymous with the mobility of capital. In order to retain high levels of investment, states must increasingly provide an investment climate deemed conducive to profit maximization by both potential and existing investors. They must, in short, internalize the preferences of capital.[2] Such preferences are conventionally assumed to be for minimal regulation and low levels of taxation.[3] The mobility of capital is, then, seen, both directly and indirectly, to exert strong downward pressures on the space for political deliberation – directly, since globalization enhances the effective bargaining power of capital, and capital is seen to exert a strong preference for market mechanisms as opposed to public regulation; and indirectly, since globalization effectively squeezes the fiscal base out of which public policy is funded.

Third, and more generally, globalization is seen to reduce the policy-making capacity and autonomy of the nation-state, resulting in a displacement of functions from public to quasi-public bodies (such as independent central banks) and from national to trans-national institutions (such as those associated with the process of European integration and more obviously global institutions such as the IMF, the WTO and the World Bank). Here commentators highlight what they identify as an increasing disparity between the level at which policy problems emerge and/or must effectively be dealt with and the still predominantly national/domestic character of the institutions from which such responses are initially sought. In short, they note, in a context of globalization, the nation-state's increasing lack of fitness for purpose. Of course, to identify a proliferation of global/trans-national problems with which the nation-state is not well placed to deal is not necessarily to point to a shortfall in the capacity to respond, especially if global/trans-national policy-making capacity is enhanced in parallel with the proliferation of problems at this level. Yet it is the gap between the pace at which the problems proliferate and that at which the policy-making capacity increases that prompts contemporary concerns. Invariably, it seems, global problems have failed to prompt co-ordinated global solutions – environmental degradation providing an ever more alarming case in point.

As this already serves to indicate, the dominant themes in the existing literature all point to an adversarial relationship between globalization and political deliberation and autonomy. In this context, it is perhaps hardly surprising that commentators like Colin Crouch (2004) should point to the emergence of 'post-democratic' politics, whilst David Marquand (2004) identifies a contemporary 'decline of the public'. Yet before rushing to endorse such a pessimistic conclusion, it is important to acknowledge that most of the themes of the literature already discussed rest on strong assumptions as to the nature, extent and consequences of globalization. Whether acknowledged as such, these are unavoidably empirical claims and, moreover, empirical claims that do not always stand up under a close consideration of the available evidence.

Yet, if we are to assess such claims, it is first important to isolate and identify as clearly as possible the mechanisms appealed to in the existing literature which suggest the corrosive effect of globalization of the space for domestic political deliberation. That brings us directly to a consideration of the so-called hyper-globalization thesis.

The hyper-globalization thesis

However influential they are, most strong variants of the globalization thesis, which present the nation-state as simply a casualty of globalization, tend to do so without pointing directly or explicitly to the mechanism or mechanisms involved (see for instance Ohmae 1990, 1995; Reich 1992). At best, it seems, they treat the existence of such mechanisms as self-evident. Yet, where such processes are alluded to, they invariably make reference to the increased bargaining power and/or mobility of capital in an era of globalization. In so doing, 'hyper-globalists' appeal, whether they are aware of it or not, to mechanisms derived from neoclassical open economy macroeconomic models (for reviews of the relevant literature, see Obstfeld and Rogoff 1996; Rødseth 2000; Ugur 2001). This is an important point, and gives a first clue as to the character of the hyper-globalization thesis. For it serves to indicate that, for such authors, it is *economic* globalization that is the principal factor limiting the capacity and autonomy of the state in the contemporary context. In short, economic globalization gives mobile international investors the upper hand over domestic political authorities.

Without going into any technical detail it is useful to examine further such open economic macroeconomics models. In particular, it is important that we

1. Establish the assumptions on which such models are predicated;
2. Assess the plausibility of such assumptions;

3. Consider the sensitivity of the conclusions derived from such assumptions (especially those relating to the extent of domestic policy-making autonomy) to modifications in the initial premises from which they are derived.

The logic of the hyper-globalization thesis is in fact very similar to that elaborated by Adam Smith in 1776.

> The . . . proprietor of stock is properly a citizen of the world, and is not necessarily attached to any particular country. He would be apt to abandon the country in which he is exposed to a vexatious inquisition, in order to be assessed a burdensome tax, and would remove his stock to some country where he could either carry on his business or enjoy his fortune at his ease. A tax that tended to drive away stock from a particular country, would so far tend to dry up every source of revenue, both to the sovereign and to the society. Not only the profits of stock, but the rent of land and the wages of labour, would necessarily be more or less diminished by its removal. (Smith 1976 [1776]: 848–9; cited in Swank 2002: 245)

The contemporary form of the argument goes something like this (see also table 3.1). In closed national economies, such as those which (supposedly) characterized the early post-war period, capital was essentially immobile and national in character; it had no 'exit' option. In such an environment, governments could impose punitive taxation regimes upon unwilling and relatively impotent national capitals, with little cost to the domestic economy (except for the tendency of capitalists to hoard rather than reinvest their profits). With open economy conditions, such as are conventionally held to characterize the contemporary era, this is no longer the case. Capital may now exit from national economic environments at minimal cost (indeed, in most neoclassical-inspired models, at zero cost).

Accordingly, by playing off the regulatory regimes of different economies against one another, capital can ensure for itself the highest rate of return on its investment. *Ceteris paribus*, capital will exit high taxation regimes for low taxation regimes, comprehensive welfare states for residual states, highly regulated labour markets for flexible labour markets, and economies characterized by strict environmental regulations and high union density for those characterized by lax environmental standards and low union density.

The process pits national economy against national economy in an increasingly intense competitive struggle. States must effectively clamber over one another in an ever more frenzied attempt to produce a more favourable investment environment for mobile ('footloose') foreign direct investors than their competitors. Yet this is not a one-shot game – and an early influx of foreign direct investment only increases the dependence of the state upon its continued 'locational competitiveness'. If investment is to be retained in such an environment, states must constantly strive to improve the investment opportunities they can offer relative to those of their competitors. Any failure to do so can only precipitate a haemorrhaging of invested funds, labour shedding and, eventually, economic crisis. In other words states must internalize and continue to internalize the preferences of capital, offering ever more attractive investment incentives, ever more flexible labour markets, and ever less restrictive environmental regulation, if they are not to be emptied of investment, economic activity and employment. Big government, if not perhaps the state itself, is rendered increasingly anachronistic – no longer a guarantor of the interests of citizens or even consumers, but a sure means to disinvestment and economic crisis.

In precisely the same way in which public choice theoretical assumptions served to rationalize and necessitate central bank independence, as we saw in the previous chapter, so stylized open economy macroeconomic assumptions here serve to rationalize and necessitate a neoliberal agenda of welfare and labour market reform.

Plausible, familiar and compelling though such a logic may well appear, it will serve us well to isolate the assumptions on which it is predicated. For, as we shall see, it is these, rather than any inexorable process of globalization, which ultimately summon the demise of domestic policy-making autonomy. They are principally fivefold and are summarized below, and each can be challenged on both theoretical and empirical grounds.

1. That capital invests where it can secure the greatest net return on that investment and is possessed of perfect information regarding the means by which to do so;
2. That markets for goods and services are fully integrated globally and that, consequently, national economies must prove themselves internationally competitive if economic growth is to be sustained;
3. That capital enjoys perfect mobility, and the cost of 'exit' (disinvestment) is zero;
4. That capital will invariably secure the greatest return on its investment by minimizing its labour costs in flexible labour markets and by relocating its productive activities to economies with the lowest rates of corporate taxation;
5. And consequently that the welfare state (and the taxation receipts out of which it is funded) represents nothing other than lost capital to mobile

asset-holders and has no positive externalities for the competitiveness and productivity of the national economy.

Each of these premises is at best dubious, at worst demonstrably false. Such assumptions, it should be noted, are justified in neoclassical economics not in terms of their accuracy, but because they facilitate the algebraic modelling of the puzzles they define. That defence, whatever one thinks of it, is simply not available to proponents of the hyper-globalization thesis, whose borrowings from neoclassical economics rarely, if ever, extend beyond the assumptions to the algebra.

Consider each assumption in turn. It may seem entirely appropriate to attribute to capital the sole motive of seeking the greatest return on its investment. And, indeed, this is perhaps the least problematic of the assumptions listed. Yet the political and economic history of capital provides little or no support for the notion that capital is blessed either with complete information or even with a relatively clear and consistent conception of what its own best interest is. Moreover, as the political economy of the advanced capitalist democracies demonstrates well, capital has a history of resisting social and economic reforms which it has later come both to rely upon and actively to defend (see for instance Swenson 2000).

The second assumption is little more than a convenient fiction, used in neoclassical macroeconomics to make possible the formal modelling of an open economy. Few if any economists would defend empirically the claim that markets for goods or services are fully integrated or clear instantly. Indeed, the degree of integration of such markets is an empirical question. It is, as such, an issue to which we return later in the chapter.

If the first two assumptions are problematic, then the third is demonstrably false, at least with respect to certain types of capital. For whilst portfolio capital may indeed exhibit almost perfect mobility in a digital economy, the same is simply not the case for capital invested in infrastructure, machinery and personnel. Consider inward foreign direct investment. Once attracted to a particular locality, foreign direct investors acquire a range of non-recuperable or 'sunk' costs – such as their investment in physical infrastructure, plant and machinery. Consequently, their exit options become seriously depleted. Whilst it is entirely 'rational' for foreign direct investors to proclaim loudly their mobility, exit is perhaps most effective as a threat.

What this in turn suggests is that predictions of the haemorrhaging of invested capital from generous welfare states are almost certainly misplaced. A combination of exit threats and concerns arising from the hyper-globalization thesis about the *likelihood* of exit may well have had an independent effect on the trajectory of fiscal and labour market reform. But there would seem no a priori reason to hold generous welfare states and high corporate taxation burdens incompatible with the attraction and retention of foreign direct investment. As we shall see presently, this is precisely what the empirical record suggests. Not only have the most generous welfare states consistently proved the most attractive locations for inward foreign direct investors (Locke and Kochan 1985; Swank 2002), but volumes of foreign direct investment (expressed as a share of GDP) are in fact positively correlated with levels of corporate taxation, union density, labour costs, and the degree of regulation of the labour market (Cooke and Noble 1998; Dunning 1988; Traxler and Woitech 2000; Wilensky 2002: 654–5). As Duane Swank notes, 'contrary to the claims of the international capital mobility thesis . . . the general fiscal capacity of democratic governments to fund a variety of levels and mixes of social protection and services may be relatively resilient in the face of the internationalisation of markets' (2002: 276). Here it is perhaps instructive to note that despite a marked tendency for direct corporate taxation to fall in recent years in line with the predictions of such neoclassical-inspired models, the overall burden of taxation on firms has in fact remained remarkably constant, rising marginally since the mid-1980s (Kiser and Laing 2001; Steinmo 2003).

No less problematic are assumptions four and five – that capital can only compete in a more intensely competitive environment on the basis of productivity gains secured through tax reductions and cost-shedding and that the welfare state is, for business, merely a drain on profits. Such assumptions are, again, difficult to reconcile with the empirical evidence. Moreover, the hyper-globalization thesis here extrapolates wildly and inappropriately from labour-intensive sectors of the international economy in which competitiveness is conventionally enhanced in this way to the global economy more generally. It fails to appreciate that foreign direct investors in capital-intensive sectors of the international economy are attracted to locations like the Northern European economies neither for the flexibility of their labour markets nor for the cheapness of the wage and non-wage labour costs that they impose, but for the access they provide to a highly skilled, reliable and innovative labour force. High wages and high non-wage labour costs (in the form of payroll taxes) would seem to be a price that many multi-national corporations regard as worth paying for a dynamic and highly skilled workforce.

As the above paragraphs perhaps serve to indicate, there is a powerful theoretical challenge to each of the assumptions on which the thesis is predicated. Yet it is important that we do not confine ourselves to a purely theoretical consideration of the hyper-globalization thesis. For it both relies upon a series of substantive claims and it generates a series of potentially testable predictions. This makes possible a more thoroughgoing empirical assessment. It is the aim of the later sections of this chapter to provide that assessment. However, before turning directly to the evidence, it is first important to consider the concept of globalization itself.

What is globalization?

Given the ubiquity of the term in the existing literature, one might be forgiven for expecting a clear (even if implicit) consensus on the meaning of globalization. Nothing could be further from the truth. Whether globalization is occurring or not is highly contested; and, indeed, what would count as evidence of globalization in the first place is scarcely less contested. The result is considerable confusion as analysts, who may in fact agree to a far greater extent than they assume on what is really going on, mistake semantic differences for more substantive analytical disagreements.

A variety of effects follow from this – not least of which is the tendency of proponents of the globalization thesis and their critics to talk past one another. Whether globalization is happening and whether the consequences often attributed to it *should* be attributed to it depend on what globalization is taken to imply – and it is here that the major differences often lie. Unremarkably perhaps, the critics (or 'sceptics', in Giddens's (1999) terminology) tend to adopt a more exacting definitional standard than the proponents of the thesis (the 'radicals', in Giddens's terms). Indeed, this is the basis of the former's contention that the globalization thesis is based on a mischaracterization of contemporary trends. The radicals, by contrast, set for themselves a rather less discriminating definitional hurdle, with the result that they interpret the very same evidence that leads their critics to challenge the globalization thesis as seemingly unambiguous evidence *for* the thesis. What makes this all the more confusing is the seeming reluctance of authors on either side of the exchange to define clearly and concisely their terminology.

One way to get at underlying or implicit understandings of globalization in such accounts is to look at the assumptions made by their proponents about the process in deriving the consequences and effects they attribute to it. This is perhaps rather easier when it is the economic consequences of globalization that are being considered – for here the assumptions made by proponents of the globalization thesis are quite often both stark and stylized. The so-called business school variant of the radical or hyper-globalization thesis is a case in point.

Here globalization is essentially synonymous with economic openness – in neoclassical economic terms, with a perfectly clearing and fully integrated global market. The effects of globalization appealed to in this literature are, in effect, logical deductions from such assumptions. This is an important point, for whatever one thinks of it, the global economy today is *not* a perfectly clearing and fully integrated market. And to the extent to which this is true, the assumptions from which the deduction proceeds are false. In other words, many of the predictions/diagnoses of the conventional globalization thesis are predicated on unrealistic and implausible assumptions – assumptions used in economic theory not for their accuracy but for their heuristic value (in modelling a perfectly integrated market) and as simplifying distortions necessary to facilitate the algebra to which economists seem professionally drawn.

This is certainly important, but it does not really get us any closer to a definition of globalization. For such authors do not offer perfect market integration on a global scale as a definition of globalization – though this *is* invariably how they operationalize the term. The question of how perfectly integrated globally a market must be to warrant analysis in such terms is, again, rarely posed; and, consequently, the question of when the degree of integration in the world economy is sufficient to justify the label 'globalization' is rarely, if ever, answered.

Yet, if it is difficult to be clear about the definition of globalization in much of the existing literature, we can at least be clear about how the term will be employed in what follows. The definition I prefer, as already indicated, is a relatively specific and exacting one; yet it is not, I would suggest, an unreasonable one if the term is to have analytical precision and utility. It is, moreover, very similar to that advanced by David Held and his colleagues. For them, 'globalization is a process (or set of processes) that embodies a transformation in the spatial organization of social relations and transactions, generating transcontinental or inter-regional flows and networks of activity, interaction and power' (1999: 16).

This definition has a double appeal. First, it is clear, concise and easily operationalized empirically (as I hope to show presently). Second, it differentiates very clearly between regionalization on the one hand and globalization on the other. It does not assume that one implies the other, and in drawing a clear division between the two, it sharpens our powers of analytical description. Regional (say, European) integration is not globalization; nor is it evidence of globalization. Similarly, the term 'globalization' cannot simply be treated as a synonym for the openness of an economy. For this is to flatten the geography of globalization. If an economy becomes more open by trading an ever growing share of its GDP, but with only one or two countries, whilst its trade volume with other countries falls, then this is not globalization. To count as evidence of globalization, the process under consideration must be genuinely *global*-izing (increasingly inter-regional and / or inter-continental in character).

Having defined our terms, we are now finally in a position to shed some empirical light on the relationship between globalization on the one hand and the policy-making autonomy of the nation-state on the other. In the sections that follow, we consider first the independent variable and then the dependent variable. The argument, in essence, is that it is difficult to see globalization as an agent laying waste the policy-making autonomy of the nation-state. There are two dimensions to this. First, it is far from self-evident that globalization describes well the trajectory of the developed world. Second, even were this conceded, the most open economies in the world are invariably those that have most systematically violated the policy strictures associated with globalization in the existing literature.

The independent variable: globalization

The debate on the extent of globalization often begins with a dispute over how we might interpret aggregate global trends in trade such as that displayed in figure 4.1. This shows, on a logarithmic scale, standardized measures of world merchandise exports and world production since the 1940s. The former is effectively a measure of world trade, the latter a measure of world output. Each data series is standardized at a value of 100 for 1995. Consequently, if – as is the case for world merchandise exports – the value in 1955 were 10, then we would have seen a tenfold increase in world merchandise exports (at standard prices) in the four decades between 1955 and 1995. Presenting the data on a logarithmic scale gives us something resembling a straight line, where otherwise we would see an exponential growth curve.

The graph shows an exponential increase in both world production and world merchandise exports since the 1940s. More significantly, it shows that over this period of time world merchandise exports have increased at a faster rate than world merchandise production. This is important, as it indicates that a greater share of world production is being traded today than at any previous point in the data series. In other words, the world economy is producing more goods, and a higher proportion of those good are being traded.

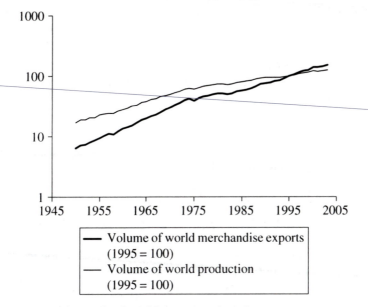

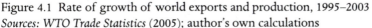

Figure 4.1 Rate of growth of world exports and production, 1995–2003
Sources: WTO Trade Statistics (2005); author's own calculations

This much is uncontested. Yet as soon as it comes to interpreting these data, the controversy begins. For proponents of the globalization thesis, data like these are clear evidence of globalization, since they show in aggregate terms the growing openness of national economies to trade. Here openness (conventionally imports plus exports as a share of GDP) is regarded as a proxy for globalization – the more open the economy, the more trade it is engaged in, and the more global it is. Yet, if we insist on a rather more discriminating definition of globalization, such as that introduced in the previous section, this will not do. The fact that trade is growing at a faster rate than production is certainly important. But it is an outcome compatible with a variety of generative mechanisms, many of which should not be labelled 'globalization'.

Their point is a simple one. In order to know whether this is evidence of globalization or not, we need to know rather more about the trading relations giving rise to these aggregate figures. In particular, we need to know whether, and if so to what extent, this aggregate increase in trade is intra-regional and/or intra-continental in character. If a sizeable and growing share of this trade is a product of regional economic integration, then it is evidence of regionalization, not globalization. Similarly, if the largest eight economies in the world (the G8) were to trade more extensively with one another, whilst the rest of the world was increasingly excluded from the privileged trading relations between these economic giants, it would almost certainly be the case that aggregate world trade would increase at a faster rate than world production. The result would be a plot much like that we see in figure 4.1. Yet we would be wrong to label this 'globalization'.

At this point proponents of the globalization thesis might respond with data like these presented in figure 4.2. This displays the global *and* regional figures for aggregate merchandise trade (here imports and exports separately). It shows that the growth in world merchandise trade is by no means confined to a handful of economies. Yet, what it does not show, and what no aggregate data of this type can show, is the extent to which such regional increases in merchandise trade are a product of regionally specific processes of economic integration as distinct from a more general global trend.

As this already begins to suggest, whether we see clear evidence of globalization or not depends very much on what we take that claim to imply. What counts as evidence of globalization in one account does not in another. If we define globalization in the terms set out in the previous section – as a set of processes generating flows that are trans-continental or inter-regional in character – then there is a strong empirical case against the globalization thesis; it comes in three parts and is summarized thus:

1. Although the period since the 1960s has undoubtedly seen a sustained process of economic integration between national economies, this is by no means unprecedented, and indeed, there is still some considerable distance to travel before pre-First World War levels are likely to be exceeded;
2. A closer, more empirical exploration of patterns of trade and investment flows reveals evidence of regionalization and what is termed 'triadization' (heightened integration between Europe, North America and Pacific Asia), but not globalization *per se*;
3. Financial integration to date has failed to produce either the anticipated convergence in interest rates across the globe or the anticipated divergence in rates of domestic savings and rates of domestic investment that one would expect in a fully integrated global capital market.

Contextualizing current levels of economic integration

In its presentation of the evidence for the globalization thesis, much of the existing literature tends to confine itself to data from the 1960s or, as in figures 4.1 and 4.2, from the 1940s. And there is little doubt that if we plot

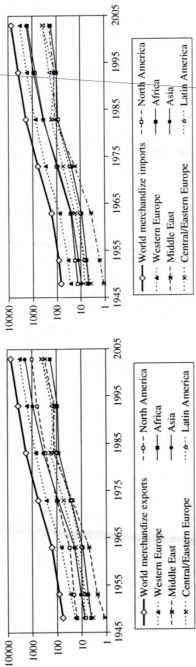

Figure 4.2 Growth in world merchandise trade, 1948–2003, in billions of US dollars

Sources: WTO Trade Statistics (2005); author's own calculations

economic data from the 1960s or even the 1940s to the present day we see clear evidence of an exponential rise in a whole range of flows between economies (such as trade and foreign direct investment) expressed as a share of global GDP. Yet it would clearly be wrong to infer from these data alone unprecedented levels of economic integration between nations.

There are, in fact, good reasons for thinking that the world economy experienced, in the inter-war period and particularly following the Great Depression of the 1930s, a significant decline in economic integration from a previous high. The question is not, then, whether levels of economic integration today are higher than they have been at any time since the 1960s, but how they compare with the previous high point in the second half of the nineteenth century.

Consider trade. figure 4.3 shows the ratio of merchandise trade to GDP at current prices for a number of advanced economies since just before the First World War. What this time-series data show is that the picture presented by proponents of the globalization thesis of an exponential growth in trade, leading to a current period of unprecedented economic integration today is in fact something of a distortion. By extending the time-frame of the analysis, we can see that the high levels of economic integration that we have witnessed since the 1980s are by no means unprecedented historically. Moreover, this is not merely confined to trade, as Hirst and Thompson's detailed mapping of capital flows over the same time period shows (1999: 28–31; see also Bairoch 1996).

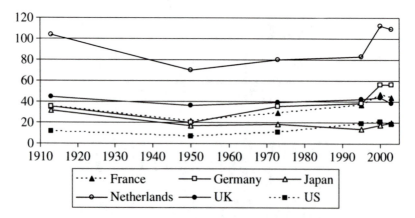

Figure 4.3 Ratio of merchandise trade to GDP at current prices
Sources: Calculated from Maddison 1987: table A-23; Hirst and Thompson 1999: 27, table 2.3; updated from World Bank, *World Development Indicators* (various years)

This may seem like something of a devastating blow to the globalization thesis – and in a sense it is. Yet it is important that we don't infer from data like these that the world economy today closely resembles that in 1913. In fact, as Hirst and Thompson are the first to concede, the composition of the trade has changed immeasurably since 1913. Trade patterns for Germany, the Netherlands and the UK in particular in the latter half of the nineteenth century and the early part of the twentieth century were dominated by colonial ties; those today are rather differently comprised. Whether they can genuinely be said to be more global is an interesting question, which takes us to the second pillar of the case against the globalization thesis.

Globalization, regionalization or triadization

The empirical evidence with respect to trade, foreign direct investment and finance reveals the term 'globalization' to be an inaccurate – and, in fact, ever more inaccurate – description of existing patterns of economic integration. There are two elements to this. First, if looked at in aggregate terms, what we observe is not a process of globalization, but one more accurately labelled 'triadization' (where the 'triad' refers to the North American, South-East Asian and European regional economies; and 'triadization' to the process of economic integration within and between these three regional economies). Second, looked at in a rather more disaggregated way, the pace of intra-regional economic integration (regionalization) exceeds in almost every case the pace of inter-regional economic integration, and hence globalization. The world economy is regional and triadic, regionalizing and even triadizing, but it is neither global nor globalizing. Far from seeing the development over time of a single global economy, trends since the 1960s have established and reinforced a core distinction between the most advanced capitalist economies the world has ever seen (the 'triad') and the rest. Whilst the triad is ever more seamlessly integrated economically and accounts for an ever growing share of world economic activity, the non-triad world is ever more excluded from most favourable trading relations with this hegemonic core. Moreover, what applies to trade also applies to foreign direct investment and finance.

Figure 4.4 uses United Nations data on foreign direct investment inflows and outflows to extend and update the earlier work of Brewer and Young (1998: 58–60). It presents the triad's total share of world accumulated inward and outward foreign direct investment for the period 1980 to 2003 (the most recently published data). What it demonstrates, as Brewer and Young's earlier work also demonstrated, is the very significant concentration of

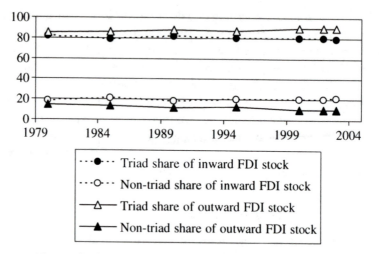

Figure 4.4 The triad's share of inward and outward FDI stock, 1980–2003
Source: Calculated from UN, *World Investment Report 2004: The Shift Towards Services*

inward foreign direct investment in the triad economies. What it also shows is that an ever higher proportion of world outward foreign direct investment stock was sourced from within the triad. Given these data, it should come as no surprise that, between 1991 and 1996, according to Hirst and Thompson (1999: 71), more than 60 per cent of all flows of foreign direct investment were conducted within and between the triad economies. Finally, the data also show that the high triadic concentration in both source and destination of world foreign direct investment is extremely stable over time. The world market, if we can indeed speak of one, for foreign direct investment would seem highly triadic in character.

Yet the triadic character of the world economy is by no means confined to foreign direct investment, however prominently it features in discussions of triadization. For instance, in 2003, despite representing scarcely 10 per cent of the world's population, the triad economies accounted for some 70 per cent of world merchandise trade, a figure almost identical to that in 1992, and significantly higher than that in 1996 (66 per cent), 1990 (64 per cent), 1980 (55 per cent) or 1970 (61 per cent) (Hirst and Thompson 1999: 73; Petrella 1996: 79; WTO Trade Statistics, 2005). Similarly, in 2001 the triad accounted for some 77 per cent of all reported international capital flows, a figure almost identical to that throughout the 1980s (Petrella 1996: 77; Bank for International Settlements 2004). The triadic character of world economic relations would seem well established and deeply entrenched.

Yet this does not exhaust the case against the globalization thesis. Indeed, arguably rather more important is the regional (rather than global or triadic) character of the process of economic integration we witness today. The work of Jeffrey Frankel is particularly significant, in this respect, though it is now expressive of a wider consensus amongst trade economists.

The issue here is less whether globalization is under way or not, as the extent to which any trend towards globalization is swamped at least in aggregate terms by rather more powerful regionalizing tendencies. Here it is important to distinguish very clearly between *intra-* and *inter-*regional processes of economic integration. By intra-regional economic integration we are referring to developments internal to a region – more specifically, in this instance, to the tendency of economies within a region to transact more business with one another. By inter-regional integration we are referring to developments across regional boundaries – more specifically, in this instance, to the tendency of economies to transact more business with partners beyond the region in which they are located. It is plausible to assume that both processes are under way, but that they are developing at different paces.

The empirical evidence is clear, and it is difficult to reconcile with the globalization thesis. The most pervasive and powerful dynamic within the international political economy is in fact intra-regionalization. This swamps any tendency to inter-regional economic integration. In other words, intra-regional trade accounts for an ever growing share of global trade. This is clearly seen from the data presented in figure 4.5, which updates and extends a similar graph in Frankel (1997: 22). It shows intra-regional trade as a proportion of total trade for a number of regional economies/regional trading areas and shows a clear tendency for the ratio of intra-regional to total trade to rise over time. That trend remains unabated in the first decade of the twenty-first century.

A similar propensity for the rate of intra-regional economic integration to exceed that for inter-regional economic integration has also been demonstrated for both inward and outward foreign direct investment (Hay 2006; Kleinknecht and ter Wengel 1998).

The degree of capital market integration

Given the significance attached to financial integration in the literature on globalization and the constraints on domestic policy autonomy that are seen to issue from it, it is hardly surprising that the third key pillar of the

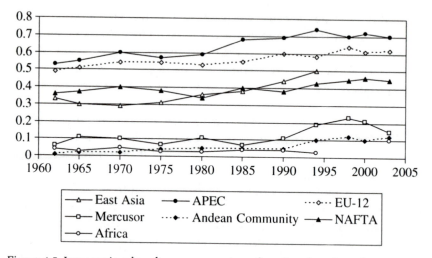

Figure 4.5 Intra-regional trade as a proportion of total trade, selected regions and regional trade areas.

Key: EU-12 = Belgium and Luxembourg, Denmark, France, Germany, Greece, Ireland, Italy, Netherlands, Portugal, Spain and United Kingdom; NAFTA = USA, Canada and Mexico; East Asia = ASEAN-6 (Brunei, Indonesia, Malaysia, Philippines, Singapore and Thailand) plus China, Hong Kong, Japan, Korea and Taiwan; Mercusor = Argentina, Brazil, Paraguay and Uruguay; APEC = East Asia-11 plus NAFTA-3 plus Australia, Chile, New Zealand and Papua New Guinea; Andean Community = Bolivia, Colombia, Ecuador, Peru and Venezuela. *Sources:* Calculated from Frankel 1997: 22–4; *WTO Trade Statistics* (2005)

critique of the globalization thesis concerns capital market integration. Space prevents a detailed consideration of what is at times a highly technical debate invariably pitting equations against logistic regressions (though for more systematic yet accessible reviews, see Hay 2005a; Watson 2001). Suffice it here to note that there are good grounds for questioning the extent to which capital markets are as integrated globally as proponents of the globalization thesis tend to imply. Indeed, the real question is whether capital markets as loosely integrated as those we see in the 'real world' are capable of generating the constraints on policy-makers' autonomy at the domestic level that the literature predicts (see for instance Mosley 2003). That is a question to which we return presently, in considering the dependent variable.

The basis of the case against the globalization of financial markets is, in essence, quite simple. It comes in two parts. The first is concerned with interest rate convergence, the second with the persistence of national savings and investment correlations. Both elements of the critique of the globalization orthodoxy work by counterposing the 'real world' performance of capital markets with what we would expect in a world of perfect market integration. Due to limits of space, we will merely consider the first.

In a fully integrated global capital market, we should expect a common international rate of interest on both short- and long-term loans to emerge relatively rapidly. For, if borrowers seek the lowest rate of interest available to them and are free to borrow across national boundaries, they will rapidly relocate their loans to those providing the most favourable terms. In order to continue to provide loans, lenders will need to offer loans competitively, at the global and not the national market rate. The result is an anticipated convergence of interest rates, any residual interest rate differential being an index of the extent to which capital markets remain less than perfectly integrated. The important point, as a growing literature testifies, is that interest rate differentials persist, and show little sign of being eroded (for a review of the literature, see Simmons 1999: 57–61). Moreover, as sceptics like Robert Zevin take some pleasure in noting, 'every available descriptor of financial markets in the late nineteenth and early twentieth century suggests that they were more fully integrated than they were before or have been since' (1992: 51–2).

Why is this so? A number of factors might be identified. First, it is not so much that capital markets have failed to integrate internationally as that it is naïve ever to expect them to conform closely to the economics textbooks' predictions of perfect market integration. Second, and perhaps more significantly, capital markets did not require for their integration the digital technology of the global age. In fact, as Hirst and Thompson have argued persuasively, it was the coming of the electronic telegraph in the 1870s – and not the switch from telegraph to telematics a century later – that was largely responsible for the raising of levels of capital market integration to those we witness today. Contemporary levels of market integration are far from unprecedented historically.

The dependent variable: state retrenchment

This brings us to the dependent variable. If globalization is a relatively poor description of both the degree and the character of the integration of the world economy, then are the rumours of the demise of domestic policy-making autonomy with which it is associated similarly exaggerated? The short answer to that question is 'yes'. In this section I seek to explain why.

The size and scope of the state

The first and most obvious point is that despite apocalyptic pronouncements of its imminent demise, the nation-state has, palpably, failed to disappear. Indeed, in terms of its *scope*, it is difficult to find much aggregate evidence of state retrenchment, let alone evaporation.

As Figure 4.6 shows, gauged in terms of the economic resources it consumes, it is difficult not to conclude that the state is very active indeed. What these data show, at best, is a slowing of the rate of growth of state expenditure as a share of national output (GDP) since the 1980s. What they do not show is any obvious sign of state retrenchment, or even evidence of a convergence between such economies in the share of GDP they expend (there being no sign of the highest levels of state expenditure falling towards the mean). What we see instead is that the state is arguably larger today, even amongst the most advanced and open economies in the world, than at any previous point in its history. Very similar inferences can be drawn from looking at the share of the total workforce employed by the state (see Hay 2005a: 247).

One caveat perhaps needs to be entered at this point. Aggregate data such as these tell us nothing about the character of state expenditure. What we do know is that the demands placed upon advanced liberal democratic states have grown in recent decades – as average unemployment levels have risen and, above all, as populations have aged. Given that these

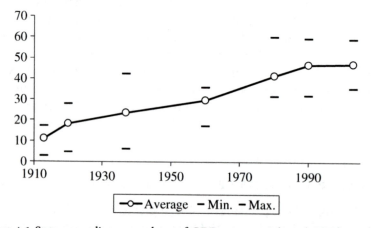

Figure 4.6 State expenditure as a share of GDP, per cent, selected OECD countries
Note: Data for France, Germany, Italy, Japan, Netherlands, Norway, Sweden, UK and US (the only OECD countries with an uninterrupted series of data)
Source: Calculated from OECD, *Economic Outlook*; Tanzi and Schuknecht 2000

states have tended to be characterized, at least since the early post-war years, by relatively inclusive and generous welfare provision, we might well attribute the scalar increase in state expenditure since the 1970s to demographic factors. Indeed, were one to modify the data to control for increases in welfare need associated with demographic change alone, one might reveal some modest degree of state retrenchment in recent years (see Hay 2006). It would certainly seem to be the case that the most developed welfare states are rather less generous today than they were in their heyday, despite the fact that welfare provision consumes a greater share of GDP than ever before.

Though this is no trivial matter, especially for benefit claimants, it is but a minor qualification. Whether or not the welfare state is more generous than it once was, globalization is compatible with far higher levels of state expenditure than the prevailing orthodoxy would seem to imply. For these states are not only amongst the largest in the world (in terms of the share of GDP they consume); they are also amongst the most exposed to the pressures of globalization in the sense that their economies are amongst the most open (in terms of trade, investment and financial flows).

The correlation between trade volume and state expenditure

This brings us to a second, and equally important, piece of the evidential puzzle. This concerns the correlation between state expenditure (again, gauged as a share of GDP) and economic openness. If the globalization thesis is accurate, we would expect to see a negative correlation between the openness of an economy to trade, investment flows and so forth and levels of state expenditure as a share of GDP ('stateness'). Yet, as a consistent body of literature now demonstrates, that expectation is confounded by the empirical record. This was first shown by David Cameron in 1978. What he demonstrated was a strong positive correlation between stateness and openness. He also demonstrated that openness was correlated positively with social democratic tenure, union power and the degree of regulation of the labour market.

That is all very well, but 1978 was a long time ago, and Cameron's data arguably pre-date by some way the full impact of globalization. This, indeed, would be a valid objection were it not for the consistency and, indeed, frequency with which Cameron's findings have subsequently been confirmed. If anything, the positive correlation he demonstrated in 1978 has only strengthened in recent years, as a now sizeable body of literature testifies (see for instance Katzenstein 1985; Rodrik 1996, 1997; Garrett

1998). Indeed, figure 4.7 shows that even the most recent data (those for the period 2000–3 for selected OECD countries) display the same clear positive correlation.

The puzzle, it would seem, is not which way the correlation goes, but how best to explain it. Dani Rodrik (1997: 53) sees high levels of state expenditure as an important reinvestment of the proceeds generated by trade – providing collective societal insurance against the risks (individual and collective) associated with dependence on export markets. Others, however, stress the more direct economic advantages to be gained by comprehensive welfare provision and high-quality public services. Such authors see high levels of state expenditure as intimately associated with the production of high-quality, high-value-added consumer goods for luxury markets by highly skilled, flexible, committed and well-educated employees in conditions of social and industrial harmony (Garrett 1998; Gough 1996; Swank 2002). Either way, it seems, high levels of state expenditure need not be a burden on competitiveness in an integrated world economy. The character of one's labour market and the generosity of one's welfare state would seem to remain matters of domestic political choice.

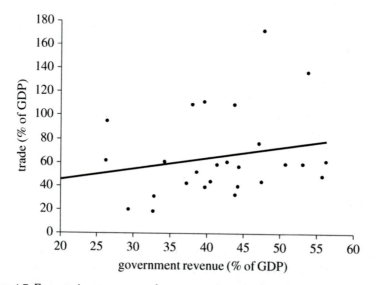

Figure 4.7 Economic openness and state spending, OECD member state averages, 2000–3
Sources: World Bank Trade Data (various years); OECD Pocketbook Data (various years); author's own calculations

Foreign direct investment and state expenditure

A strong positive correlation between trade volume and state expenditure is certainly damaging to the globalization thesis, but economic globalization is by no means reducible to trade. It is important, then, that we examine the evidence with respect to foreign direct investment and financial flows more generally, before concluding that the thesis is flawed.

Figure 4.8 plots the average volume of inbound foreign direct investment for the period 2000–3 against the average level of government revenue (as a share of GDP) over the same time period. It reveals a strong and positive correlation between volumes of inbound foreign direct investment and government revenue.

This is an important result, and one again borne out by a substantial body of literature (Cooke and Noble 1998; Dunning 1988; Traxler and Woitech 2002; Wilensky 2002). It shows that the picture with respect to trade is not the exception to the rule. It also adds further support to the view that high levels of state expenditure may in fact contribute to the competitiveness of the economy, rather than placing a burden upon it. Yet, as with all aggregate data, it cannot present us with a complete picture. For that we need a rather more disaggregated view of the evidence. For a long time, at least with respect to foreign direct investment, that was simply not available to us. But in recent years a new body of literature has emerged which sheds considerable light on the motivations behind the investment decisions of multi-national corporations.

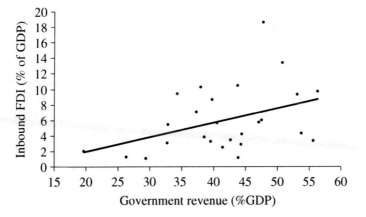

Figure 4.8 Inbound foreign direct investment and state revenue, OECD member state averages, 2000–3
Sources: World Bank Trade Data (various years); OECD Pocketbook Data (various years); author's own calculations

Notable here is the recent work of William N. Cooke and Deborah S. Noble. Their research examines the preferences, as revealed in exhibited investment behaviour, of US multi-nationals (1998). Their findings are in stark contrast to the prevailing globalization orthodoxy – as is their approach. Instead of making strong a priori assumptions about the rationality exhibited by foreign direct investors in their investment behaviour, Cooke and Noble infer investors' motivations and preferences from *actual* investment decisions. For instance, they do not simply assume that investors will be put off by high levels of corporate taxation, but instead examine the determinants of investment behaviour. In contrast to the vast majority of the existing literature, their approach is inductive and evidential, rather than deductive and abstract. Their principal findings can be summarized as follows.

1. Proximity and access to market are the single greatest determinants of investment location. Irrespective of their taxation and/or labour market regimes, affluent economies are likely to provide prime targets for foreign direct investors. Whilst investors might not like it, higher levels of corporate taxation would seem to be a price such investors are prepared to pay for market access.
2. The next most critical determinant of locational competitiveness is the skill and educational attainment level of the host economy's workforce. For the advanced liberal democracies (though not developing economies, where the correlation goes in the opposite direction), there is a strong positive correlation (which remains once market access/proximity is controlled for) between skill levels and foreign direct investment volumes. States able to supply their citizens with high levels of skill can expect to attract high levels of foreign direct investment to their shores.
3. Finally, there is no evidence that the degree of regulation of the labour market (the extent to which it is difficult to hire and fire workers, for instance, and the compensation payable to those made redundant) or non-wage labour costs (such as employers' pensions and national insurance contributions) suppress levels of inbound foreign direct investment. If anything, the converse is the case, with a positive correlation observed between the number of International Labour Organisation standards ratified and foreign direct investment volume.

On the basis of evidence like this, the notion that globalization is corrosive of the welfare state, let alone of the nation-state itself, would seem somewhat perverse.

Appeasing financial markets

The globalization thesis would not appear that strong if it were based solely on a consideration of the empirical evidence with respect to trade and foreign direct investment. Yet it might easily be resuscitated by a consideration of the constraints imposed on policy-makers at the national level by financial markets. Yet here again there is something of a disparity between the assumptions made about such actors and empirical evidence of their behaviour.

Again, until recently we were largely reliant on such stylized models of financial market actors' rationality in a context of ever more closely integrated and global financial markets. Yet, in recent years a rather more inductive and evidential approach to the behaviour of financial market actors has started to develop, paralleling that described in the previous section with respect to foreign direct investment. Notable here is the work of Layna Mosley (2003).

Mosley's methodology is, in the context of the existing literature, highly innovative. Rejecting deductive approaches which build from a priori assumptions about financial market actors' preferences, she develops an alternative inductive approach. This is based on an exhaustive series of interviews with fund managers, designed to solicit their expressed preferences. But she does not simply substitute such expressed preferences for the existing literature's assumed preferences in building an alternative and equally stylized model of financial market behaviour. Instead, she compares the preferences of fund managers as revealed in real investment decisions with their rationalization of their conduct to her in their responses to interview questions. Any anomalies are further explored in interviews. The results are extremely illuminating. They reveal a rather different rationality on the part of fund managers from that assumed in almost all of the existing literature.

In particular, Mosley's findings challenge the assumptions in the existing literature about financial market actors' information. Thus, although the liberalization of financial markets has undoubtedly increased the potential damage that investors can inflict upon an economy (through speculative assaults on its currency, for instance), capital market participants are far less well informed or, indeed, discriminating in their political risk assessment than has previously been assumed. Far from being blessed with near complete information about relevant economic policy decisions in the states in whose currencies their assets are denominated, capital market actors' knowledge base is actually very limited. As Mosley shows in some detail, their investment decisions are in fact informed by an assessment of a very small number of key variables, typically just two – the rate of inflation and the level of government debt. For the advanced liberal democracies in particular, provided that inflation is (deemed to be) under control and levels of government debt are not deemed excessive, the economy is unlikely to be considered a political risk for investment. As Mosley explains:

> Governments are pressured strongly to satisfy financial market preferences in terms of overall inflation and government budget deficit levels but retain domestic policymaking latitude in other areas. The means by which governments achieve macropolicy outcomes, and the nature of government policies in other areas, do not concern financial market participants . . . [G]overnments retain a significant amount of policy autonomy and political accountability. If, for domestic reasons, they prefer to retain traditional social democratic policies, for instance, they are quite able to do so. (2003: 305)

This is a most important finding, suggesting, as it does, that although financial markets have great potential power to punish macroeconomic policy choices that incur their wrath, and great disciplining power as a consequence, they are in fact far more tolerant of policy diversity than has conventionally been assumed. The most recent literature (see also Swank 2002) simply does not find any evidence to substantiate the claim that social-democratic economic governance, welfare state expansion and the era of big government are rendered anachronistic by virtue of financial market integration.

The rhetoric and reality of the globalization thesis

The preceding sections certainly serve to do some considerable damage to the prevailing orthodoxy that has come to surround the term 'globalization'. Despite the proliferation of the language of globalization and despite the ubiquitous nature of the assumption that we live in an era of globalization, definitive evidence of a single and ever more closely integrated world economy is remarkably elusive. Indeed, as the literature on international economic integration has become more and more empirical, it has become more and more sceptical about the extent of globalization. This is not to argue that the world economy is, in aggregate terms, not more closely integrated than ever before. But it is to suggest that the terms 'regionalization' and, indeed, 'triadization' better describe the character of that process of integration than the far more popular term 'globalization'.

The picture with respect to the dependent variable is not so very different. Despite the often apocalyptic pronouncements of the inexorable demise of the nation-state at the hand of globalization, there is plenty of evidence of its continued activity and, indeed, its continued efficacy. Governments make choices, and those choices continue to matter for the welfare of their citizens. Again, as the literature has become more and more empirical in content, it has become increasingly sceptical as to the corrosive impact of globalization on the policy-making autonomy of the nation-state.

That is all well and good, and it would be tempting to conclude from this that globalization does indeed have nothing to do with the space for democratic deliberation and, ultimately, depoliticization, disenchantment and disengagement. Yet we would be quite wrong to draw this inference. For there is one very important way in which, notwithstanding the empirical evidence we have considered, globalization continues to exert a powerful influence on policy-making autonomy and the capacity for democratic deliberation at the national level. That is through the *idea* of globalization. Quite simply, if policy-makers believe that their autonomy is greatly diminished and that, in an era of globalization, their policy choices must be driven by the perceived imperatives of competitiveness, they will deny themselves the political autonomy they might otherwise enjoy. The resulting loss of the capacity for democratic political deliberation is no less significant – nor is the depoliticization that ensues.

Indeed, this, I suggest, describes depressingly accurately the situation we now face. Just as policy-makers in the advanced liberal democracies have increasingly come to internalize and project on to themselves the most pessimistic of public choice assumptions about their own motivations and conduct, so too they have come to embrace the most pessimistic of assumptions about their very capacity to act. This has served to unleash a tide of depoliticizing dynamics as policy-makers have, effectively, questioned their integrity, their professional competence, and their capacity to make policy – and have off-loaded their responsibilities to others in the process. When our political elites seem to hold such pessimistic assumptions about their competence, credibility and autonomy, is it any wonder that as citizens of the polities they serve we have come to share in their crisis of political confidence and competence? Is it any wonder that we participate in formal political processes increasingly reluctantly, and in ever smaller numbers?

As this suggests, although the state today consumes a greater share of global GDP than at any previous point in its history, and although economic openness is in fact positively correlated with most indices of state expenditure and activity, the so-called era of globalization has undoubtedly precipitated a crisis of confidence in the capacity and autonomy of domestic policy-makers. In this respect, globalization has much to do with it. Yet, the evidence reviewed in this chapter would suggest that the state is in fact a rather more potent force, or at least a rather more *potentially* potent force, than we tend these days to give it credit for. But it remains the case that if the state is not perceived to have the capacity that it once enjoyed to influence events, it is unlikely to play as considerable a role in the shaping of societal destinies as it might.

For some, that is a good thing, and it is certainly true that the nation-state has, in its still relatively brief history, done an awful lot of harm to an awful lot of people. But the nation-state still remains the natural vessel of democratic deliberation in a world of complex interdependence, and if it increasingly cedes to the market and to independent authorities its undoubted capacity for governance, we will have lost much of our collective ability to hold power to account democratically. If the analysis of this chapter and this book is correct, there is no inevitability about this; the choice is ours.

5

Why Do We Hate Politics?

In this volume I have sought to provide a distinctive account of the origins of the contemporary condition of political disenchantment. I have done so by developing a fresh perspective on the concepts of politics, politicization and depoliticization in – and perhaps *for* – an age of political disaffection and disenchantment. The resulting approach to political analysis and to the question of why we hate politics has been unapologetically unconventional. I have not sought to concentrate on what politics *should* be like, though I have had a fair amount to say about what it *might* be like. Instead, I have adopted a rather more inductive approach – reflecting on the concept of politics by looking at the practices we label 'political', the characteristics we attribute to those practices when we appeal to them as political, and the attitudes towards politics and the political that this reveals. What this shows, all too clearly, is how low our expectations of (formal) politics now are, and how frequently, nonetheless, politics still fails to live up to those expectations. If this is the contemporary political condition, then it does not make for a very edifying spectacle. 'Politics' is a dirty word, a term that has come to acquire a whole array of almost entirely negative associations and connotations in contemporary discourse. Politics is synonymous with sleaze, corruption and duplicity, greed, self-interest and self-importance, interference, inefficiency and intransigence. It is, at best, a necessary evil, at worst an entirely malevolent force that needs to be kept in check.

The contemporary condition of political disaffection is, of course, by no means unprecedented historically. Yet it is difficult to think of a period of modern history in which the term has acquired quite such an array of negative connotations in public discourse. What makes this all the more remarkable is that this most recent demonization of the political should coincide with the first time in human history when democracy might legitimately claim to be the dominant form that politics – at least formal politics – takes. Democracy is, of course, a *bon mot* in almost all contemporary political discourse. Indeed, democracy is now invariably cast as the ideal which politics subverts. Democracy is an ethereal principle beyond reproach, politics a

sordid and grubby practice beyond redemption. It is the paradoxical coincidence of the global ascendancy and diffusion of the idea of democracy and
the contemporary condition of disaffection and (formal) political disengagement that I have principally sought to explore in this book.

In this brief conclusion I reflect on the implications of that exploration
for our understanding of politics and the political today. These reflections
are organized into four sections. In the first I seek to isolate the principal
determinants of the contemporary condition of political disaffection and
disengagement that I have sought to diagnose, before turning, in the
second, to the problem of attributing responsibility and blame. The third
section reflects further on the nature of the explanation for political disenchantment offered in this volume. In particular, it problematizes the simple
supply-side / demand-side distinction on which I have thus far drawn. The
fourth and final section considers the implications of the argument for the
reanimation of the political, for the political re-engagement of the public,
and for the agenda of contemporary political analysis.

The 'politics *we* deserve' or the 'levels of political participation *they* deserve'?

As we saw in chapter 1, the contemporary condition of political disaffection
and disengagement has attracted a vast literature by more or less anxious
analysts, commentators and practitioners. Some have bemoaned the
decline of civic virtue in contemporary societies, arguing that political
disaffection and disengagement are part of a broader societal malaise.
Others have discerned a rather more innocent process whereby the rise of
post-material values has generated a better-educated, more savvy, less deferential and more critical electorate less inclined to vote out of habit or out
of simple respect for political authority, and less likely to be taken in by politics as a consequence. Still others have attributed the decline in electoral
participation largely to the cumulative consequences of the lowering of the
voting age and the effect this has had in enfranchising those least well integrated into social networks. Yet what is immediately striking – though
rarely noted – about all of this literature is its almost exclusive emphasis on
what I have termed 'demand-side factors'.

In all of these accounts, it is not politics or the 'supply' of political goods
that has changed, but the receptiveness or 'demand' of citizens for the political goods on offer. This is obviously a convenient message for politicians
who, to the extent to which declining formal political participation can be
read as a demand-side phenomenon, are absolved of all responsibility. Yet

to allow such a view to remain unchallenged is to exclude from consideration a variety of potentially plausible supply-side factors, for which political culpability might not so easily be displaced. It is almost as if the existing
literature proceeds from the premise that *citizens get the politics they deserve.*

My approach has been entirely different. In so far as it can be summarized in an equivalent premise, it is that *democratic polities get the levels of
political participation they deserve.* To be fair, this is not so much a premise as
a heuristic. It has served as an analytical device for gaining a fresh perspective on a complex set of issues that we have become accustomed – too
accustomed, perhaps – to viewing in a certain way. It immediately serves to
highlight a range of potential supply-side factors largely absent from the
existing literature. Much of this volume – most directly chapters 3 and 4 –
has been concerned to explore further and to elucidate the potential
explanatory influence of these factors. The resulting argument is, I think,
in the context of the existing literature distinctive. It can be stated relatively
simply, though the devil is undoubtedly in the detail.

What we expect from politics is dependent to a considerable extent on
the assumptions we project on to politicians and public officials – about
both their motivations and their capacity to influence events. And those
assumptions have changed decisively in recent years. It is not at all difficult
to show that such assumptions are, today, profoundly pessimistic ones; nor
is it difficult to show that this is still a relatively recent phenomenon.
Unremarkably perhaps, it parallels the rise of political disaffection and disengagement. Politicians are assumed today not to be selfless representatives
of those who elected them, or benevolent guardians of the public good, or
even partisan advocates of a particular cause. They are, instead, self-serving
and self-interested rational utility-maximizers. They are, moreover, increasingly seen to be powerless and ineffective in the face of processes beyond
their control.

This is a very distinctive conception both of the motivations of political
actors and of their capacity to act. And it is not at all surprising that such a
view should be associated with declining levels of formal political participation. Explaining its origins, I have argued, is crucial to accounting for the
contemporary condition of political disaffection and disengagement. That
is no easy task, however. The profound similarities between the assumptions
projected on to politicians in contemporary public discourse, on the one
hand, and those that politicians project on to themselves, on the other, provided an initial clue. Indeed, an examination of the public political rationale
offered for the depoliticization of policy-making revealed the internalization by political elites of a similarly instrumental conception of the motiva-

tions of political actors. In so doing, it suggested the potential source of such ideas in public choice theory, a body of theory that has come to acquire phenomenal influence since the 1980s in steering the trajectory of public policy.

In chapter 3 I charted the influence of public choice theory since that time, showing how the internalization of the assumption of instrumental rationality on the part of political actors has led, in a variety of policy domains, to a series of processes of depoliticization. I also showed how an equivalent set of assumptions had been incorporated into the politics of electoral competition through the growing influence of political marketing techniques. In so doing, I suggested the alarmingly cumulative consequences of seemingly innocent assumptions. For, assuming electoral competition to be analogous to that between rival businesses for market share, I argued, may have served to turn the rational voter paradox into something of a self-fulfilling prophecy. However rational it is for parties-as-businesses to appeal to the narrow self-interest of the median voter-as-consumer, we should not forget that voting in such a scenario is an irrational act – since political goods are indivisible, and since the stakes of the contest will have been effectively reduced to zero by the process of median convergence.

In chapter 4 I developed a parallel argument for the influence of ideas about globalization on the diminished capacity for democratic political deliberation at the national level. I reviewed, thoroughly and systematically, the evidence for globalization itself and for its widely assumed corrosive impact on domestic policy-making autonomy, challenging both the descriptive accuracy of the term 'globalization' and the extent to which policy-making autonomy has indeed been eroded at the domestic level. Yet I suggested that, in one sense less significant than whether policy-making autonomy has actually been eroded, is whether it is perceived to have been eroded. For whether policy-making autonomy is denied to policy-makers by globalization or whether it is something they deny themselves by virtue of the ideas they hold about globalization, it is denied. The capacity for democratic political deliberation is correspondingly eroded.

Who is to blame?

So who is to blame for this? Three potential candidates logically present themselves from the argument I have sought to develop: the electorate, those competing for their votes, and, more strangely perhaps, academic political commentators. In fact, though each has come to play a decisive role in the demonization of the political, blame cannot easily be apportioned among them. But in so far as my argument absolves any of these potential suspects of responsibility, it is the electorate – though often the immediate agent of political disaffection and disengagement – that it exonerates most clearly. I do not 'blame' potential voters for their invariably cynical, negative and pessimistic assumptions about the motivations and capacities of political actors. Yet I do argue that such assumptions are, almost certainly, unwarranted; that they have had, and continue to have, an alarmingly cumulative and corrosive impact upon democratic political culture and the capacity of political elites to deliver collective / public goods; and that our reasons for holding such assumptions have precious little to do with the 'reality' of politics itself. It would, of course, be nice if we trusted, and felt able to trust, politicians – both to do good and to have the capacity to do good – rather more than we do. Moreover, the capacity of the latter to do good would almost certainly be enhanced were they so trusted. But they are not, and that they are not is not something for which the electorate can be held responsible.

So, are politicians themselves to blame? If democratic polities get the levels of (formal) political participation they deserve, as I have argued, and levels of democratic participation are alarmingly low, as I have also argued, then surely if anyone is to blame it is those who put themselves forward for high office? This may well seem like a logical inference to draw from the preceding remarks. But it is not the argument I make. In projecting no less bleak, no less instrumental, and no less pessimistic assumptions about both their motivations and their capacity to act on to political actors and public servants, they have certainly conspired in the demonization of the political. Moreover, informed by such assumptions, they have further denuded the political, discharging and off-loading their responsibilities to those less directly and publicly accountable for their decisions. In so doing they have significantly undermined not only their own capacity to deliver collective public goods, but also the collective societal capacity for public deliberation. Yet their motivations for so doing, however misconceived, have been largely genuine. Indeed, somewhat ironically, the very process of depoliticization in which they have engaged as a consequence of holding such assumptions indicates just how wrong they were to project on to themselves such narrowly instrumental motivations in the first place.

No, if we are to explain and attribute responsibility for the contemporary condition of disaffection and disengagement, then we must look beyond the relationship between the electorate and those they elect – to the origins of the ideas and assumptions that both project on to political actors. As I have argued, there is nothing unprecedented culturally about the projection of instrumental self-interest on to political elites. Such assumptions have a very long and distinguished history. They can be seen in Machiavelli and, indeed, in the Madisonian and Jeffersonian traditions which underpin the US Constitution. Yet it is in public choice theory that they have been explored most systematically, and it is in public choice theory that they have been given their contemporary inflection. Moreover, it is public choice theory that has directly informed the pervasive and at times quite conscious and deliberate depoliticization of democratic governance to which disaffection and disengagement would seem a most natural reaction. Yet it would be wrong to attribute all responsibility and blame for contemporary political disenchantment to public choice theorists. Indeed, the search for someone to blame may well be part of the problem here. Knowing at whom to point the finger may be well be comforting, but it gets us no closer to reanimating the political and re-engaging citizens in the democratic process. The contemporary condition of political disaffection and disengagement is perhaps better seen as the result of an unfortunate series of cumulative, mutually reinforcing, yet largely unintended consequences, in which public choice theoretical assumptions have undoubtedly played a crucial role. Such assumptions may never have been very realistic, are arguably no more realistic today than they have ever been, and have had, and continue to have, a series of profoundly debilitating consequences for the supply of public goods. Yet they have found, and continue to find, a receptive audience. And for that we are all partly to blame.

Problematizing the supply-side/demand-side distinction

Thus far I have tended to present the alternative explanation of political disaffection and disengagement that I have sought to develop in this volume as a supply-side corrective to a pervasive demand-side orthodoxy. That is certainly simple and neat, but, as briefly hinted at in the conclusion to chapter 1, it is perhaps just a little too simple and a little too neat. Moreover, given the above remarks about the cumulative consequences of innocent analogies, especially economic ones, the language of supply and demand might be seen as somewhat inappropriate in this context. These two points are in fact closely connected, as we shall see.

It is certainly the case that my reflections on the problem of the decline in political participation have been motivated, to a considerable extent, by a desire to place at centre stage the content and character of contemporary public policy. That, in turn, was motivated by a certain frustration that so much of the existing literature should start and finish with citizens – putting them in the dock, as it were, for their apparent political disinterest, rather than asking whether the quality of the 'political goods' on offer might not have something to do with it. In that respect my approach does indeed search for a supply-side alternative to a demand-side consensus.

But is that what I have provided? Arguably not. In seeking to explain declining formal political participation, I have undoubtedly pointed to a range of supply-side factors – most obviously a variety of forms of depoliticization. I have suggested that privatization, the contracting-out of public services, the marketization of public goods, the displacement of policy-making autonomy from the formal political realm to independent authorities, the rationalization and insulation from critique of neoliberalism as an economic paradigm, and the denial of policy choice (for instance, in discerning the imperatives of competitiveness in an era of globalization) are all forms of depoliticization. Each serves, effectively, to diminish and denude the realm of formal public political deliberation; each might be seen as a legitimate cause of political disaffection and disengagement (at least from formal politics). Moreover, the increasing adoption of a range of political marketing techniques has also resulted in a narrowing of the field of electoral competition (at least in policy terms), the depoliticization of whole areas of public policy, a tendency to remove questions of policy content, especially those involving significant institutional reform from electoral scrutiny, and a compensating politicization of the personality traits of candidates for high office. Again, each of these is a supply-side factor, and each might credibly be linked to declining levels of formal political participation.

Yet such supply-side factors are important in determining levels of formal political participation only in so far as they influence potential voters and the choices they make (whether consciously or subconsciously). As I argued in chapter 1, a focus on the demand side is here inevitable, since ultimately it is the electorate, not those who stand for office, who must choose whether or not to participate. And, as that in turn suggests, if we are to explain trends in formal political participation (or any other form of participation for that matter), we cannot avoid considering the attitudes and perceptions of potential participants. In other words, supply-side factors matter only in so far as they result in a change in the *demand* for the political goods on offer. In that sense, this remains a demand-side account, albeit one rather more sensitive to the supply-side factors that so often underpin such changes in demand than in many conventional accounts.

Yet, not all of the factors that I have pointed to as of potential explanatory significance can be traced back to the supply side in this way. This is particularly true of general societal assumptions about, and attitudes towards, politics and the political. As I have sought to demonstrate, these underpin declining formal political participation and the contemporary condition of political disaffection and disengagement more generally. Yet it would be extremely dangerous to see these as a simple reflection of changes in political reality, as it were. Indeed, and as I have sought at various points to suggest, arguably they have rather more to do with changes in intellectual fashion than with changes in the moral fibre of political actors. As citizens of democratic polities, we increasingly project instrumental assumptions on to political actors and public officials. But that does not make it right to do so, the potentially self-fulfilling consequences of assuming the worst of those we elect notwithstanding. In public discourse the term 'politics' is, indeed, increasingly synonymous with duplicity, greed, corruption, interference and inefficiency. But it seems distinctly unlikely that this is because today's breed of politicians are any more sinful that their predecessors. Altogether more likely is that we have simply got into the habit of viewing them, and their conduct, in such terms. And if we look hard enough, we are likely to find plenty of behaviour consistent with such pessimistic assumptions. Moreover, the more we look, the more we will reinforce that increasingly intuitive tendency. The contemporary condition of political disaffection and disengagement is, at least in part, a consequence of that unfortunate habit. Yet, what makes it harder to kick than it might otherwise be is that it seems to be a habit that politicians have also got into.

As this may suggest, it is time that we rejected the overly parsimonious language of supply and demand. Politics is more complicated than that, and the distorted depiction of politics that emerges from viewing it in narrowly economistic terms is responsible for much that I have sought to challenge in this volume. The distinction between supply-side and demand-side determinants of political disaffection has served its purpose. In particular, it has drawn attention to certain important lacunae in the existing literature that I have sought to fill. But there is a danger that it might now become an impediment to the further development of that literature – a literature whose task from now on must surely be to analyse rather more effectively the complex relationships between the ideas and assumptions we project on to politics on the one hand and the practices and processes on to which those ideas and assumptions are projected on the other.

Politics and human nature

This brings us finally to the implications of the argument I have sought to develop for the potential reanimation of the political, the political re-engagement of the public that this would entail, and, more prosaically perhaps, the agenda of contemporary political analysis.

It is tempting to conclude by suggesting that politics is what we make of it. And, to an extent, that is true. It is certainly the case, as I have sought to demonstrate, that what we can expect from, and what we are likely to get out of, politics are both dependent to a considerable extent on the assumptions about human nature that we project on to political actors. And, by extension, we are today expecting less from, and getting less out of, politics than we might by virtue of the assumptions we project on to political actors. Indeed, that is something of an understatement. If we assume the worst of political actors – and, by and large, we do – then our capacity for collective public deliberation and our capacity to provide a range of collective public goods – such as security, welfare and a sustainable environment – are significantly attenuated as a consequence. Politics is a social activity, and like most social activities, it works best in situations of co-operation and trust. If we assume that others cannot be trusted, or we assume (as in the precautionary principle) that they must first demonstrate themselves trustworthy before we will reciprocate, then we foreclose the very possibility of deliberation, co-operation and the provision of collective goods. In short, we disavow politics.

In a sense that is a choice. Moreover, in so far as it is a choice, this is an optimistic conclusion. But it is not a simple choice. Tempting though it might be to encourage us to think nicer thoughts about politics and politicians – on the basis that what politics is capable of depends on the assumptions we project on to political actors – that will not do. My argument is not that we should trust politicians and public servants more. We trust them as much as we feel able to, and that is the way it is. My point is subtly different. I ask merely that we consider rather more the cumulative consequences of the assumptions we project on to politics and political actors before we plump for them. In short, we should politicize such assumptions and seek to make them the subject of public deliberation. If we come to revise the narrowly instrumental conception of human nature that we currently project on to political actors in that process, all well and good. For what it is worth, I hope we do. If we do not, it is difficult to see how the contemporary condition of political disaffection and disengagement that I have sought both to describe and explain in this volume can be alleviated.

All I can hope for is that we acknowledge that we have a choice in the first place.

What of the implications for political analysis? The first point that might be noted here is rather obvious. It would seem reasonable to assume that contemporary political analysis has, or certainly should have, something of a stake in the contemporary condition of political disaffection and disengagement – and not just in the sense that political disaffection might serve to diminish the supply of students for the courses it provides! As noted in chapter 1, political analysts surely bear a certain responsibility towards their subject matter – they are, after all, not neutral, disinterested and dispassionate analysts, but participant observers. As such, one might expect them to display a certain concern at the extent of contemporary political disaffection and disengagement. Again, my argument is not that political analysts should spend their time proselytizing for a more positive depiction of current political trends. Rather, I suggest, they should be more concerned to show that politics can be about more than the pursuit of individual utility, and that the depiction of politics in such terms is both a distortion and a denial of the capacity for public deliberation and the provision of collective goods. These are defining features of politics, and they deserve a resolute defence from political analysts.

Finally, we still know remarkably little about what motivates actors to engage politically, and what animates and drives their political behaviour. We know very little, too, about the cognitive processes in and through which we come to attribute motivations to the behaviour we witness, or how we come to develop and revise the assumptions about human nature that we project on to others. If politics depends ultimately on our capacity to trust one another, if such trust in contemporary societies is increasingly conditional, increasingly fragile and in increasingly short supply, and if that is due in part to the increasing influence of a conception of human nature as narrowly instrumental and self-interested, then there can be no more important questions for political analysts than these. It is, moreover, increasingly urgent that we find some answers to these questions before politics is thoroughly depoliticized . . . and we are left with nothing to analyse.

Notes

Chapter 1 Political Disenchantment

1 As we shall see presently, there are those for whom declining levels of formal political participation are to be welcomed – as an indication of a more educated, less deferential, more savvy and correspondingly more cynical, critical and sanguine electorate. Most commentators would nonetheless concede that declining levels of political participation in ostensibly democratic political systems are not in themselves reassuring trends.

2 This is, of course, a rather idealized view, as the argument of later chapters will make very clear. The problem, in essence, is that just as collective action problems exist between corporations in a (hypothetical) closed national economy, so too they exist between states in an integrated world economy. In the absence of collectively binding international agreements that are rigidly monitored and policed, individual states will resist imposing upon their national economies exacting environmental standards and the costs to competitiveness that these might entail. The politics required to deal with this latter variety of collective action problem (one of 'global governance' in contemporary parlance) must be genuinely trans-national in scope and scale.

3 In a way this parallels Joseph Schumpeter's (1942) rightly famous suggestion that the rationalizing culture of liberal democracy with which contemporary capitalism is associated gives voice to intellectuals who serve systematically to scrutinize it, contributing in so doing to our sense of political disenchantment.

4 Actually, this too might be seen as something of a simplification. For arguably it is the ability of this relatively timeless critique of politics to acquire resonance with the experience of contemporary political practice that gives it access to positions of political power in the first place. Thus, rather than its influence reflecting the extent to which it has already acquired access to political power, its access to political power might be seen as conditional upon its ability to shape or mould impressions of politics.

5 On the almost systematic misrepresentation of Machiavelli's writings on 'politics' (a term he used sparingly and quite specifically), see especially Viroli 1992.

6 The equation of the ruler with the common good is also a central element of the iconography of the period. This is graphically and most powerfully demonstrated in Lorenzetti's famous fresco of 'good government' in Siena's Palazzo Publico (see Rubinstein 1958; Skinner 1978: i. 59).

7 It is here interesting to note that, etymologically, 'the state' and 'status' are synonymous.

8 The use of the term 'liberal republican', rather than the now more conventional term 'liberal democratic', is deliberate. For Madison, though keen to build the American polity on the basis of representative institutions, was quite reticent about referring to such institutions as democratic. This, for him, implied (decidedly Greek) connotations of direct rule – the dangers of which the US system of checks and balances was deliberately intended to prevent.

9 One important demographic fact complicates this otherwise relatively simple picture: namely, that the societies in which we live and vote are ageing. The reasons for this are twofold. First, and most obviously, we are tending to live longer. As a consequence, the voting life of those with the highest propensity to vote is being extended. Yet, even were this not the case, the average age of the voting population in most advanced liberal democracies would be rising, since birth rates from the 1970s have tended to fall. Taken together, these two factors have, in fact, served significantly to attenuate the effect of youth political disaffection and disengagement on aggregate turnout levels. For, all things being equal, we would expect an ageing society to be character-ized by rising not falling levels of political participation – the precise opposite of the exhibited trend.

10 Even habituated non-participants in formal politics, it would seem, still feel some sense of political obligation to participate and, indeed, a certain level of guilt at their non-participation. Such feelings are likely to be even stronger amongst 'recently lapsed' former participants. This would seem to account for the consistent tendency for levels of political participation to be over-reported in survey responses.

11 For an excellent and far more thorough analysis of these trends see Dalton 2004: 49–54.

12 And, albeit it to a lesser extent, a similar observation might be made of the French repub-lican tradition.

13 As Putnam himself concedes, 'no general and simultaneous decline in social capital throughout the industrial/post-industrial world over the last generation' can be observed (2002: 410).

14 In fact, as the recent research of Russell J. Dalton reveals (2004: 70–1), this is something of a simplification. At the level of the individual, statistically significant correlations can be observed between indices of social group membership and a variety of measures of political support. Similarly positive associations can be found between levels of social and political trust (though cf. Newton 1999; Newton and Norris 2000, which find no such relationship). The point, however, is that since levels of social capital and social trust are stable, whilst levels of political participation and trust are falling, the former cannot explain the longitudinal decline in the latter.

15 Given his description of social-scientific research as akin to solving *The Murder on the Orient Express* (Putnam 2000: 184), in that innumerable suspects present themselves, and there is often more than one perpetrator, one might be forgiven for expecting a more inclusive attitude towards potential explanatory variables in his recent work. And, to an extent, that is indeed what we see. However, to date that spirit of inclusiveness seems only to extend to demand-side factors.

16 Being one step closer to an explanation is, nonetheless, clearly better than being one step further away – and, in social and political analysis in particular, often constitutes a very significant achievement in its own right. I am indebted to an anonymous reader for pressing me on this important point.

17 Like-minded, that is, at least in the sense that they prefer the same candidate or party.

18 An assumption, it might be noted in passing, certainly no easier to reconcile with rational choice theory.

19 It is, of course, always easier to 'predict' outcomes that have already happened. Nonetheless, it is a very significant achievement to be able to construct a statistical model that is capable of predicting, to this level of accuracy, levels of turnout over a forty-year period in a large number of countries.

20 Indeed, given the inertial character of participation levels amongst generational cohorts, this is presumably precisely what Franklin would expect.

21 Franklin's data are here suggestive. They show that young cohorts of potential voters are more likely to vote if they are in full-time education or regard themselves as religious. On the other hand, they are actually less likely to vote if they are regular church-goers

(2004: 159–61). The point, however, is that none of these data cast any light on the degree to which newly enfranchised voters are members of extensive social networks.

Chapter 2   Politics, Participation and Politicization

1 For the proponents of such a view of politics, notably public choice theorists, that is precisely the point. Convinced that actors are motivated solely by considerations of self-interest, they proceed to show that politics as conventionally understood – the delivery of collective or public goods – is either impossible or, at best, a fortuitous accident. Consequently, the extent to which we continue to define politics in terms of the provision of such goods is the extent to which we continue to delude ourselves. This is an argument to which we return in much greater detail in the following chapter. Suffice it for now to note that if we refuse to accept that actors are motivated solely by self-interest, then a rather different view of politics emerges.

2 To associate politics with the capacity for agency is not, of course, to deny that such a capacity is displayed in arenas – such as the market – conventionally described in non-political terms. Indeed, if anything, it is to point to the potential value of a political analysis of arenas such as the market, complementing the modes of analysis (here, economic) with which they are more conventionally associated.

3 As we shall see presently, however, it is by no means a neutral definition and is not compatible with a number of the definitions in the two lists above.

4 As is ever the case, there are exceptions – notably the provision, in some US states, for referenda to be held when the public demands them.

5 This is not, of course, to suggest that wedding invitations (whether accompanied by an official wedding present list or not) do not come with their own sense of obligation and duty. An offer which cannot be refused is, of course, not an offer at all. The old aphorism almost certainly applies – there is no such thing as a free lunch. On the implicitly contractual nature of the 'gift relationship' see Mauss 1954; Titmuss 1971.

6 Though the term 'anti-globalization' is appropriate in the sense that it was – as it remains – the protestors' chosen badge of self-identification, it is potentially misleading. For, as much as anything else, such protestors sought to draw attention to, and to seek redress for, the distortion of the terms of trade between North and South. In effect, they were identifying protectionist tendencies in the terms of international trade associated with the desire to protect the interests and trade balances of the developed world at the expense of developing economies. As such, their protests might better be characterized as pro-globalization rather than anti-globalization. In effect, what they sought to demonstrate and expose was the uneven character of the process of globalization and the uneven distribution of any efficiency gains associated with it. Ironically, in so doing, they endorsed the core contention of neo-Ricardian free-trade economics – that the globalization of trade is good for us since it leads to efficiency gains. This, of course, is precisely the same mantra that underpins the so-called Washington consensus – the ostensible target of the protestors' resistance.

7 Whatever their motivations for so doing, should a sufficiently large proportion of eligible voters fail to vote, the legitimacy of the government elected, and indeed the electoral process itself, may be called into question. If, as I have suggested they can be, actions may be judged political in terms of their consequences, then failing to remember to vote or not being bothered to vote are political acts.

8 It is, of course, an empirical question which poses almost intractable methodological problems. For respondents who may well feel a certain moral or political obligation to vote are likely to under-report both their electoral non-participation and the extent to which a simple failure to remember to vote is responsible.

9 Whilst religion has often played a key role in policing the boundaries between the realms of necessity or fate and contingency or choice, it would be entirely wrong to present religion as a realm of depoliticized fate. Conceptions of free will and choice are crucial to many religions, and are often powerfully politicizing.

10 On the complex role played by both religion and secularization in the development of the modern state, see Crone (1989); G. Gill (2003); Hall and Ikenberry (1989); Hay and Lister (2006: 4–6).

11 This does not of course mean that science has had no role to play in processes of depoliticization. Indeed, that is an issue to which we return presently.

12 This is not, of course, to suggest that the principal motive underpinning the development of regionally co-ordinated policies (most obviously those of the European Union) is the depoliticization that might result from the displacement of political responsibility to trans-national bodies. That is an unduly cynical view, for which there is scant evidence. It is also to overlook the considerable potential to increase policy-making capacity (if not domestic autonomy) associated with policy co-ordination at the regional level.

13 The 2006 leadership contest for the UK's Liberal Democratic Party clearly shows that this point is still some way off, with two of the four initially declared candidates for the leadership being subject to intensive and sustained media speculation regarding their sexual orientation. Indeed, Mark Oaten, the party's then Home Affairs spokesman was forced to withdraw his candidacy and to resign from his shadow ministerial post when he was informed by journalists from the tabloid newspaper *The News of the World* that they would be running the story that he had regularly paid for sex with a male prostitute. The leadership contest was itself precipitated by the resignation of Charles Kennedy following a public admission of his widely publicized drink problem.

14 For attempts to map such appeals comparatively, see Hay and Rosamond 2002; Hay and Smith 2004.

Chapter 3   The Domestic Sources of Depoliticization

1 I am greatly indebted to Jim Buller and Matthew Flinders for their help in tracking down many of the references cited in this paragraph.

2 The principal problem in relying on the market to provide such goods is that many of them are either 'non-excludable', 'non-rival', or both. This makes it very difficult to redeem the cost of their provision from all (potential) beneficiaries/users. A non-excludable good is one that, if it is provided to one, is effectively provided to all. A 'non-rival' good is one whose availability is not reduced by its use – in other words, it is not, strictly speaking, consumed at all. The classic example of both is the provision of street lighting. This is non-excludable in the sense that, regardless of who pays for it, all benefit. It is similarly non-rival in the sense that the use made of it by one does not diminish its provision to others.

3 It is now more conventional for public choice theorists to declare themselves agnostic about the specific utility function to be maximized in any given context, insisting that the term 'rationality' refers only to the efficiency with which means are deployed in the service of given preferences. However, it is the case that, even today, most game-theoretic modelling within this tradition draws on a remarkably narrow set of utility functions, which seem to correspond closely to a simple conception of material self-interest and to be preserved from one game to the next and from one author to the next. Capital maximizes profit, political parties the chance of their election or re-election, public servants the budgets of their bureaux, and so forth.

4 It is generally assumed that rational actors will take account of the consequences of their action for others only in so far as those consequences have (or are anticipated to have) knock-on implications for their own ability to maximize their personal utility in the future.

5 The scare-quotes are important here, for if public choice theorists are right to assume that bureaucrats, for instance, are motivated by utility-maximizing rational self-interest, they are not public servants at all – for in so far as they serve anyone, they serve themselves, sacrificing their ability to deliver collective or public goods on the altar of narrow personal advantage.

6 As we saw in chapter 1, there is some considerable evidence to substantiate this – with electoral turnout in the US, for instance, rising significantly in the early 1980s.

7 On the seeming paradox of the 'free economy and the strong state' see esp. Gamble 1988.

8 Whilst there is something of a natural affinity between public choice theory and neoliberalism, it would be wrong to see this as extending to all rational choice theory. The natural affinity with neoliberalism arises from the projection of the assumption of narrow instrumentality on to public servants (elected or otherwise). And that is distinctive of public choice theory. Indeed, contemporary rational choice theory is increasingly agnostic about the specific utility functions of political actors, and is by no means wedded, as a consequence, to the view of public servants as purely self-interested.

9 Table 3.1 is, of course, by no means exhaustive in its consideration of the rational / public choice theoretical antecedents of neoliberalism – the role of transaction cost economics, in particular, might also be acknowledged.

10 Though Arrow does not in fact restrict himself to considering the possibility of the democratic aggregation of societal preferences, it is his answer to this more specific question that is responsible for the status of *Social Choice and Individual Values* as the founding work of public choice theory.

11 Arrow is often misunderstood as demonstrating that all putatively democratic preference aggregations are either arbitrary or dictatorial. That he does not do. What he does show is that if individuals have at least three alternatives, and if they are unconstrained in their choices, then specific distributions of societal preferences *may* arise that cannot be aggregated in a democratic fashion. In short, he shows that preference distributions may be such that no democratic aggregation is possible.

12 The degree to which the ascendant economic paradigm was genuinely 'Keynesian' is a matter of some contention in the literature (compare e.g. Booth 1983, 1984 with Tomlinson 1984). Suffice it for now to note that, however it is labelled, it did not provide a simple or effective solution to the problem of 'stagflation'.

13 This is not, of course, to deny the strong and negative correlation widely observed for OECD countries between indices of central bank independence and post-war average inflation rates (e.g. Alesina and Summers 1993; Franzese 2002: 202–4). The point, though, is that in the absence of evidence from time-series data linking the granting of independence with improved anti-inflationary performance, it would be wrong to draw strong causal inferences from such a correlation, however robust. Indeed, the available empirical evidence suggests that credibility and predictability flow primarily from *achieving* low inflation, and not from replicating the institutional template seen as most conducive for so doing in standard neoclassical economic models.

14 It is important to note that a strategy for maximizing the total share of the vote received by a party is likely to be very different from that designed merely to ensure the 30–40 per cent of the popular vote required for electoral victory in most advanced liberal democratic polities today.

15 Interestingly enough, not much is made of this in the existing public choice literature. Indeed, Downs himself seems to take the view that the competitive nature of the electoral process guarantees, serendipitously, that individually rational action on the part of the parties does not translate into a collectively irrational outcome. 'Median voter convergence' is seen, as Dunleavy and O'Leary note, as an ideal outcome, since it is the best single approximation of what a majority of the citizens want (1987: 28).

Chapter 4   The Global Sources of Depoliticization

1 As we saw in the previous chapter, the presumed necessity of central bank independence can be summoned without any appeal to the logic of globalization.

2 Of course, it is not only capital that is mobile in a globally integrated market. In so far as labour is both mobile and scarce – and in some sectors of the international economy it is certainly both – its preferences, too, must be accommodated if the supply of this essential factor of production is to meet demand. With a few rare exceptions, however, the mobility of labour has not featured prominently in accounts of the economic imperatives issuing from globalization (though see e.g. Rogowski 1989). This is largely because of the emphasis placed in the existing literature upon the differential mobility of capital and labour. Yet two further factors are also likely to have proved significant: first, the stigmatized and rather undifferentiated public discourse which surrounds immigration in most of the world's leading economies, and second, the rather greater political clout and influence of those advocating ostensibly capital-friendly reforms. The latter, of course, are more likely to stress the mobility of capital and the imperatives issuing from it over those issuing from the mobility of labour.

3 The notion that capital is motivated politically by strong deregulatory preferences is, of course, a crude generalization and one, as we shall see in later sections, that is difficult to reconcile with the expressed preferences of capital (as revealed by investment behaviour). Regulation may well bring with it a certain sense of security on the part of (say, financial) investors, suggesting at minimum the existence of complex trade-offs in capital's own assessment of the merits of regulation versus deregulation. The simple point, however, is that in most stylized accounts of globalization, such complex trade-offs are simply not acknowledged, and capital's preferences are assumed to be both simple and fixed.

References

Alesina, Alberto (1989) 'Politics and Business Cycles in Industrial Democracies', *Economic Policy*, 8, 57–98.

Alesina, Alberto, and Summers, Laurence (1993) 'Central Bank Independence and Macroeconomic Performance: Some Comparative Evidence', *Journal of Money, Credit and Banking*, 25 (2), 151–63.

Almond, Gabriel, and Verba, Sidney (1963) *The Civic Culture*. Princeton: Princeton University Press.

Amadae, S. M. (2003) *Rationalising Capitalist Democracy: The Cold War Origins of Rational Choice Liberalism*. Chicago: University of Chicago Press.

Arrow, Kenneth (1951) *Social Choice and Individual Values*. New York: Wiley.

Bairoch, Peter (1996) 'Globalisation Myths and Realities: One Century of External Trade and Foreign Investment', in R. Boyer and D. Drache (eds), *States Against Market: The Limits of Globalisation*. London: Routledge.

Bank for International Settlements (2004) *Triennial Central Bank Survey of Foreign Exchange and Derivatives Market Activity in April 2004*. Monetary and Economic Department, BIS.

Berman, Sheri, and McNamara, Kathleen R. (1999) 'Bank on Democracy: Why Central Banks Need Public Oversight', *Foreign Affairs*, 7, 2–8.

Birch, Anthony H. (2001) *Concepts and Theories of Modern Democracy*, 2nd edn. London: Routledge.

Blinder, Alan S. (1997) 'Is Government Too Political?', *Foreign Affairs*, 77 (6), 115–26.

Boggs, Carl (2000) *The End of Politics*. New York: Guilford Press.

Booth, A. (1983) 'The Keynesian Revolution in Economic Policy-Making', *Economic History Review*, 36, 101–23.

Booth, A. (1984) 'Defining the "Keynesian Revolution" in Economic Policy-Making', *Economic History Review*, 37, 263–7.

Brewer, T. L., and Young, S. (1998) *The Multilateral Investment System and Multinational Enterprises*. Oxford: Oxford University Press.

Bryant, Raymond L., and Goodman, Michael K. (2004) 'Consuming Narratives: The Political Ecology of "Alternative Consumption"', *Transactions of the Institute of British Geographers*, 29, 344–66.

Buchanen, James M. (1988) 'Market Failure and Political Failure', *Cato Journal*, 8, 1–13.

Buchanen, James M., and Wagner, Robert E. (1977) *Democracy in Deficit*. New York: Basic Books.

Buchanen, James M., and Wagner, Robert E. (1978) *The Consequences of Mr Keynes*. London: Institute for Economic Affairs.

Buller, Jim, and Flinders, Matthew (2005) 'The Domestic Origins of Depoliticisation in the Area of British Economic Policy', *British Journal of Politics and International Relations*, 7 (4), 526–44.

Burnham, Peter (2001) 'New Labour and the Politics of Depoliticisation', *British Journal of Politics and International Relations*, 3 (2), 127–49.

Cameron, David R. (1978) 'The Expansion of the Public Economy: A Comparative Analysis', *American Political Science Review*, 72 (4), 1243–61.

Citrin, Jack (1974) 'Comment', *American Political Science Review*, 16, 431–53.

Cooke, William N., and Noble, Deborah S. (1998) 'Industrial Relations Systems and US Foreign Direct Investment Abroad', *British Journal of Industrial Relations*, 36 (4), 581–609.

Crick, Bernard (2000) *In Defence of Politics*, 5th edn. London: Continuum.

Crone, Patricia (1989) *Pre-Industrial Societies*. Oxford: Blackwell.

Crouch, Colin (2004) *Post-Democracy*. Cambridge: Polity.

Crozier, Michel J., Huntingdon, Samuel P., and Watanuki, Joji (1975) *The Crisis of Democracy: Report on the Governability of Democracies to the Trilateral Commission*. New York: New York University Press.

Dalton, Russell J. (2000) 'Value Change and Democracy', in S. Pharr and R. D. Putnam (eds), *Disaffected Democracies*. Princeton: Princeton University Press.

Dalton, Russell J. (2004) *Democratic Challenges, Democratic Choices: The Erosion of Political Support in Advanced Industrial Democracies*. Oxford: Oxford University Press.

Dalton, Russell J., and Wattenberg, Martin P. (eds) (2000) *Parties without Partisans: Political Change in Advanced Industrial Democracies*. Oxford: Oxford University Press.

Denver, David, Hands, Gordon, and McAllister, Iain (2004) 'The Electoral Impact of Constituency Campaigning in Britain, 1992–2001', *Political Studies*, 52 (2), 289–306.

Deth, Jan van, and Scarborough, Elinor (eds) (1995) *The Impact of Values*. Oxford: Oxford University Press.

Dowding, Keith (2005) 'Is it Rational to Vote? Five Types of Answer and a Suggestion', *British Journal of Politics and International Relations*, 7 (3), 442–59.

Downs, Anthony (1957) *An Economic Theory of Democracy*. New York: Harper Collins.

Downs, Anthony (1967) *Inside Bureaucracy*. Boston: Little, Brown.

Dunleavy, Patrick, (1991) *Democracy, Bureaucracy and Public Choice*. Hemel Hempstead: Harvester Wheatsheaf.

Dunleavy, Patrick, and Hood, Christopher (1994) 'From Old Public Administration to New Public Management', *Public Money and Management*, 14 (3), 9–16.

Dunleavy, Patrick, and O'Leary, Brendan (1987) *Theories of the State: The Politics of Liberal Democracy*. London: Macmillan.

Dunn, John (2000) *The Cunning of Unreason: Making Sense of Politics*. London: Harper Collins.

Dunning, John H. (1988) 'The Eclectic Paradigm of International Production: An Update and Some Possible Extensions', *Journal of International Business Studies*, 19 (1), 1–32.

Dyson, Kenneth (ed.) (2002) *European States and the Euro: Europeanisation, Variation and Convergence*. Oxford: Oxford University Press.

European Commission (2001) *European Governance: A White Paper*. COM 428. Brussels: The European Commission.

European Policy Forum (2000) *Making Decisions in Britain*. London: European Policy Forum.

Feigenbaum, Harvey, Henig, Jeffrey, and Hamnett, Christopher (1998) *Shrinking the State: The Political Underpinnings of Privatisation*. Cambridge: Cambridge University Press.

Flinders, Matthew (2004) 'Delegated Governance in the European Union', *Journal of European Public Policy*, 11 (3), 520–44.

Frankel, Jeffrey A. (1991) 'Quantifying International Capital Mobility in the 1980s', in D. Bernheim and J. Shoven (eds), *National Saving and Economic Performance*. Chicago: University of Chicago Press.

Frankel, Jeffrey A. (1997) *Regional Trading Blocs: In the World Economic System*. Washington: Institute for International Economics.

Franklin, Mark N. (2002) 'The Dynamics of Electoral Participation', in L. LeDue, R. G. Niemi, and P. Norris (eds), *Comparing Democracies, vol. 2: New Challenges to the Study of Elections and Voting*. London: Sage.

Franklin, Mark N. (2004) *Voter Turnout and the Dynamics of Electoral Competition in Established Democracies since 1945*. Cambridge: Cambridge University Press.

Franzese, Robert J. Jr (2002) *Macroeconomic Policies of Developed Democracies*. Cambridge: Cambridge University Press.

Gamble, Andrew (1988) *The Free Economy and the Strong State*. London: Macmillan.

Gamble, Andrew (2000) *Politics and Fate*. Cambridge: Polity.

Garrett, Geoffrey (1998) *Partisan Politics in the Global Economy*. Cambridge: Cambridge University Press.

Garrett, Geoffrey (2001) 'Globalization and Government Spending Around the World', *Studies in Comparative International Development*, 35 (4), 3–29.

Geys, Benny (2006) 'Rational Theories of Voter Turnout: A Review', *Political Studies Review*, 4 (1), 16–35.

Giddens, Anthony (1994) *Beyond Left and Right: The Future of Radical Politics.* Cambridge: Polity.

Giddens, Anthony (1999) *The Runaway World.* London: Profile Books.

Gill, Graeme (2003) *The Nature and Development of the Modern State.* Basingstoke: Palgrave.

Gill, Stephen (2000) 'Towards a Postmodern Prince? The Battle in Seattle as a Moment in the New Politics of Globalisation', *Millennium*, 29 (1), 131–40.

Gough, Ian (1996) 'Competitiveness and the Welfare State', *New Political Economy*, 1 (2), 209–32.

Green, Donald P., and Shapiro, Ian (1994) *Pathologies of Rational Choice Theory: A Critique of Applications in Political Science.* New Haven: Yale University Press.

Hall, John A., and Ikenberry, G. John (1989) *The State.* Minneapolis: University of Minnesota Press.

Hall, Peter A. (1999) 'Social Capital in Britain', *British Journal of Political Science*, 29 (3), 417–61.

Hall, Peter A. (2002) 'Great Britain: The Role of Social Capital and the Distribution of Social Capital', in R. D. Putnam (ed.), *Democracies in Flux: The Evolution of Social Capital in Contemporary Society.* Oxford: Oxford University Press.

Hall, Peter A., and Soskice, David (eds) (2001) *Varieties of Capitalism.* Oxford: Oxford University Press.

Hamilton, A., Jay, J., and Madison, J. (1901) *The Federalist.* New York: The Colonial Press.

Hauptmann, Emily (1996) *Putting Choice before Democracy: A Critique of Rational Choice Theory.* Albany, NY: State University of New York Press.

Hay, Colin (1996) 'Narrating Crisis: The Discursive Construction of the Winter of Discontent', *Sociology*, 30 (2), 253–77.

Hay, Colin (1999) *The Political Economy of New Labour.* Manchester: Manchester University Press.

Hay, Colin (2001) 'The Crisis of Keynesianism and the Rise of Neoliberalism in Britain: An Ideational Institutionalist Approach', in J. L. Campbell and O. K. Pedersen (eds.), *The Rise of Neoliberalism and Institutional Analysis.* Princeton: Princeton University Press.

Hay, Colin (2002) *Political Analysis.* Basingstoke: Palgrave.

Hay, Colin (2005a) 'Globalisation's Impact on States', in J. Ravenhill (ed.), *Global Political Economy.* Oxford: Oxford University Press.

Hay, Colin (2005b) 'The Normalising Role of Rationalist Assumptions in the Institutional Embedding of Neoliberalism', *Economy and Society*, 33 (4), 500–27.

Hay, Colin (2006) 'What's Globalisation Got to Do with it? Economic Interdependence and the Future of European Welfare States', *Government and Opposition*, 41 (1), 1–22.

Hay, Colin, and Lister, Michael (2006) 'Introduction: Theories of the State', in C. Hay, M. Lister, and D. Marsh (eds), *The State: Theories and Issues*. Basingstoke: Palgrave.

Hay, Colin, and Rosamond, Ben (2002) 'Globalisation, European Integration and the Discursive Construction of Economic Imperatives', *Journal of European Public Policy*, 9 (2), 147–67.

Hay, Colin, and Smith, Nicola J. (2004) 'The Political Discourse of Globalisation and European Integration in the UK and Ireland', *West European Politics*, 28 (1), 124–59.

Held, David, McGrew, Anthony, Goldblatt, David, and Perraton, Jonathan (1999) *Global Transformations: Politics, Economics and Culture*. Cambridge: Polity.

Heywood, Andrew (1994) *Political Ideas and Concepts: An Introduction*. Basingstoke: Palgrave.

Hindmoor, Andrew (2006) 'Public Choice Theory', in C. Hay, M. Lister, and D. Marsh (eds), *The State: Theories and Issues*. Basingstoke: Palgrave.

Hirst, Paul, and Thompson, Grahame (1999) *Globalisation in Question*, 2nd edn. Cambridge: Polity.

Hood, Christopher (1991) 'A Public Management for All Seasons?', *Public Administration*, 69 (1), 3–19.

Hughes, Owen E. (2003) *Public Management and Administration*, 3rd edn. Basingstoke: Palgrave.

Inglehart, Ronald (1990) *Culture Shift*. Princeton: Princeton University Press.

Inglehart, Ronald (1997) *Modernisation and Postmodernisation*. Princeton: Princeton University Press.

Inglehart, Ronald (1999) 'Postmodernisation Erodes Respect for Authority, but Increases Support for Democracy', in P. Norris (ed.), *Critical Citizens*. Oxford: Oxford University Press.

Inoguchi, Takashi (2002) 'Broadening the Basis of Social Capital in Japan', in R. D. Putnam (ed.), *Democracies in Flux: The Evolution of Social Capital in Contemporary Society*. Oxford: Oxford University Press.

Kaldor, Mary (2000) 'Civilising Globalisation? The Implications of the "Battle" in Seattle', *Millennium*, 29 (1), 105–14.

Katzenstein, Peter J. (1985) *Small States in World Markets*. Ithaca, NY: Cornell University Press.

Katzenstein, Peter J. (2000) 'Confidence, Trust, International Relations and Lessons from Smaller Democracies', in S. Pharr and R. D. Putnam (eds), *Disaffected Democracies*. Princeton: Princeton University Press.

King, Anthony (1975) 'Overload: Problems of Governing in the 1970s', *Political Studies*, 23 (2/3), 284–96.

King, Desmond S. (1987) *The New Right: Politics, Markets and Citizenship*. London: Macmillan.

Kiser, Edgar, and Laing, Aaron M. (2001) 'Have We Overestimated the Effects of Neoliberalism and Globalisation? Some Speculations on the Anomalous

Stability of Taxes on Business', in J. L. Campbell and O. K. Pedersen (eds), *The Rise of Neoliberalism and Institutional Analysis*. Princeton: Princeton University Press.

Kleinknecht, Alfred, and ter Wengel, Jan (1998) 'The Myth of Economic Globalisation', *Cambridge Journal of Economics*, 22, 637–47.

Klingemann, Hans-Dieter (1999) 'Mapping Political Support in the 1990s: A Global Analysis', in P. Norris (ed.), *Critical Citizens: Global Support for Democratic Governance*. Oxford: Oxford University Press.

Klingemann, Hans-Dieter, and Fuchs, Dieter (eds) (1995) *Citizens and the State*. Oxford: Oxford University Press.

Kydland, F. E., and Prescott, E. C. (1977) 'Rules Rather than Discretion: The Inconsistency of Optimal Plans', *Journal of Political Economy*, 85 (3), 473–92.

Lasswell, Harold (1958) *Politics: Who Gets What, When and How*. New York: Meridian.

Lawson, Kay, and Merkl, Peter (eds) (1988) *When Parties Fail: Emerging Alternative Organisations*. Princeton: Princeton University Press.

Lees-Marshment, Jennifer (2001) *Political Marketing and British Political Parties: The Party's Just Begun*. Manchester: Manchester University Press.

Leftwich, Adrian (2004) 'Thinking Politically: On the Politics of Politics', in A. Leftwich (ed.), *What is Politics?* 2nd edn. Cambridge: Polity.

Locke, Richard M., and Kochan, Thomas (1985) 'The Transformation of Industrial Relations? A Cross-National Review of the Evidence', in R. Locke, T. Kochan, and M. Piore (eds), *Employment Relations in a Changing World*. Cambridge, Mass.: MIT Press.

McLaughlin, Kathleen, Osborne, Stephen P. and Ferlie, Ewan (eds) (2002) *The New Public Management: Current Trends and Future Prospects*. New York: Routledge.

Maddison, Angus (1987) 'Growth and Slowdown in Advanced Capitalist Economies: Techniques of Quantitative Assessment', *Journal of Economic Literature*, 25 (2), 649–98.

Maloney, Ross (2006) 'Karl Polanyi, Neo-Polanyians and Resistance to Globalisation's Market Mentality' (unpublished Ph.D. thesis, University of Birmingham).

Maloney, William (2006) 'Political Participation: Beyond the Electoral Arena', in P. Dunleavy, R. Heffernan, P. Cowley, and C. Hay (eds), *Developments in British Politics*, vol. 8. Basingstoke: Palgrave.

Margetts, Helen (2000) 'Political Participation and Protest', in P. Dunleavy, A. Gamble, I. Holliday, and G. Peele (eds), *Developments in British Politics*, vol. 6. Basingstoke: Palgrave.

Marquand, David (2004) *Decline of the Public*. Cambridge: Polity.

Marsh, David, (ed.) (1998) *Comparing Policy Networks*. Buckingham: Open University Press.

Marsh, David, and Rhodes, R. A. W. (eds) (1992) *Policy Networks in British Government*. Oxford: Oxford University Press.

Mauss, Marcel (1954) *The Gift: The Form and Reason for Exchange in Archaic Societies*. London: Cohen and West.

Moravcsik, Andrew (1998) *The Choice for Europe: Social Purpose and State Power from Messina to Maastricht*. Ithaca, NY: Cornell University Press.

Mosley, Layna (2003) *Global Capital and National Governments*. Cambridge: Cambridge University Press.

Mueller, Dennis C. (2003) *Public Choice*, vol. 3. Cambridge: Cambridge University Press.

Newton, Kenneth (1999) 'Social and Political Trust in Established Democracies', in P. Norris (ed.), *Critical Citizens*. Oxford: Oxford University Press.

Newton, Kenneth, and Norris, Pippa (2000) 'Confidence in Political Institutions: Faith, Culture or Performance?', in S. Pharr and R. D. Putnam (eds), *Disaffected Democracies*. Princeton: Princeton University Press.

Nicholson, Peter P. (2004) 'Politics and the Exercise of Force', in A. Leftwich (ed.), *What is Politics?* Cambridge: Polity.

Niskanen, William A. (1971) *Bureaucracy and Representative Government*. Chicago: Aldine.

Nordhaus, William D. (1975) 'The Political Business Cycle', *Review of Economic Studies*, 42, 169–90.

Norris, Pippa (ed.) (1999a) *Critical Citizens: Global Support for Democratic Governance*. Oxford: Oxford University Press.

Norris, Pippa (1999b) 'Conclusions: The Growth of Critical Citizens and Its Consequences', in *Critical Citizens: Global Support for Democratic Governance*. Oxford: Oxford University Press.

Norris, Pippa (2000) 'The Impact of Television on Civic Malaise', in S. Pharr and R. D. Putnam (eds), *Disaffected Democracies*. Princeton: Princeton University Press.

Norris, Pippa (2002) *Democratic Phoenix: Reinventing Political Activism*. Cambridge: Cambridge University Press.

Obstfeld, Maurice, and Rogoff, Kenneth (1996) *Foundations of International Macroeconomics*. Cambridge, Mass.: MIT Press.

Offe, Claus, and Fuchs, Susanne (2002) 'A Decline of Social Capital? The German Case', in R. D. Putnam (ed.), *Democracies in Flux: The Evolution of Social Capital in Contemporary Society*. Oxford: Oxford University Press.

Ohmae, Kenichi (1990) *The Borderless World*. London: Collins.

Ohmae, Kenichi (1995) *The End of the Nation State*. New York: Free Press.

Ordeshook, Peter C. (1996) 'Engineering or Science: What is the Study of Politics?', in J. Friedman (ed.), *The Rational Choice Controversy: Economic Models of Politics Reconsidered*. New Haven: Yale University Press.

O'Toole, Therese, Marsh, David, and Jones, Su (2003a) 'Political Literacy Cuts Both Ways: The Politics of Non-Participation among Young People', *Political Quarterly*, 74 (3), 349–60.

O'Toole, Therese, Lister, Michael, Marsh, David, Jones, Su, and McDonagh, Alex (2003b) 'Tuning Out or Left Out? Participation and Non-Participation among Young People', *Contemporary Politics*, 9 (1), 45–61.

Paldam, Martin (1997) 'Political Business Cycles', in Dennis C. Mueller (ed.), *Perspectives on Public Choice*. Cambridge: Cambridge University Press.

Parry, Geraint, Moyser, George, and Day, Neil (1992) *Political Participation and Democracy in Britain*. Cambridge: Cambridge University Press.

Pateman, Carole (1970) *Participation and Democratic Theory*. Cambridge: Cambridge University Press.

Pattie, Charles, Seyd, Patrick, and Whiteley, Paul (2003a) 'Citizenship and Civic Engagement: Attitudes and Behaviour in Britain', *Political Studies*, 51, 443–68.

Pattie, Charles, Seyd, Patrick, and Whitely, Paul (2003b) 'Civic Attitudes and Engagement in Modern Britain', *Parliamentary Affairs*, 56, 616–33.

Pattie, Charles, Seyd, Patrick, and Whitely, Paul (2004) *Citizenship in Britain: Values, Participation and Democracy*. Cambridge: Cambridge University Press.

Petrella, Ricardo (1996) 'Globalisation and Internationalisation: The Dynamics of the Emerging World Order', in R. Boyer and D. Drache (eds), *States Against Market: The Limits of Globalisation*. London: Routledge.

Pettit, Philip (2004) 'Depoliticising Democracy', *Ratio Juris*, 17 (1), 52–65.

Pissarides, Christopher A. (1980) 'British Government Popularity and Economic Performance', *Economic Journal*, 90, 569–81.

Pollitt, Christopher, and Bouckaert, Geert (2000) *Public Management Reform: A Comparative Analysis*. Oxford: Oxford University Press.

Posen, Andrew S. (1993) 'Why Central Bank Independence Does Not Cause Low Inflation: There is No Institutional Fix for Politics', in R. O'Brien (ed.), *Finance and the International Economy*, vol. 7. Oxford: Oxford University Press.

Posen, Andrew S. (1998) 'Central Bank Independence and Disinflationary Credibility: A Missing Link?', *Oxford Economic Papers*, 50 (3), 335–9.

Price, Simon, and Sanders, David (1993) 'Modelling Government Popularity in Postwar Britain: A Methodological Example', *American Political Science Review*, 37 (1), 317–34.

Putnam, Robert D. (1993) *Making Democracy Work: Civil Traditions in Modern Italy*. Princeton: Princeton University Press.

Putnam, Robert D. (1995) 'Bowling Alone: America's Declining Social Capital', *Journal of Democracy*, (Jan.), 65–78.

Putnam, Robert D. (2000) *Bowling Alone: The Collapse and Revival of American Community*. New York: Simon and Schuster.

Putnam, Robert D. (2002) 'Conclusions', in R. D. Putnam (ed.), *Democracies in Flux: The Evolution of Social Capital in Contemporary Society*. Oxford: Oxford University Press.

Rancière, Jacques (1995) *On the Shores of Politics*. London: Verso.

Reich, Robert (1992) *The Work of Nations*. New York: Vintage Books.

Riker, William H., and Ordeshook, Peter C. (1968) 'A Theory of the Calculus of Voting', *American Political Science Review*, 62, 25–42.

Rodrik, Dani (1996) *Why Do More Open Economies Have Bigger Governments?* NBER Working Paper no. 5537, Cambridge, Mass.: National Bureau of Economic Research.

Rodrik, Dani (1997) *Has Globalisation Gone Too Far?* Washington: Institute for International Economics.

Rødseth, Asbjorn (2000) *Open Economy Macroeconomics*. Cambridge: Cambridge University Press.

Rogowski, Ronald (1989) *Commerce and Coalitions*. Princeton: Princeton University Press.

Rothstein, Bo (2002) 'Social Capital in the Social Democratic State', in R. D. Putnam (ed.), *Democracies in Flux: The Evolution of Social Capital in Contemporary Society*. Oxford: Oxford University Press.

Rubinstein, Nicolai (1958) 'Political Ideas in Sienese Art: The Frescoes by Ambrogio Lorenzetti and Taddeo di Bartolo in the Palazza Publico', *Journal of the Warburg and Courtauld Institutes*, 21, 179–207.

Scarrow, Susan E. (2000) 'Parties without Members? Party Organisation in a Changing Electoral Environment', in R. J. Dalton and Wattenberg, M. P. (eds), *Parties without Partisans: Political Change in Advanced Industrial Democracies*. Oxford: Oxford University Press.

Scharpf, Fritz W. (2000) 'Interdependence and Political Legitimation', in S. Pharr and R. D. Putnam (eds), *Disaffected Democracies*. Princeton: Princeton University Press.

Scholte, Jan-Aart (2000) 'Cautionary Reflections on Seattle', *Millennium*, 29 (1), 115–21.

Schumpeter, Joseph (1942) *Capitalism, Socialism and Democracy*. New York: Harper and Row.

Self, Peter (1993) *Government by the Market*. London: Macmillan.

Simmons, Beth A. (1999) 'The Internationalisation of Capital', in H. Kitschelt, P. Lange, G. Marks, and J. D. Stephens (eds), *Continuity and Change in Contemporary Capitalism*. Cambridge: Cambridge University Press.

Skinner, Quentin (1978) *Foundations of Modern Political Thought*, 2 vols. Cambridge: Cambridge University Press.

Smith, Adam (1976 [1776]) *An Inquiry into the Nature and Causes of the Wealth of Nations*. Oxford: Oxford University Press.

Sparks, A. W. (1994) *Talking Politics: A Wordbook*. London: Routledge.

Steinmo, Sven (2003) 'The Evolution of Policy Ideas: Tax Policy in the Twentieth Century', *British Journal of Politics and International Relations*, 5 (2), 206–36.

Stokes, Donald (1962) 'Popular Evaluations of Government', in H. Cleveland and H. D. Lasswell (eds), *Ethics and Bigness*. New York: Harper.

Strøm, Kaare, Müller, Wolfgang C., and Bergman, Torbjörn (2003) *Delegation and Accountability in Parliamentary Democracies*. Oxford: Oxford University Press.

Swank, Duane (2002) *Global Capital, Political Institutions and Policy Change in Developed Welfare States*. Cambridge: Cambridge University Press.

Swenson, Peter (2000) *Capitalists against Markets*. Oxford: Oxford University Press.

Tanzi, Vito, and Schuknecht, Ludger (2000) *Public Spending in the 20th Century: A Global Perspective*. Cambridge: Cambridge University Press.

Titmuss, Richard M. (1971) *The Gift Relationship*. London: Harper Collins.

Tomlinson, Jim (1984) 'A "Keynesian Revolution" in Economic Policy-Making?', *Economic History Review*, 37, 258–62.

Traxler, Franz, and Woitech, Birgit (2000) 'Transnational Investment and National Labour Market Regimes: A Case of "Regime Shopping"?', *European Journal of Industrial Relations*, 6 (2), 141–59.

Tullock, Gordon (1965) *The Politics of Public Bureaucracy*. Washington: Public Affairs Press.

Ugur, Mehmet (ed.), (2001) *Open Economy Macroeconomics: A Reader*. London: Routledge.

Vickers, John, and Yarrow, George (1988) *Privatisation: An Economic Approach*. Cambridge, Mass.: MIT Press.

Vihinen, Lea, and Lee, Hyung-Jong (2004) 'Fair Trade and the Multilateral Trading System', *OECD Trade Directorate*. Paris: OECD.

Viroli, Maurizio (1992) *From Politics to Reason of State: The Acquisition and Transformation of the Language of Politics, 1250–1600*. Cambridge: Cambridge University Press.

Walsh, Kieran (1995) *Public Services and Market Mechanisms: Competition, Contracting and the New Public Management*. Basingstoke: Palgrave Macmillan.

Watson, Matthew (2001) 'International Capital Mobility in an Era of Globalisation: Adding a Political Dimension to the "Feldstein–Horioka Puzzle"', *Politics*, 21 (2), 81–92.

Weale, Albert (2004) 'Politics as Collective Choice', in A. Leftwich (ed.), *What is Politics?* Cambridge: Polity.

Whiteley, Paul, and Seyd, Patrick (2003) 'How to Win a Landslide by Really Trying: The Effects of Local Campaigning on Voting in the 1997 British General Election', *Electoral Studies*, 22 (3), 301–24.

Wilensky, Harold L. (2002) *Rich Democracies: Political Economy, Public Policy and Performance*. Berkeley: University of California Press.

World Bank (2000) *Bolivia: From Patronage to Professional State*. Report no. 20115-BO.

Wuthnow, R. (2002) 'United States: Bridging the Privileged and the Marginalised?', in R. D. Putnam (ed.), *Democracies in Flux: The Evolution of Social Capital in Contemporary Society*. Oxford: Oxford University Press.

Zevin, Robert (1992) 'Are World Financial Markets More Open? If So, Why and with What Effects?', in T. Banuri and J. B. Schor (eds), *Financial Openness and National Autonomy: Opportunities and Constraints*. Oxford: Oxford University Press.

Index